Beginning Game Programming, Third Edition

Jonathan S. Harbour

Course Technology PTR
A part of Cengage Learning

COURSE TECHNOLOGY
CENGAGE Learning

Australia • Brazil • Japan • Korea • Mexico • Singapore • Spain • United Kingdom • United States

HILLSBORO PUBLIC LIBRARIES
WITHDRAWN
Member of Washington County
COOPERATIVE LIBRARY SERVICES

COURSE TECHNOLOGY
CENGAGE Learning™

Beginning Game Programming,
Third Edition
Jonathan S. Harbour

Publisher and General Manager,
Course Technology PTR: Stacy L. Hiquet

Associate Director of Marketing: Sarah Panella

Manager of Editorial Services: Heather Talbot

Marketing Manager: Jordan Casey

Senior Acquisitions Editor: Emi Smith

Project Editor: Jenny Davidson

Technical Reviewer: Joshua Smith

PTR Editorial Services Coordinator: Jen Blaney

Interior Layout Tech: Macmillan Publishing
Solutions

Cover Designer: Mike Tanamachi

CD-ROM Producer: Brandon Penticuff

Indexer: Sharon Shock

Proofreader: Sandi Wilson

© 2010 Course Technology, a part of Cengage Learning.

ALL RIGHTS RESERVED. No part of this work covered by the copyright herein may be reproduced, transmitted, stored, or used in any form or by any means graphic, electronic, or mechanical, including but not limited to photocopying, recording, scanning, digitizing, taping, Web distribution, information networks, or information storage and retrieval systems, except as permitted under Section 107 or 108 of the 1976 United States Copyright Act, without the prior written permission of the publisher.

For product information and technology assistance, contact us at
Cengage Learning Customer & Sales Support, 1-800-354-9706

For permission to use material from this text or product, submit all requests online at **www.cengage.com/permissions** Further permissions questions can be emailed to **permissionrequest@cengage.com**

Anim8or, audacity, DirectX SDK, Mappy, and Pro Motion are all open-source programs. All trademarks are the property of their respective owners.

Library of Congress Control Number: 2009924510

ISBN-13: 978-1-4354-5427-9

ISBN-10: 1-4354-5427-8 A1211953   9/09

Course Technology, a part of Cengage Learning
20 Channel Center Street
Boston, MA 02210
USA

Cengage Learning is a leading provider of customized learning solutions with office locations around the globe, including Singapore, the United Kingdom, Australia, Mexico, Brazil, and Japan. Locate your local office at: **international.cengage.com/region**

Cengage Learning products are represented in Canada by Nelson Education, Ltd.

For your lifelong learning solutions, visit **courseptr.com**

Visit our corporate website at **cengage.com**

Printed in Canada
1 2 3 4 5 6 7 11 10 09

For My Mother,
Vicki Myrlene Harbour

FOREWORD

"I want to be a game designer, how do I get a job?" This is a question I field very often when I do interviews or talk to students. I've even been accosted by the parents of an apparently gifted teenager as I left the stage with my band. My usual answer is, "so what have you designed?" The vast majority of the time, I am given a long explanation about how the person has lots of great ideas, but is in need of a team to make them a reality. My response to this is to try to explain how everyone I work with has great ideas, but only a small percentage of them are designers.

I don't mean to be harsh, but the reality is that there are no successful companies out there that will give someone off the street a development team for 18+ months and a multimillion dollar budget without some sort of proof of concept. What sets someone like Sid Meier (legendary game designer with whom I'm honored to work at Firaxis Games) apart is his ability to take an idea and make something fun out of it. Of course, Sid now gets large teams to do his projects, but he always starts the same way—a team of one cranking out prototypes cobbled together with whatever art and sound he can either dig up or create himself. It's these rough proofs of concept that allow people uninvolved with the creation process to immediately see the fun in a given idea, and that's what gets you a budget and a team. Every budding designer should take note and ask, "What would Sid do?"

That's when a book like this is invaluable. I became acquainted with Jonathan a couple of years ago when I picked up the original version of this book at the bookstore at the Game Developer's Conference. A programmer buddy of mine helped me pick it out from among numerous similar books. He thought it was very well written and thought the emphasis on DirectX would be very applicable to what we do at Firaxis. Another buddy mentioned that he had read Jonathan's work on programming the Game Boy Advance and was very impressed. In my opinion, they gave me great advice and I enjoyed myself immensely while working through the book. While reading, I noticed that Jonathan was a big fan of our game, *Sid Meier's Civilization III*. I contacted him because I have worked on numerous *Civ* titles and we have kept in contact ever since.

The beauty of a book like this is that it takes away all of the excuses. It provides an excellent introduction into game programming. It takes you by the hand and walks you through the seemingly complex process of writing C code making use of DirectX. Before you know it, you'll have a fully usable framework for bringing your ideas to life. You are even provided with tools to create your own art and sound to help dress up the game. In other words, you will have all the tools you need to start making prototypes and prove that you are much more than just someone with great ideas. Believe me; taking this crucial next step will put you at the top of the heap of people looking for jobs in the industry. You will have the ability to stand out and that's vital when so many people are clamoring for work in game development.

So, what would Sid do? Well, when he was prototyping *Sid Meier's Railroads!* last year, he wrote the entire prototype in C. He didn't have an artist (they were all busy on another title at the time), so he grabbed a 3D art program, made his own art, and threw it in the game—often using text labels to make sure players knew what things were in the game. He used audio files from previous Firaxis games and the Internet, and sprinkled them around to enhance the player's experience. He created something—in a fairly short amount of time—that showed our publisher and others just how much fun the game was going to be. And he did it on his own . . . just like the "old days" when he worked from his garage.

So what should you do? Well, if you want to get a job in the industry as a game designer or even if you just want to make a cool game to teach math to your daughter, you should buy this book. Jump in and work through the exercises and develop the beginnings of your own game library—Sid has some code he's used since the Commodore 64 days. Let your imagination run wild and then find ways to translate your ideas into something people can actually play.

Whatever you do, just do *something*. It's the one true way to learn and develop as a designer and it is your ticket to finding game designer fulfillment and maybe even a job. And if Sid wasn't Sid, and didn't already have all of those tools at his disposal, it just might be what he would do too.

Barry E. Caudill
Executive Producer
Firaxis Games
2K Games
Take 2 Interactive

ACKNOWLEDGMENTS

I am most thankful to my wife, Jennifer, for her enduring patience. I am grateful to the hard working people at Course Technology for doing such a fine job. Many thanks especially to Jenny Davidson, Joshua Smith, and Emi Smith. I believe you will find this a gem of a game programming book due to all of their efforts. Any mistakes found herein are mine alone.

ABOUT THE AUTHOR

Jonathan S. Harbour, an associate professor at University of Advancing Technology (www.uat.edu), has written about and teaches many programming topics including: DirectX, Allegro, Python, LUA, DarkBASIC, multi-player networking, XNA Game Studio, and Java. He teaches proprietary courses covering Nintendo GameCube (Dolphin SDK); Nintendo GBA and Nintendo DS (DevKitPro); Sony PlayStation 2 (TOOL); Xbox 360 (XNA SDK); and cell phones (Java ME). His last book, *Advanced 2D Game Development,* was published in 2008, and he is currently working on a new project involving multi-threading. He lives in Arizona with his wife, Jennifer, and four mini gamers: Jeremiah, Kayleigh, Kaitlyn, and Kourtney. He can be reached at www.jharbour.com/forum.

CONTENTS

WELCOME TO THE ADVENTURE!

Welcome to the adventure that is game programming! I have enjoyed playing and programming games for many years, and probably share the same enthusiasm for this once-esoteric subject that you do. Games, and by that I mean PC games, were once found within the realm of Geek Land, where hardy adventurers would explore vast imaginary worlds and then struggle to create similar worlds on their own; meanwhile, out in the real world, people were living normal lives: hanging out with friends, flirting with girls (or guys), going to the movies, cruising downtown.

Why did we choose to miss out on all that fun? Because we thought it was more fun to stare at pixels on the screen? Precisely!

But one man's pixel is another man's fantasy world or outer-space adventure. And the earliest games in "gaming" were little more than globs of pixels being shuffled around on the screen. Our imaginations filled in more details than we often realized when we played the primitive games of the past.

So, what's your passion? Or rather, what's your favorite type of game? Is it a classic arcade shoot-em-up, a fantasy adventure, a real-time strategy game, a role-playing game, a sports-related game? I'd like to challenge you to design a game *in your mind* while reading this book, and imagine how you might go about creating that game as you delve into each chapter. This book was not written to give you a "warm fuzzy" feeling about game development, with a few patchy code listings and directions on where to go next. I really take the subject quite seriously and prefer to give you a sense of completion upon finishing the last chapter. This is a self-contained book to a certain degree, in that what you will learn is applicable toward your own early game projects. What you will learn here will allow you to write a complete game with enough quality that you may feel confident to share it with others.

This book will teach you how to write DirectX code in the C++ language. Game programming is a challenging subject that is not just difficult to master; it is difficult just to get started. This book takes away the mystery of game programming using the tools of the trade: C++ and DirectX. You will learn how to harness the power of Windows and DirectX to render graphics in both 2D and 3D.

You will learn how to write a simple Windows program. From there, you will learn about the key DirectX components: Direct3D, DirectSound, DirectInput, and D3DXSprite. You will learn how to make use of these key DirectX components while writing simple code that is easy to understand, at a pace that will not leave you behind. Along the way, you will put all of the new information gleaned from each chapter into a game library that you can reuse for future game projects. After you have learned all that you need to know to write a simple game, you will see how to create a side-scrolling shoot-em-up game!

Where to Begin?

My philosophy for game development is neither limited nor out of reach for the average programmer. I want to really get down to business early on and not have to explain every function call in the standard C++ library. So you will want to begin learning C++ right now if you are not familiar with the language. There are certainly a lot of great products you can use that are as powerful (or more so) as language used in this book. There are products like Blitz Basic (see *Game Programming for Teens* by Maneesh Sethi) and DarkBASIC (see *DarkBASIC Pro Game Programming, Second Edition* by Jonathan Harbour and Joshua Smith). These are two examples of game development tools that provide you with a complete package: compiler, editor, game library/engine, and the ability to produce a standalone Windows/DirectX game without the need for a runtime library of any kind. If you are fairly new to the C++ language or have no experience with it at all, I strongly suggest that you read a C++ language primer first.

Game programming is not something that you just pick up after reading a single book. Although this book has everything you need to write simple 2D and 3D games (and granted it does cover a lot of useful information in that regard), no single volume can claim to cover everything because game development is a complex subject. I am confident that you will manage to follow along and grasp the concepts in this book just fine without one, but a C++ primer will give you a very good advantage before getting into Windows and DirectX programming. This book spends no time at all discussing the C++ language; it jumps right into Windows and DirectX code fairly quickly, followed by a new subject in each chapter!

This book was written in a progressive style that is meant to challenge you at every step, and relies on repetition rather than memorization. I don't cover a difficult subject just once and expect you to know it from that point on. Instead, I just present similar code sections in each program so you'll get the hang of it over time. The learning curve here is modeled after driving a car: once you have learned to use the accelerator and brake pedals, the actual process of learning to drive comes from practice. You wouldn't dare attempt to compete in a NASCAR race after simply reading a driving book, would you? Of course not! But after many hours behind the wheel, you would at least be qualified to drive around the track.

What Will You Learn?

This book will teach you how to write a Windows program, and from there, the sky's the limit! You will learn about DirectX; you will dive into Direct3D head-first and learn all about surfaces, textures, meshes, 3D models, and that is just the beginning! You will learn how to interface with your computer's hardware using DirectX components, and use those hardware devices in your games!

Since this book is dedicated to teaching the basics of game programming, it will cover a lot of subjects very quickly, so you'll need to be on your toes! I use a casual writing style to make the subjects easy to understand and use repetition rather than memorization to nail the points home. You will learn by doing and you will not struggle with any one subject, because you will practice each topic several times throughout the book. Each chapter builds on the one before, but may be considered independent, so if there is any one subject that you are very interested in at the start, then feel free to skip around. However, the game framework built in this book does refer back to previous chapters, so I recommend reading it one chapter at a time.

Let's Talk About Compilers

The programs in this book were written with Microsoft Visual C++ 2008. Although there are many Windows compilers on the market, very few of them will compile the programs in this book due to the DirectX SDK, which was written with and for Visual C++.

The projects on the CD-ROM included with this book are in Visual C++ 2008 format, since that is the standard compiler at this time. A free compiler called Dev-C++ 5.0 is available from Bloodshed Software, and is fully capable of compiling Windows and DirectX code. The same holds true for the free Turbo C++ 2006, which also supports DirectX via a custom third-party library. (For more information, visit www.jharbour.com/forum for instructions on how to use these compilers—since the subject is beyond the scope of this book.)

If you are using Visual C++ 2005, the previous version, then the code will still compile, but you will need to create the projects on your own—since 2005 and 2008 are not compatible.

The free version of Visual C++ 2008, called the Express Edition, is available for download from Microsoft at http://www.microsoft.com/express/product/. This compiler is not limited in any way, even though it's free!

Advice

I recommend using Visual C++ 2008 for DirectX programming, because it is the latest and greatest compiler, and is certain to support every feature of DirectX for the foreseeable future. In fact, XNA Game Studio 3.1 also uses Visual C++ 2008 should you wish to delve into Xbox 360 programming.

What's Your Skill Level?

This chapter moves along at a brisk pace, so if you already have some experience writing Windows code, it shouldn't bore you. On the other hand, if you have never written a Windows program before, this may be a bit of a challenge for you because I'm going to assume that you already have some familiarity with the C++ language. I just want you to be prepared! If you picked up this book thinking that it would teach you absolutely everything you need to know to write a computer game using the C++ language, and all you'll need to know about Windows and DirectX to boot, well, you may be in for a surprise, because we only have time to cover the key topics—not DirectX *and* the C++ language! I'm going to assume that you have already studied the basics of the language at least. We have *so* much information to cover in this book—if I don't move along at a pretty good pace, we'll never get into the good stuff, like loading and drawing 3D models!

I remember how, when I was just getting started, I had assumed that so much of the work involved in a computer program is done automatically (or rather, was handled by the O/S). It's quite a shock when you realize that *nothing* is given to you—that *you* must write all the code to get anything at all to come up on the screen. Now, it isn't as bad as it was in the early years of the PC, when MS-DOS was the most common O/S (up until the mid-1990s). Back then, you really did have to screw with the video card registers and literally program it using very low-level assembly language.

Note

I have a huge book on that subject by Michael Abrash called *Graphics Programming Black Book* (no longer in print). Michael developed his graphics coding wizardry *before* he was hired as a graphics consultant by studios such as Valve, id Software, and Croteam, and he was the ultimate graphics programming guru! To read some of Michael's commentary about programming *Quake*, visit http://www.bluesnews.com/abrash/index.htm.

As compilers became more powerful, standard operating system libraries that abstracted the computer system hardware and raised it up a notch became available. No longer did programmers have to write all the interface code to the hardware (if you have been playing games for a long time, you may remember how convoluted some of the older MS-DOS game installs used to be). Back in the MS-DOS days, game programmers had to write their own video card and sound card drivers! Imagine that! If you want some classic examples, look up *Dungeon Keeper* and *Jedi Knight*. Instead, Windows, the device drivers, and DirectX provide a layer of abstraction over the hardware.

You can focus on the design and programming of your game rather than spending so much time writing hardware interface code (which was the subject of all game programming books in the early days, when game design was unheard-of). I suspect that these limitations in the operating system are what limited game development to the realm of the ultra-guru and prevented many aspiring game designers from getting into the business in the '80s and early '90s. You simply had to be technical, as well as creative, to succeed at that time. But when Microsoft released DirectX for Windows 95, and then continued to improve it over the next ten years, it took all of that complexity and simplified it down to a common game API—application programming interface. The new features added to each new version of DirectX (a result of all the advances in 3D graphics technology) greatly enhanced the original version of DirectX, which was designed to bring gaming to

Windows in a big way. However, during the intervening years, DirectX has grown to become immensely large and complicated, and again we are faced with barriers to entry once again.

Of course, it is better to have DirectX (on the right side of the teeter-totter) because you don't have to make use or even look into all the advanced features if you don't need them for your game. That's the good news, really; if you want the power, it's available, but you can learn the basics and start seeing progress with simple games very quickly.

Conventions Used in This Book

The following styles are used in this book to highlight portions of text that are important. You will find note, tip, and caution boxes here and there throughout the book.

Advice

This is what an advice pop-out looks like. Advice pop-outs provide additional information related to the text.

Book Summary

This book is divided into four parts:

- **Part I: Introduction to Game Programming with Windows and DirectX.** This first section provides all the information you will need to get started writing Windows code. By the time you have completed these first three chapters, you will have a solid grasp of how a Windows program works and how to initialize Direct3D.

- **Part II: The Game Programming Toolbox.** This section is the meat and potatoes of the book, providing solid tutorials on all of the relevant components of DirectX, including functions for loading images; manipulating sprites; polling keyboard, mouse, and Xbox 360 controller; playing sound effects; rendering 3D models; and other core mechanics of any game.

- **Part III: Game Project.** This part includes a single chapter containing an example side-scrolling shoot-em-up game.

- **Part IV: Appendices.** This final part includes the four appendices.

PART I

INTRODUCTION TO GAME PROGRAMMING WITH WINDOWS AND DIRECTX

This first part introduces the Windows API (the Application Programming Interface), which is a foundation that you'll need before moving on to DirectX. The first two chapters will give you an overview of how Windows works by explaining how to write a simple Windows program, how the Windows messaging system works, and how to create a non-interrupting message loop (which gives a Windows program its power). The next chapter introduces DirectX wherein you will learn how to create a Direct3D rendering device and set up the rendering system.

- Chapter 1: Getting Started with Windows
- Chapter 2: Listening to Windows Messages
- Chapter 3: Initializing Direct3D

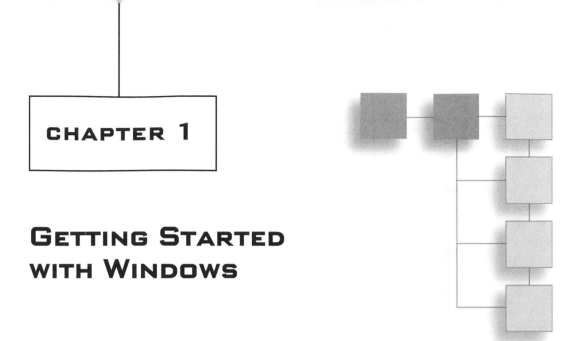

CHAPTER 1

GETTING STARTED WITH WINDOWS

Game programming is one of the most complicated forms of computer programming you will ever have the pleasure of endeavoring to master. Games are as much works of art as they are grand technical achievements. Many technically fantastic games go unnoticed and unappreciated, while less technically savvy games go on to widespread fame and bring fortune to their makers. Regardless of your ultimate goals as a game programmer, this is one of the most enjoyable hobbies that you could ever take up, and the results will both frustrate and exhilarate you at the same time—I hope you're ready for the adventure that is about to begin! This chapter provides the crucial information necessary to get started writing Windows games; it leads into the next two chapters, which provide an overview of the mechanics of a Windows program.

In this chapter, I am going to show you what a simple Windows program looks like. This is valuable information that you will need in the following three chapters, which build on this knowledge to take you into the world of DirectX. These introductory topics will come back to haunt you later on if you have not mastered them, as the chapters to follow will rely on your basic understanding of how Windows works. It will be very helpful if you have some experience writing Windows programs already, but I won't assume that you do. Instead, I'll just cover the basics of a Windows program—all that is necessary to start writing DirectX code.

Windows programming is actually quite fun once you get the hang of it! While some of the code might look like an alien language, it will soon be very familiar to you. If you feel even a little bit overwhelmed by any subject in this chapter, don't worry too much because repetition in later chapters will nail the points home for you. This chapter focuses on showing you how to write a simple Windows program, create the project, type in the code, and compile and run it. Here is what you will learn:

- How to put game programming into perspective.

- How to choose the best compiler for your needs.

- How to create a Win32 Application project.

- How to write a simple Windows program.

An Overview of Windows Programming

If you are new to Windows programming, then you're in for a treat, because Windows is a fun operating system to use for writing games. (This was not always the case in the past though!) First of all, there are so many great compilers and languages available for Windows. Second, it's the most popular operating system in the world, so any game you write for Windows has the potential to become quite popular. The third great thing about Windows is that we have the amazing DirectX SDK at our disposal. Not only is DirectX the most widely used game programming library in *existence*, it is also easy to get into. Now, don't misunderstand my meaning—DirectX is easy to learn, but *mastering* it is another matter. I will teach you how to use it—and wield it, so to speak—to create your own games. Mastering it will require a lot more work and knowledge than this single book provides. Studying DirectX is a very worthwhile thing to spend your time on, especially if you want to get up to date with the latest research in game development (since most articles and books on game development today focus on DirectX).

Before you can start writing DirectX code, you will need to learn how to write a simple Windows application and learn how Windows handles messages. So let's start at the beginning. What *is* Windows?

Windows is a multi-tasking, multi-threaded operating system. What this means is that Windows can run many programs at the same time, and each of those programs can have several threads running as well. As you might imagine, this operating system architecture works well with multi-core processors such as the Intel Core2 and i7 processors.

Advice

For reference, the programs (and screenshots) featured in this book were developed on a PC with an Intel Core2Quad Q6600 processor, 2GB DDR2 RAM, Nvidia 8800GT 512MB DDR3 video card. At the time of this writing, this is an upper-middle class PC in performance.

"Getting" Windows

Few operating systems will scale as well as Windows from one version to the next. The numerous versions of Windows that are in use—primarily Windows Vista and Windows XP, at the time of this writing—are so similar that programs can be written for one version of Windows that will run almost without change on other versions of Windows. For instance, a program compiled with Microsoft Visual C++ 6.0 back in 1998 under Windows NT 4.0 or Windows 98 will still run on the latest version of Windows XP and Vista. You may even have a few games in your game library that came out in the late 1990s that supported an early version of DirectX (for instance, DirectX 8.0); don't be surprised if such games will still run on a new PC. This is a very good thing because we can rely on the platform running our code for years to come. This is one area where console game developers have satisfaction that is lacking among Windows PC game developers, because you can rely on a console system not changing, while PCs change very rapidly, causing technical issues for some games after only a year or two in some cases.

So we have established that Windows programs have a lot of longevity (also known as "shelf life" in the software industry). What can Windows really do?

Advice

Whenever I refer to "Windows" in this book, I'm including every recent version of Windows that is relevant to the topic at hand—that is, PCs and game programming. This should include all previous, current, and future versions of Windows that are compatible. For all practical purposes, this really is limited just to 32-bit programs. You may assume any reference to "Windows" from here on includes all such versions: Windows XP, 2003, Vista, and Windows 7. As a case in point, the previous two editions of this book were developed using Windows 2000 and Windows XP, respectively, and the source code has required little or no changes in these last five years.

Windows programming can be simple or complex, depending on the type of program you are writing. If you have a development background with experience writing applications, then you probably have a good understanding of how complex a graphical user interface (GUI) can be to program. All it takes is a few menus, a few forms, and you will find yourself inundated with dozens (if not hundreds) of controls with which you must contend. Windows is very good as a multi-tasking operating system because it is message-driven. Object-oriented programming proponents would argue that Windows is an object-oriented operating system. In fact, it isn't. The latest version of Windows today functions almost exactly the same way that early versions of Windows (such as the old Windows 286, Windows 3.0, and so on) functioned, in that *messages* drive the operating system, not objects. The operating system is similar to the human nervous system, although not nearly as intricate or complicated. But if you simplify the human nervous system in an abstract way, you'll see impulses moving through the neurons in the human body from the senses to the brain, and from the brain to the muscles.

Advice

Although 64-bit computing is the wave of the future, it will not be as big of an issue for programmers as the 16-to-32 bit transition was, because the processors, operating systems, and development tools have been evolving in unison, with the result being that the transition will go largely unnoticed (as it has already).

Understanding Windows Messaging

Let's talk about a common scenario to help with the analogy of comparing an operating system to the human nervous system. Suppose that some *event* is detected by nerves on your skin. This event might be a change of temperature or something may have touched you. If you touch your left arm with a finger of your right hand, what happens? You "feel" the touch. Why? When you touch your arm, it is not your arm that is feeling the touch, but rather, your brain. The sense of "touch" is not felt by your arm, per se, but rather, your brain localizes the event so that you recognize the source of the touch. It is almost as if the neurons in your central nervous system are queried as to whether they participated in that "touch event." Your brain "sees" the neurons in the chain that relayed the touch message, so it is able to determine where the touch occurred on your arm. Now touch your arm, and move your finger back and forth on your arm. What do you sense is happening? It is not a constant "analog" measurement, because there are a discrete number of touch-sensitive neurons in your skin. The sense of motion is, in fact, digitally relayed to your brain. Now you might refute my claim here by saying that the sense of pressure is analog. We are getting into some abstract ideas at this point, but I would pose that the sense of pressure is relayed to your brain in discrete increments, not as a capacitive analog signal.

How is this subject related to Windows programming? The sense of touch is very similar to the way in which Windows messaging works. An external event, like a mouse click, causes a small electrical signal to pass from the mouse to the USB port into the system bus, which might be thought of as the nervous system of the computer. From there, the signal is picked up by the operating system (Windows) and a message is generated and passed to applications that are running (like your game). Your program, then, is like a conscious mind that reacts to that "sense of touch." The subconscious mind of the computer (the operating system that handles all of the logistics of processing events) "presented" this event to your program's awareness.

Advice

It seems that over time, our advanced information systems tend to mimic the natural world, and when we have finally built the ultimate supercomputer, it may end up resembling a human brain.

There is yet another issue at hand. We humans don't have two brains, after all. Remember my comment about technology mimicking biological brains? Well, most processor builders today are heading in the direction of incorporating multiple processor cores into a single silicon chip. Multi-core systems are already the norm today, rather than the exception (which was not the case when the first edition of this book was published in 2004!).

DirectX 9, 10, or 11?

DirectX 10 has already been available for two years at the time of this writing, and DirectX 11 is already in the early stages of testing. In fact, the DirectX SDK included on the CD-ROM contains one such early version of Direct3D 11. What does this mean for those of us who are still programming games with DirectX 9 (which this book focuses on)?

The reason for the continued widespread support for DirectX 9 is that it supports Windows XP, which is still the most widely used version of Windows (since the vast majority of individuals and businesses have not upgraded to Vista yet). DirectX 10 and later code will not run on Windows XP, while DirectX 9 code will run on any modern version of Windows—which accounts for the continued popularity of DirectX 9.

You can *continue* to write DirectX 9 code even when Windows 7 is officially launched with DirectX 11, because the DirectX SDK will continue to provide all of the header files, library files, and DLL files needed to compile and run DirectX 9, 10, and 11 programs for the foreseeable future.

Multi-Tasking

First and foremost, Windows is a *preemptive* multi-tasking operating system. This means that your PC can run many programs at the same time. Windows accomplishes this feat by running each program for a very short amount of time, counted in milliseconds, or thousandths of a second. This jumping from one program to another very quickly is called *time slicing*, and Windows handles time slicing by creating a virtual address space (a small "simulated" computer) for each program in memory. Each time Windows jumps to the next program, the state of the current program is stored so that it can be brought back again when it is that program's turn to receive some processor time. This includes processor register values and any data that might be overwritten by the next process. Then, when the program comes around again in the time-slicing scheme, these values are restored into the processor registers and program execution continues where it left off.

Advice

If this sounds like a wasteful use of processor cycles, you should be aware that during those few microseconds, the processor is able to run a few million instructions. Modern processors already run at the gigaflop level, able to easily crunch a billion math calculations in a short "time slice."

The Windows operating system might be thought of as having a central nervous system of its own—based on events. When you press a key, a message is created for that *keypress* event and circulated through the system until a program picks it up and uses it. I should clarify a point here, as I have brought up "circulation." Windows 3.0, 3.1, and 3.11 were *non-preemptive* operating systems that technically were just very advanced programs sitting on top of 16-bit MS-DOS. These early versions of Windows were more like MS-DOS shells than true operating systems, and, thus, were not able to truly "own" the entire computer system. You could write a program for Windows 3.x and have it completely take over the system, without freeing up any processor cycles for other programs. You could even lock up the entire operating system if you wanted to. Early Windows programs had to release control of the computer's resources in order to be "Windows Logo" certified (which was an important marketing issue at the time).

Windows 95 was the first 32-bit version of Windows and was a revolutionary step forward for this operating system family in that it was a *preemptive* operating system.

What this means is that the operating system has a very low-level core that manages the computer system, and no single program can take over the system, which was the case under Windows 3.x. *Preemptive* means that the operating system can preempt the functioning of a program, causing it to pause, and the operating system can then allow the program to start running again later. When you have many programs and processes (each with one or more threads) begging for processor time, this is called a time-slicing system, which is how Windows works. As you might imagine, having a multi-processor system is a real advantage when you are using an operating system such as this.

A multi-core Intel or AMD system is a great setup for a game developer. For one thing, SMP (symmetric multiprocessing) processors usually have more internal cache memory. The more processing power the better! While you may have had to shut down most running applications while playing or developing a game in the past, a modern multi-core system can easily handle many applications running at the same time while you are working on a game and you will not notice any drag on the system. Of course, a ton of memory helps too—at least 2GB of RAM for game development. While you're at it, buy the fastest memory chips your system can handle because speed is better than size when it comes to computer hardware!

Figure 1.1 shows an overview of how non-preemptive multi-tasking works. Note how each program receives control over the processor and must then explicitly

Non-Preemptive Multi-Tasking

Figure 1.1
Non-preemptive multi-tasking requires the voluntary release of control by each program. The O/S is very limited in control over applications.

Preemptive Multi-Tasking

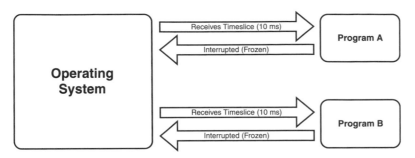

Figure 1.2
A preemptive multi-tasking O/S has full control over the system and allocates slices of time for each running process and thread.

release control in order for the computer system to function properly. Such programs must also be careful about using too much time; in essence, non-preemptive O/S programs must voluntarily share the processor.

Figure 1.2 shows how preemptive multi-tasking works. As you can see, the diagram is similar to Figure 1.1 (so it is easy to compare), but the O/S now controls everything and need not wait for the programs to "play nicely" and share processor time. The O/S will simply suspend a program after an allotted number of milliseconds of time-slice and then give the program more processor time after looping through all processes and threads running in the system.

Multi-Threading

Multi-threading is the process of breaking up a program into multiple, independent parts that might work together to accomplish a task (or that might perform completely independent tasks). This is not the same as multi-tasking on the system level. Multi-threading is sort of like multi-multi-tasking, where each program has running parts of its own, and those small program fragments are oblivious of the time-slicing system performed by the operating system. As far as your main Windows program and all of its threads are concerned, they all have complete control over the system and have no "sense" that the operating system is slicing up the time allotted to each thread or process. Therefore, multi-threading means that each program is capable of delegating processes to its own mini-programs. For instance, a chess program might create a thread to think ahead while the player is working on his next move. The "thought" thread would continue to update moves and counter-moves while waiting for the player. While this might just as easily be accomplished with a program loop that thinks while waiting for user input, the ability to delegate the process out to a thread might have significant benefits for a program.

Just as an example, you can create two threads in a Windows program and give each thread its own loop. As far as each thread is concerned, its loop runs endlessly and it runs extremely fast, without interruption. But at the system level, each thread is given a slice of processor time. Depending on the speed of the processor and operating system, a thread may be interrupted 50, 100, or even 1000 times per second, but will be oblivious to the interruption. (Imagine yourself falling asleep and being awakened many times during the night while trying to get some rest! Unlike a human, a computer does not notice!) Figure 1.3 illustrates the relationship between program, processes, and threads.

Advice

Multi-threaded programming is a fascinating subject, and worth your time to learn about! I covered this subject briefly in *Game Programming All In One, Third Edition* (ISBN 1-59863-289-2). I explained how to use the Posix Threads library which makes multi-threading a snap. That may be a good next step after you've finished this book. I've found that most beginners can learn the Allegro game library very quickly. If you're up for a bigger challenge, look for my new book on this subject titled *Multi-Threaded Game Engine Design* (ISBN 1-4354-5417-0)—but be prepared for a huge programming workout if you aren't already proficient with C++ and DirectX!

Multi-threading is very useful for game programming. The many tasks involved in a game loop might be delegated into separate threads that will execute independently, each one communicating with the main program. A thread might

Figure 1.3
A multi-threaded program might feature multi-threaded processes and independent threads.

be set up to handle screen updates automatically. All the program would have to do then is make sure the double buffer gets updated at a specified time with all of the objects on the screen, and the thread will do the work on a regular basis—perhaps even with timing built in so that the game will run at a uniform speed regardless of the processor. Most of the popular game engines are multi-threaded, meaning that they inherently support multiple processors. This is a boon for gamers who have forked over the additional cost for a multi-core system! What is even more useful is when a standalone game server (which is often provided with popular online games so that players can run their own games) supports multiple processors, because it takes a lot of processing power to handle large games with many players. A dual-processor game server is even more capable of handling a large allotment of players.

Advice

A double buffer is sort of a bitmap image in memory that you can use to draw the graphics for your game, and this image is then copied to the screen resulting in a very smoothly rendered display.

Event Handling

At this point, you might be asking yourself, "How does Windows keep track of so many programs running at the same time?" Windows handles the problem, first of all, by requiring that programs be event-driven. Secondly, Windows uses system-wide messages to communicate. Windows messages are small packets of data sent by the operating system to each running program with three primary features—window handle, instance identifier, and message type—telling that program that some event has occurred. The events will normally involve user input, such as a mouse click or key press, but might be from a communications port or a TCP/IP socket used by a networking library (which is used in multi-player games).

Each Windows program must check every message that comes in through the message handler to determine whether the message applies to that program. Messages that are not identified are sent along to the default message handler, which puts them back into the Windows messaging stream, so to speak. Think of messages as fish—when you catch a fish that is too small or that you don't like, you throw it back. But you keep the fish that you want. It is similar in the Windows event-driven architecture; if your program recognizes a message that it wants to keep, that message is taken out of the message stream and no other program will see it.

Once you have experimented with Windows programming and have learned to handle some Windows messages, you will see how it was designed for applications, not games. The trick is learning to "tap into" the Windows messaging system and inject your own code, such as a Direct3D initialization routine or a function call to refresh the screen. All of the actions in a game are handled through the Windows messaging system; it is your job to intercept and deal with messages that are relevant to your game. You will learn how to write a Windows program in the next chapter, and will learn more about Windows messaging in the next couple of chapters.

A Quick Overview of DirectX

I've covered a lot of information in a short amount of time on Windows theory, just to get to this point—where I can introduce you to DirectX. You've probably heard a lot about DirectX, because it is a buzzword that many people use in the industry, but that few in the mainstream truly understand. We're not going to begin writing any DirectX code just yet, but I do want you to see how it works with Windows. DirectX provides an interface to the low-level hardware interface of a Windows PC, providing a consistent and reliable set of functions for games that do not rely on the Windows API or GDI (which means DirectX is much faster). Figure 1.4 shows how DirectX works with the Windows API.

DirectX is closely integrated into Windows and will not work with any other O/S, as it relies on the basic libraries in the Windows API to function. Here is a rundown of the DirectX components:

- **Direct3D** is the rendering component that provides access to the video card and graphics processing unit (GPU) to render 2D and 3D graphics. This is the most important component.

- **DirectSound** is the obsolete audio component formerly used to play digital samples loaded from wave files, using its multi-channel audio mixer. It is still included for backward compatibility.

- **XACT** is the new audio system that supplements DirectSound, and is also used for audio in the XNA Game Studio SDK.

- **DirectInput** is the device input component used to access the peripherals such as the keyboard, mouse, and joystick, with support for unusual hardware such as flight sticks and steering wheels.

Figure 1.4
DirectX 9 works with the Windows API.

- **XInput** is a new component used to access an Xbox 360 controller connected to a Windows PC. Although most Windows users do not have one of these controllers plugged in, it is very popular with XNA Game Studio programmers.

- **DirectPlay** is the older networking component that is no longer supported but still included for backward compatibility.

Advice

XNA Game Studio is an SDK and plug-in for Visual Studio that makes it possible to program games for the Xbox 360 console, as well as for Windows. The latest version at the time of this writing is 3.1. XNA developers can publish their games on the XNA Creator's Club website and offer them for sale on Xbox Live Arcade.

What Is Direct3D?

Since Direct3D is the most important component of DirectX, let's focus on it for a moment. Direct3D handles all of the 2D and 3D rendering in a game. I'll teach you to use Direct3D beginning in Chapter 3. In later chapters, you will learn how to load a bitmap file into memory as a texture and then draw the texture (in 2D mode), as well as apply the texture when rendering a 3D object (called a mesh).

I have to admit, I'm a huge fan of 2D games, especially turn-based strategy games and classic arcade-style games like the older *Sid Meier's Civilization* series (although the latest incarnation—*Civilization Revolution* for Xbox 360 and Nintendo Wii—is fully realized in 3D). You can still program a 2D game using Direct3D, or use 2D bitmaps and sprites to enhance a 3D game. You will need to display information on the screen that must be done with a 2D font, so learning how to draw 2D graphics is a necessity. For the short term, a brief overview of 2D textures and sprites will help you to understand the Direct3D when we explore 3D programming later on. As a case in point, *Civilization Revolution* for Nintendo DS is a 2D game.

Just to keep things on track, let me reiterate an important goal: to develop an understanding of 2D and 3D graphics and the knowledge needed to create games. My intent is not to try to make you into an expert game programmer, just to give you enough information (and enthusiasm!) to take yourself to the next level and learn more about this subject. We will eventually get into 3D models, texturing, lighting, and all the other subjects needed to write a simple 3D game, but we will stick with the old-school fixed function pipeline—a phrase that means we will be doing 3D rendering without any vertex or pixel shaders (a program that runs on the GPU instead of the CPU). What I'm getting at is that I want you to have *fun* with the material, and not get bogged down in the details! Because the details of 3D game programming are huge and complex, the average beginner's eyes tend to glaze over when hearing about vertex buffers and texture coordinates. I can relate, because it takes time to build up to details like that when you're just getting started!

It is possible to just jump in and start writing Direct3D code at this point, but sooner or later you'll need to learn the basics of Windows programming and get some exposure to `WinMain` and the other Windows core functions, as this is at the core of a DirectX program.

The Basics of a Windows Program

Are you ready to get started writing Windows programs? Good! Now we will learn to write a real Windows program in C++. Every Windows program includes a function called `WinMain` at minimum. Most Windows programs also include a message handler function called WinProc that receives messages (such as key presses and mouse movement). If you were writing a full-blown Windows application (for instance, a commercial software product like *3ds Max* or *Microsoft Word*), then you would have a very large and complicated WinProc function in the program to handle the many program states and events. But in a DirectX program, you don't really have to mess with events because your main interest lies with the DirectX interfaces that provide their own functions for dealing with events. DirectX is mostly a *polled* SDK, in that you must ask for data rather than having it thrown at you (which is the case with WinProc). For instance, when you start learning about DirectInput, you'll find that keyboard and mouse input is mainly gathered by calling functions to see what values have changed.

Creating Your First Win32 Project

Every new project will be similar, so once you have learned to create a new project in Visual C++, then you'll be able to use the same strategy to create all the projects in the rest of the book. What is a project, you may ask? Well, a project is a file, really, that manages all the source code files in a program. All of the simple programs in this book will have a single source code file (at least until we build the game framework), but most real games have many source code files. You might have source code files for your Direct3D routines, DirectInput code, XACT code, and so on, and you'll also have the main code for the game itself. The project keeps track of all the source code files, and is managed from within the IDE of your compiler. For the sake of simplicity, rather than referring to Visual Studio 2005 or 2008 or a later version, I'll just use the general term "Visual C++."

Advice

Important! If you are new to Visual C++ and do not know how to download and install the software, let alone how to create a new project, please refer to Appendix A for complete instructions on how to set up the compiler. I have created this appendix to cut down on the amount of repeated information in each chapter. Rather than explain how to create each project separately, I will refer you to this appendix.

Let's create a new project in Visual C++. Open the File menu, choose New, Project, as shown in Figure 1.5. The version shown here is Visual C++ 2008, which is the latest version at the time of this writing.

Open the Visual C++ item in the list on the left, and then select Win32 to narrow down the types of project templates listed. The project template that you will want to choose is "Win32", which is what I have selected in Figure 1.6. Try not to

Figure 1.5
Opening the New Project dialog in Visual C++.

get lost in the list of project templates; stick to the "Win32" types to avoid confusion.

Next, while still in the New Project dialog, you will need to enter the name of your new project into the Name field near the bottom. In my dialog shown in Figure 1.7, you can see that I have entered the name of "HelloWorld" into this field. Do the same for your project name, then press the OK button to proceed.

Next up is the Application Wizard dialog. Click the Application Settings tab on the left to bring up the dialog shown in Figure 1.8. Note that from the choices, I've selected "Windows application" and "Empty project". Always create an "empty project" so that you can add your own files to the project, because the Application Wizard produces too many files by default that we don't need, and that just clutters our DirectX projects. This is the standard that I will use in this and all future projects.

Figure 1.6
Creating a new Win32 project.

Figure 1.7
Entering the project name for the new project.

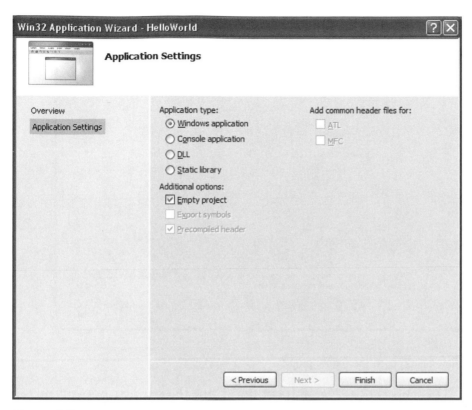

Figure 1.8
Choosing the settings for the new project using the Application Wizard.

Advice

Try not to let file extensions confuse you. All modern C++ compilers use the .cpp file extension, regardless of whether you are writing C or C++ code. For the sake of simplicity, I use the .cpp extension, although the trend in years past was to use the .c extension. Due to the way in which modern compilers work, it is just easier to use .cpp, because the .c extension causes some problems when compiling DirectX programs.

Now that you have a new project ready to go, let's take a look at a complete (but simple) Windows program, so you can better understand how it works. Since we haven't added a new file to the project yet, let's do that now.

If you have a completely blank project (as expected), you'll need to add a source file to the project. You can do so by opening the File menu and selecting New to bring up the New file dialog (the same dialog you used to create the new project). There are several other ways to add a new source file to the project as well. You can open the Project menu and select Add New Item, or you can right-click the project name in the Solution Explorer (the list of files on the right side of the

Figure 1.9
Adding a new file, main.cpp, to the empty project.

Visual C++ IDE) and choose the same option from the context pop-up menu. Look for the C++ Source File item in the list and give the file a name (I recommend main.cpp), as shown in Figure 1.9.

After you have added the new source file, the project will look something like that in Figure 1.10.

Here is the source code for the HelloWorld program. This is a complete Windows program! You see, Windows programming doesn't really have to be all that difficult when you strip out all the application stuff—like menus that aren't needed for writing games. This is an overly simplistic example, though, because this program only does one thing—displays a message box—and then quits.

```cpp
// Beginning Game Programming, 2nd Edition
// Chapter 1 - HelloWorld program
#include <windows.h>
int WINAPI WinMain(HINSTANCE hInstance, HINSTANCE hPrevInstance,
  LPSTR lpCmdLine, int nShowCmd)
{
  MessageBox(NULL, "Motoko Kusanagi has hacked your system!",
    "Public Security Section 9", MB_OK | MB_ICONEXCLAMATION);
}
```

Figure 1.10
The new main.cpp source file has been added to the project and is waiting for your source code.

This program simply displays a dialog box on the screen, shown in Figure 1.11. Let's compile and run the program so you can see for yourself. Press the F5 key now.

What happens? Oh, no, your first program results in a compiler error, even if you typed in the program exactly right! This is to be expected. Visual C++ is a large and complex piece of software which we need to learn to use. Figure 1.11 shows the error in the Output window.

Now let's resolve this error. It has to do with the character set, which can be either ANSI (8-bit) or Unicode (16-bit). Unicode is important for localization—a software engineering term that refers to converting the text in a program to other languages. Not all languages need Unicode characters, but some do—like Mandarin and Japanese. We could write all of our code to support Unicode character strings, with funky code that is not part of the C++ standard (like the

Figure 1.11
The compiler error in the Output window of our HelloWorld program.

infamous "L" character and TCHAR). But we want to write standards-compliant software, which means avoiding Microsoft funk as much as possible. Why? We are not concerned with compiling code for any operating system other than Windows, so what difference does it make if we use Unicode or not? While it's true that our DirectX code will only run on Windows systems, we may not always be using Visual C++ to compile that code! There are other compilers! I have used Turbo C++ and Dev-C++ to compile DirectX code on many an occasion, and prefer to keep my code as flexible and versatile as possible. That means not limiting my code with any unusual workarounds. Instead, let's convert the project to ANSI and ignore the whole Unicode issue altogether. Open the Project menu and choose the HelloWorld Properties option to bring up the Project Properties dialog.

After closing the dialog, try running the program again by pressing the F5 key. You should be rewarded with a message box. What is the most important thing

Figure 1.12
Changing the default character set used by the project to disable Unicode errors.

you should glean from this example? That `WinMain` does not *need* to be a big, complex hodge-podge of app code.

Advice

When you compile a program with Visual C++, the executable file is located in a folder called Debug (inside your project's folder).

Now that you've seen what a very simple Windows program looks like, let's delve a little further into the magical realm of Windows programming and learn to create a real window and draw stuff on it. Using `MessageBox` was a bit of a cheat!

Figure 1.13
Output from the HelloWorld program.

What you really want is your very own window, which you'll create next. In the tradition of climbing the learning curve, I'll expand this little example a bit and show you how to create a standard program window and draw on it in the next project. This is the next step before you will be ready to use Direct3D.

Understanding WinMain

As you have just learned, every Windows program has a function called WinMain. WinMain is the Windows equivalent of the main function in console C++ programs, and is the initial entry point for a Windows program. The most important function in your program will be WinMain, but after you have set up the messaging calls you will probably not come back to WinMain while working on other parts of the program.

WinMain hasn't changed much since 16-bit Windows 3.1, which dates back to 1992! WinMain is the boss, the foreman, and handles the top-level part of the program. The job of WinMain is to set up the program, and then to set up the main message loop for the program. This loop processes all of the messages received by the program. Windows sends these messages to every running program. Most of the messages will not be used by your program, and so the O/S doesn't even send some messages to your program. Usually, WinMain will send messages over to another function called WinProc, which works closely with WinMain to process user input and other messages. See Figure 1.14 for a comparison of WinMain and WinProc.

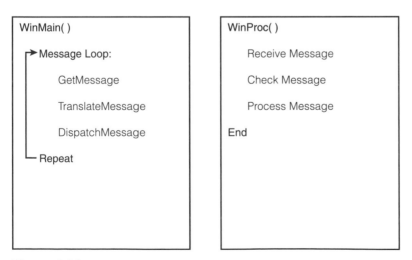

Figure 1.14
WinMain and WinProc work hand-in-hand to handle application events (such as painting the screen and responding to mouse clicks).

The WinMain Function Call

The function call of WinMain looks like this:

```
int WINAPI WinMain( HINSTANCE hInstance,
        HINSTANCE hPrevInstance,
        LPTSTR   lpCmdLine,
        int      nCmdShow )
```

Let's go over these parameters:

- **HINSTANCE hInstance.** The first parameter identifies the instance of the program being called, as a program may be run several times. The Windows architecture is such that program code actually runs in a single memory space to conserve memory, while program data and variables are stored in individual memory spaces. The hInstance parameter tells the program which instance is trying to run. For the first instance, you will want to initialize the program (covered later). But if the program is run multiple times in Windows, the general practice is to just kill the new instance (also covered later).

- **HINSTANCE hPrevInstance.** The second parameter identifies the previous instance of the program and is related to the first parameter. If hPrevInstance is NULL, then this is the first instance of the program. You will want to check the value of hPrevInstance before initializing the current instance. This is absolutely critical to game programming! You will never want to have two instances of your game running at the same time.

- **LPTSTR lpCmdLine.** The third parameter is a string that contains the command-line parameters passed to the program. This could be used to tell the program to use certain options, such as "debug," which might be used to dump program execution to a text file. Usually a Windows program will use a settings (INI) file for program parameters used for runtime. But there are many cases where you would use program parameters; an image viewer, for instance, will often be passed the name of a picture file to display.

- **int nCmdShow.** The last parameter specifies how the program window is to be displayed.

You might have noticed that WinMain returns a value with the words int WINAPI in front of the function call. This is also standard practice and goes back to Windows 3.x. A return value of zero indicates that the program never made it to the main loop and was terminated prematurely. Any non-zero value indicates success.

A Complete WinMain

Listed below is more of a standard version of WinMain that you will often see in app code. I will explain each part of the function following the code listing presented here:

```
int WINAPI WinMain(HINSTANCE hInstance,
        HINSTANCE hPrevInstance,
        LPSTR   lpCmdLine,
        int     nCmdShow)
{
  // declare variables
  MSG msg;

  // register the class
  MyRegisterClass(hInstance);

  // initialize application
  if (!InitInstance (hInstance, nCmdShow)) return FALSE;

  // main message loop
  while (GetMessage(&msg, NULL, 0, 0))
  {
    TranslateMessage(&msg);
    DispatchMessage(&msg);
  }
  return msg.wParam;
}
```

WinMain couldn't get much simpler than this, considering that the function processes the Windows messages for your program (I'll explain the new stuff shortly!). Even the simplest of graphics programs will need to process messages. Believe it or not, doing something as simple as printing "Hello World" on the screen requires that you wait for a message to come along for painting the screen. Infuriating, isn't it? Message handling does take some getting used to if you are used to just calling a function when you need something (like displaying text on the screen) done. Fortunately, we won't spend much time in the basics of Windows because soon I'll take you into the realm of DirectX. Once you have initialized Direct3D and have a game loop running, there's usually no need to go back and edit any of the code in WinMain.

Now let me explain what is going on inside WinMain in the following paragraphs. You are already familiar with the function call, so let's move along to the real code. The first section declares the variables that will be used within WinMain:

```
// declare variables
MSG msg;
```

The MSG variable is used by the GetMessage function later to retrieve the details of each Windows message. Next, the program is initialized with the following:

```
// register the class
MyRegisterClass(hInstance);

// initialize application
if (!InitInstance (hInstance, nCmdShow))
  return FALSE;
```

This code uses the hInstance variable passed to WinMain by Windows. The variable is then passed on to the InitInstance function. InitInstance is located further down in the program, and basically checks to see if the program is already running and then creates the main program window. I will go over the MyRegisterClass function shortly. Finally, let's look at the main loop that handles all of the messages in the program:

```
// main message loop
while (GetMessage(&msg, NULL, 0, 0))
{
  TranslateMessage(&msg);
  DispatchMessage(&msg);
}
```

The while loop in this part of WinMain will continue to run forever unless a message to kill the program comes along. The GetMessage function call looks like this:

```
BOOL GetMessage( LPMSG lpMsg,
        HWND hWnd,
        UINT wMsgFilterMin,
        UINT wMsgFilterMax )
```

Let's decipher the parameters:

- **LPMSG lpMsg.** This parameter is a long pointer to a MSG structure that handles the message information.

- **HWND hWnd.** The second parameter is a handle to a specific window's messages. If NULL is passed, then GetMessage will return all of the messages for the current instance of the program.

- **UINT wMsgFilterMin** and **UINT wMsgFilterMax.** These parameters tell GetMessage to return messages in a certain range. The GetMessage call is the most crucial line of code in the entire Windows program! Without this single line in WinMain, your program will be sensory-deprived, unable to respond to the world.

The two core lines of code within the GetMessage loop work to process the message returned by GetMessage. The Windows API Reference states that the TranslateMessage function is used to translate virtual-key messages into character messages, and then sent back through the Windows messaging system with DispatchMessage. These two functions will jointly set up the messages that you will expect to receive in WinProc (the window callback function) for your game window, such as WM_CREATE to create a window and WM_PAINT to draw the window. I will cover WinProc in the next chapter. If you feel confused about Windows messaging, don't worry about it, because this is just a precursor to working with DirectX; once you have written a Windows message loop, you will not need to deal with it again and can focus on your DirectX code. Now let's take a break for a moment and continue learning about WinMain in the next chapter.

What You Have Learned

In this chapter, you have learned the basics of Windows programming in preparation for DirectX coding! Here are the key points:

- You learned the basics of what makes Windows tick and how you might tap into the Windows system with your own programs.

- You learned some basic Windows programming concepts.

- You learned about the importance of `WinMain`.

- You wrote a simple Windows program that displayed text in a message box.

Review Questions

Here are some review questions that will help you to think outside the box and retain some of the information covered in this chapter. The answers to these questions can be found in the appendix.

1. What type of multi-tasking does Windows 2000 and XP use, preemptive or non-preemptive?

2. What compiler is primarily featured in this book (although the programs are compatible with any Windows compiler)?

3. What scheme does Windows use to notify programs that events have occurred?

4. What is the process called wherein a program uses multiple, independent parts that might work together to accomplish a task (or that might perform completely independent tasks)?

5. What is Direct3D?

6. What does the `hWnd` variable represent?

7. What does the `hDC` variable represent?

8. What is the main function in a Windows program called?

9. What is the name of the window event callback function?

10. What function is used to display a message inside a program window?

On Your Own

These exercises will challenge you to learn more about the subjects presented in this chapter and will help you to push yourself to see what you are capable of doing on your own.

Exercise 1. The HelloWorld program displays a simple message in a text box with an exclamation point icon. Modify the program so that it will display a question mark icon instead.

Exercise 2. Now modify the HelloWorld program so that it will display your name in the message box.

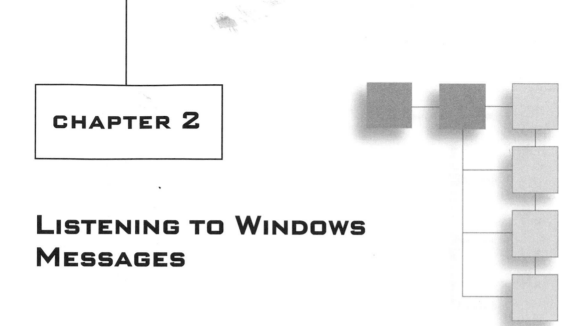

CHAPTER 2

LISTENING TO WINDOWS MESSAGES

The previous chapter briefly explained WinMain and WinProc while demonstrating a simple Windows program. This chapter studies Windows messaging and the main loop in more detail, going over a complete windowed program that displays something on the screen. You will learn how the window handle and device context work to produce output in a window. This will reinforce your grasp of the basic Windows programming model; it will also give you a glimpse of the Windows GDI (graphical device interface) and show you why it is better suited for applications rather than games (for which we have DirectX!). This chapter moves on to explore real-time game loops—specifically, how to get a real-time loop out of `WinMain`. You will learn a few new tricks in this chapter that will get the real-time loop going in preparation for DirectX in the next chapter. By the time you have finished this chapter, you will have learned how to write a game loop that will drive the rest of the code in the book. So pay attention!

Here's the gist of it:

- How to create a window.

- How to draw text on the window.

- How to draw pixels on the window.

- How the `WM_PAINT` event works in the `WinProc` callback function.

- How to create a real-time game loop.

- How to call other game-related functions from `WinMain`.

- How to use the `PeekMessage` function.

- How to draw bitmaps using the GDI.

Writing a Full-Blown Windows Program

Okay, let's use the new information you learned in the last chapter and use it to write a slightly more complicated program that actually creates a standard window and draws text and graphics on the window. The first program you wrote in the last chapter was lame! Now we'll work on some real Windows code. Sounds pretty simple, right? Well, it is! There's a lot of startup code when you need to draw on a window, so let's learn by example.

Create a new Win32 project called "WindowTest" and add a new main.cpp file to the project. I want to give you a complete listing for a more fully functional Windows program, after which we will reverse-engineer the program and explain each line of code in detail. See if you can figure out what's going on as you type in the program. If you would prefer to not type in the program, you can open the project from the CD-ROM in \sources\chapter02\WindowTest (and don't worry, I won't call you lazy).

Advice

Reminder: Please refer to Appendix A for complete instructions on how to set up Visual C++ to alleviate the need to explain how to create and configure new projects.

Figure 2.1
The WindowTest program.

Advice

Every chapter includes a ready-to-go Visual C++ project with an empty C++ file called main.cpp that you can quickly open and use for a new project. I recommend you make a copy of the sample project folder for each new project that you will create while working through a chapter.

After you have compiled and run the program, you should see output like that in Figure 2.1. Oops, not sure how to compile the program? No problem, let me show you. The easiest way is to press F5 to build and run the program (assuming there are no errors). If you want to just compile the code, press Ctrl+Shift+B (for build). This is the "professional" way to test your code—build first to ensure there are no errors before running with F5. You can also perform these actions from the Build menu and the Debug menu.

```
/**
    Beginning Game Programming, Third Edition
    Chapter 2
    WindowTest program
**/

#include <windows.h>
#include <iostream>
using namespace std;

const string ProgramTitle = "Hello Windows";
```

```
/**
 ** The window event callback function
 **/
LRESULT CALLBACK WinProc(HWND hWnd, UINT message, WPARAM wParam, LPARAM lParam)
{
    string text = "Hello Windows!";

    switch (message)
    {
        case WM_PAINT:
        {
            //get the dimensions of the window
            RECT rt;
            GetClientRect(hWnd, &rt);

            //start drawing on device context
            PAINTSTRUCT ps;
            HDC hdc = BeginPaint(hWnd, &ps);

            //draw some text
            DrawText(hdc, text.c_str(), text.length(), &rt, DT_CENTER);

            //draw 1000 random pixels
            for (int n=0; n<3000; n++)
            {
                int x = rand() % (rt.right - rt.left);
                int y = rand() % (rt.bottom - rt.top);
                COLORREF c = RGB(rand()%256, rand()%256, rand()%256);
                SetPixel(hdc, x, y, c);
            }

            //stop drawing
            EndPaint(hWnd, &ps);
        }
        break;

        case WM_DESTROY:
            PostQuitMessage(0);
            break;
    }
    return DefWindowProc(hWnd, message, wParam, lParam);
}
```

```
/**
 ** Helper function to set up the window properties
 **/
ATOM MyRegisterClass(HINSTANCE hInstance)
{
    //set the new window's properties
    WNDCLASSEX wc;
    wc.cbSize = sizeof(WNDCLASSEX);
    wc.style         = CS_HREDRAW | CS_VREDRAW;
    wc.lpfnWndProc   = (WNDPROC)WinProc;
    wc.cbClsExtra    = 0;
    wc.cbWndExtra    = 0;
    wc.hInstance     = hInstance;
    wc.hIcon         = NULL;
    wc.hCursor       = LoadCursor(NULL, IDC_ARROW);
    wc.hbrBackground = (HBRUSH)GetStockObject(WHITE_BRUSH);
    wc.lpszMenuName  = NULL;
    wc.lpszClassName = ProgramTitle.c_str();
    wc.hIconSm       = NULL;
    return RegisterClassEx(&wc);
}


/**
 ** Helper function to create the window and refresh it
 **/
bool InitInstance(HINSTANCE hInstance, int nCmdShow)
{
    //create a new window
    HWND hWnd = CreateWindow(
        ProgramTitle.c_str(),        //window class
        ProgramTitle.c_str(),        //title bar
        WS_OVERLAPPEDWINDOW,         //window style
        CW_USEDEFAULT,CW_USEDEFAULT, //position of window
        640, 480,                    //dimensions of the window
        NULL,                        //parent window (not used)
        NULL,                          //menu (not used)
        hInstance,                   //application instance
        NULL);                       //window parameters (not used)

    //was there an error creating the window?
    if (hWnd == 0) return 0;
```

```
//display the window
ShowWindow(hWnd, nCmdShow);
UpdateWindow(hWnd);

return 1;
}




/**
 ** Entry point for a Windows program
 **/
int WINAPI WinMain(HINSTANCE hInstance,
                   HINSTANCE hPrevInstance,
                   LPSTR     lpCmdLine,
                   int       nCmdShow)
{
    //create the window
    MyRegisterClass(hInstance);
    if (!InitInstance (hInstance, nCmdShow)) return 0;

    // main message loop
    MSG msg;
    while (GetMessage(&msg, NULL, 0, 0))
    {
        TranslateMessage(&msg);
        DispatchMessage(&msg);
    }
    return msg.wParam;
}
```

Okay, well that's the complete listing for the WindowText program, your first complete Windows program that features a standard program window. Now let's reverse-engineer it and see what makes a Windows program tick, shall we?

Understanding InitInstance

InitInstance is the first function called by WinMain to set up the program. InitInstance basically just creates the program window. This code could be just inserted into WinMain, but it is more convenient to have it in a separate function (this has something to do with dealing with multiple instances, when you run a program more than once). Note that InitInstance is not a primary Windows function like WinMain, but simply a "helper" function to which you could give a different name if you wished. The instance handle is a global variable used in the program to keep track of the main instance. I will show you what the function call looks like and what a typical InitInstance should do. You shouldn't treat this as the law, though, because it's just a standard practice, not a requirement.

The InitInstance Function Call

The function call for InitInstance looks like this:

```
bool InitInstance( HINSTANCE hInstance,
                   int       nCmdShow )
```

Let's go over the parameters here:

- **HINSTANCE hInstance.** The first parameter is passed by WinMain with the program instance that it receives from Windows. InitInstance will check this with the global instance to see if the new instance needs to be killed (the usual procedure in Windows). When this happens, the main instance of the program is set as the foreground window. To the user, it will seem as if running the program again just brought the original instance forward.

- **int nCmdShow.** The second parameter is passed to InitInstance by WinMain, which receives the parameter from Windows. The most common values for this parameter include SW_HIDE and SW_SHOW, and are often sent by Windows based on events in the operating system (such as a power down).

The InitInstance function returns a bool value, which is either 1 (true) or 0 (false), and simply tells WinMain whether startup succeeded or failed. Note that WinMain does not send InitInstance any of the command-line parameters. If you want to process the lpCmdLine string, then you can either create a new function to handle it or just process the parameters inside WinMain, which is how it is usually done.

The Structure of InitInstance

Quite often in application programming it is recommended that you use a resource table for string handling. Resource strings are really a matter of preference (and I, for one, do not use them). There is the possibility that you will want to port the text in your games to another language, and this is where storing strings as resources will come in handy. In general practice, however, it's not commonly used. The code to display a simple message from a resource causes a program to look up every string used, which slows down the program and adds a lot of clutter to the code, especially from the point of view of a beginner.

The InitInstance function is pretty simple, as shown here. I will explain each section of the function after the code listing that follows:

```
bool InitInstance(HINSTANCE hInstance, int nCmdShow)
{
    //create a new window
    HWND hWnd = CreateWindow(
        ProgramTitle.c_str(),         //window class
        ProgramTitle.c_str(),         //title bar
        WS_OVERLAPPEDWINDOW,          //window style
        CW_USEDEFAULT,CW_USEDEFAULT, //position of window
        640, 480,                     //dimensions of the window
        NULL,                         //parent window (not used)
        NULL,                          //menu (not used)
        hInstance,                    //application instance
        NULL);                        //window parameters (not used)


    //was there an error creating the window?
    if (hWnd == 0) return 0;

    //display the window
    ShowWindow(hWnd, nCmdShow);
    UpdateWindow(hWnd);

    return 1;
}
```

Note that until this section of code, there was actually no user interface for the program at all! The main window that is created with the CreateWindow function becomes the window used by your program. The whole point of InitInstance is to create the new window needed by this application and display it. The list of parameters for CreateWindow includes comments that describe what each parameter does. After the window has been created (and verified), the last few lines of code are used to actually display the newly created window:

```
ShowWindow(hWnd, nCmdShow);
UpdateWindow(hWnd);
```

The hWnd value is passed to these functions by the CreateWindow function. At the point of creation, the window existed in Windows but was not yet visible.

UpdateWindow tells the new window to draw itself by sending a WM_PAINT message to the window handler. Oddly enough, the program talks to itself quite often in this manner; this is common in Windows programming. The final line in InitInstance returns a value of 1 (true) back to WinMain:

```
return 1;
```

If you recall, WinMain took this return value very seriously! If InitInstance doesn't like something that is going on, WinMain will end the program:

```
if (!InitInstance (hInstance, nCmdShow)) return 0;
```

Returning a value from within WinMain, whether it is 1 (true) or 0 (false), will terminate the program immediately. If InitInstance returns a value of 1, recall that WinMain will then go into the message handling while loop, and the program will start to run.

Understanding MyRegisterClass

MyRegisterClass is a very simple function that sets up the values for the main window class used by your program. The code in MyRegisterClass could have easily been placed inside WinMain. In fact, all of this stuff could have been crammed into WinMain and Windows would not have complained. But it makes the program a bit easier to understand when the initialization code for a Windows program is segregated into recognizable (and standard) helper functions, at least at the learning stage. WinMain calls InitInstance and sets up the program window by calling MyRegisterClass. This is another optional helper function that is not required (although you must insert the code *somewhere*, so why not just use it?). You also may rename the function if you want, and Windows won't mind.

The MyRegisterClass Function Call

MyRegisterClass is passed two parameters by InitInstance so that it can set up the window class settings:

```
ATOM MyRegisterClass( HINSTANCE hInstance )
```

You are already familiar with both of these parameters. hInstance is the very same instance passed to InitInstance by WinMain. This variable gets around! As you recall, hInstance stores the current instance of the running program, and is copied into a global variable in InitInstance. The second parameter is easy enough to follow, as it was set up in InitInstance as a char * with an initial window class name (in this case, "Hello World"). Recall also that this can be a Unicode string.

Advice

The *ATOM* data type returned by `MyRegisterClass` is defined as a *WORD*, which is further defined as an *unsigned short* in one of the Windows header files. Why not just use *unsigned short* in the first place? Beats me. You can if you want! I'll bet no one at Microsoft even remembers where this *ATOM* thing came from.

The Point of MyRegisterClass

What's the point of this function? `MyRegisterClass()` is listed below again for reference. I will explain the function in detail following the code listing. These properties are pretty standard fare for a Windows program. The reason why I don't care very much is that we will usurp the window when DirectX takes over. So, who cares what special properties the window uses when it's destined to be soon overrun with hardware polygons? But, at this early stage, it's important to cover all the bases. I learned Windows programming from the master, Charles Petzold. Now, in an indirect way, *so are you*!

```
ATOM MyRegisterClass(HINSTANCE hInstance)
{
    //set the new window's properties
    WNDCLASSEX wc;
    wc.cbSize = sizeof(WNDCLASSEX);
    wc.style         = CS_HREDRAW | CS_VREDRAW;
    wc.lpfnWndProc   = (WNDPROC)WinProc;
    wc.cbClsExtra    = 0;
    wc.cbWndExtra    = 0;
    wc.hInstance     = hInstance;
    wc.hIcon         = NULL;
    wc.hCursor       = LoadCursor(NULL, IDC_ARROW);
    wc.hbrBackground = (HBRUSH)GetStockObject(WHITE_BRUSH);
    wc.lpszMenuName  = NULL;
    wc.lpszClassName = ProgramTitle.c_str();
    wc.hIconSm       = NULL;
    return RegisterClassEx(&wc);
}
```

First, `MyRegisterClass` defines a new variable, `wc`, of type `WNDCLASS`. Each member of the structure is defined in `MyRegisterClass` in order, so there is no need to list the struct.

The window style, wc.style, is set to CS_HREDRAW | CS_VREDRAW. The pipe symbol is a method for combining bits. The CS_HREDRAW value causes the program window to be completely redrawn if a movement or size adjustment changes the width. Likewise, CS_VREDRAW causes the window to be completely redrawn when the height is adjusted.

The variable, wc.lpfnWinProc, requires a little more explanation, as it is not simply a variable, but a long pointer to a callback function. This is of great importance, as without this value setting, messages will not be delivered to the program window (hWnd). The callback window procedure is automatically called when a Windows message comes along with that hWnd value. This applies to all messages, including user input and window repaint. Any button presses, screen updates, or other events will go through this callback procedure. You may give this function any name you like, such as BigBadGameWindowProc, as long as it has a return value of LRESULT CALLBACK and the appropriate parameters.

The struct variables wc.cbClsExtra and wc.cbWndExtra should be set to zero most of the time. These values just add extra bytes of memory to a window procedure, and you really do not need to use them.

wc.hInstance is set to the hInstance parameter passed to MyRegisterClass. The main window needs to know what instance it is using. If you really want to confuse your program, set each new instance to point to the same program window. Now that would be funny! This should never happen because new instances of your game should be killed rather than being allowed to run.

wc.hIcon and wc.hCursor are pretty self-explanatory. The LoadIcon function is normally used to load an icon image from a resource, and the MAKEINTRESOURCE macro returns a string value for the resource identifier. This macro is not something that is commonly used for a game (unless the game needs to run in a window).

wc.hbrBackground is set to the handle for a brush used for drawing the background of the program window. The stock object, WHITE_BRUSH, is used by default. This may be a bitmap image, a custom brush, or any other color.

wc.lpszMenuName is set to the name of the program menu, also a resource. I will not be using menus in the sample programs in this book.

wc.lpszClassName is set to the szWindowClass parameter passed to MyRegisterClass. This gives the window a specific class name and is used for message handling along with hWnd.

Finally, MyRegisterClass calls the RegisterClassEx function. This function is passed the WNDCLASS variable, wc, that was set up with the window details. A return value of zero indicates failure. If the window is successfully registered with Windows, the value will be passed back to InitInstance.

Whew—how about that to rack your brain?! I don't expect you to remember all of this information right now, but it is always a good idea as a game programmer to understand how everything works so you can get the most out of the hardware you're working on.

Advice

The code in the InitInstance and MyRegisterClass functions does not *absolutely* need to be in separate functions. We could just put this code directly in WinMain, which is exactly what we will do in later chapters. At this point, it's helpful to understand Windows programming in small stages.

Exposing the Secrets of WinProc

WinProc is the window callback procedure that Windows uses to communicate events to your program. A callback function is a function that gets called back. (I'll bet you already figured that out for yourself.) Recall that MyRegisterClass set up the WNDCLASS struct that was passed to RegisterClassEx. Once the class is registered, the window can then be created and displayed on the screen. One of the fields in the struct, lpfnWinProc, is set to the name of a window callback procedure, typically called WinProc. This function will handle all of the messages sent to the main program window. As a result, WinProc will typically be the longest function in the main program source code file. Figure 2.2 shows how WinProc handles event messages.

The WinProc Function Call

The window callback function looks like this:

```
LRESULT CALLBACK WinProc( HWND hWnd,
                          UINT message,
                          WPARAM wParam,
                          LPARAM lParam )
```

Program Event Handler

Figure 2.2
The WinProc callback function handles events related to the application.

You will want to get to know this function, because it is the key to initializing Direct3D. The parameters are simple and straightforward, and represent the real "engine" of a windows program. Recall that this information was retrieved earlier by the GetMessage function in WinMain. Do not confuse InitInstance with WinProc, though. InitInstance is only run once to set the options, after which WinProc takes over, receiving and handling messages.

Let's take a look at the parameters for WinProc:

- **HWND hWnd.** The first parameter is the window handle. Typically in a game, you will create a new handle to a device context, known as a hDC, using the hWnd as a parameter. Before DirectX came along, the window handle had to be retained since it was used any time a window or control was referenced. In a DirectX program, the window handle is only used to create the window initially.

- **UINT message.** The second parameter is the message that is being sent to the window callback procedure. The message could be anything, and you might not even need to use it. For this reason, there is a way to pass the message along to the default message handler (discussed in the next section).

- **WPARAM wParam** and **LPARAM lParam.** The last two parameters are the high and low bit value parameters passed along with certain command messages. I'll explain this in the next section.

The Big WinProc Secret

One goal of the helper functions developed in upcoming chapters is to help with things like initialization and message handling in WinProc. The functions in our game library will handle the window messages in a separate source code file to segregate the Windows core code from your game code (which makes it easier to use).

Here is a simple version of a window callback procedure, with an explanation following:

```
LRESULT CALLBACK WinProc(HWND hWnd, UINT message, WPARAM wParam, LPARAM lParam)
{
    string text = "Hello Windows!";
    switch (message)
    {
        case WM_PAINT:
        {
            //get the dimensions of the window
            RECT rt;
            GetClientRect(hWnd, &rt);

            //start drawing on device context
            PAINTSTRUCT ps;
            HDC hdc = BeginPaint(hWnd, &ps);

            //draw some text
            DrawText(hdc, text.c_str(), text.length(), &rt, DT_CENTER);

            //draw 1000 random pixels
            for (int n=0; n<3000; n++)
            {
                int x = rand() % (rt.right - rt.left);
                int y = rand() % (rt.bottom - rt.top);
                COLORREF c = RGB(rand()%256, rand()%256, rand()%256);
                SetPixel(hdc, x, y, c);
            }

            //stop drawing
            EndPaint(hWnd, &ps);
        }
        break;
```

```
        case WM_DESTROY:
            PostQuitMessage(0);
            break;
    }
    return DefWindowProc(hWnd, message, wParam, lParam);
}
```

As you are already familiar with the parameters, I'll get right down to business. This function can be broken down into two main parts, the declaration and the `switch` statement, which is like a large nested `if` statement. Within the `switch` statement, there are also two main parts, case statements for a command message and for regular messages. A command will use the last two parameters of `WinProc`, `wParam`, and `lParam`, while regular messages usually do not need the parameters.

The `PAINTSTRUCT` variable, `ps`, is used in the `WM_PAINT` message handler to start and stop a screen update, sort of like unlocking and then locking the device context while making updates (so the screen is not garbled in the process). The variable, `hdc`, is also used in the `WM_PAINT` message handler to retrieve the device context of the program's window. The other variables are used to display the message on the screen (`szHello`) and draw pixels on the window (`x`, `y`, `n`, and `c`).

Following the variable declarations is the `switch(message)` statement. This is basically an easy way to handle multiple messages, and is far better than using nested `if` statements. `switch` is far better able to handle a large number of conditional tests, which is why it is used in `WinProc` to check the messages.

Let me explain `WM_DESTROY` first. The `WM_DESTROY` message identifier tells the window that it is time to shut down; your program should gracefully close down by removing objects from memory and then call the `PostQuitMessage` function to end the program. When you take the next step and start writing Direct3D code, this will be the only message of concern, as `WM_PAINT` is not needed in a Direct3D program.

Okay, now back to the first message identifier, `WM_PAINT`. This is definitely the most interesting message for game programming because this is where the window updates are handled. Take a look at the code for `WM_PAINT` again:

```
//get the dimensions of the window
GetClientRect(hWnd, &rt);

//start drawing on device context
hdc = BeginPaint(hWnd, &ps);
```

```
//draw some text
DrawText(hdc, text.c_str(), text.length(), &rt, DT_CENTER);

//draw 1000 random pixels
for (n=0; n<3000; n++)
{
    x = rand() % (rt.right - rt.left);
    y = rand() % (rt.bottom - rt.top);
    c = RGB(rand()%256, rand()%256, rand()%256);
    SetPixel(hdc, x, y, c);
}

//stop drawing
EndPaint(hWnd, &ps);
break;
```

The BeginPaint function is called to lock the device context for an update (using the window handle and PAINTSTRUCT variables). The call to GetClientRect retrieves the program window's rectangular area into a RECT variable. This is used by DrawText to center the message in the window. Note that BeginPaint returns the device context for the program window. This is necessary at every refresh because, although it is uncommon, the device context is not guaranteed to be constant while the program is running (for instance, imagine that memory runs low and your program is filed away into virtual memory and then retrieved again—such an event would almost certainly generate a new device context).

The only line that actually does something to the user interface is the third line, which calls DrawText. This function displays a message at the destination device context. The DT_CENTER parameter at the end tells DrawText to center the message at the top center of the passed rectangle. Of course, there is also the section of code that draws pixels on the screen. Did you know that if you resize the window, all the pixels will be redrawn? Go ahead and try it! Pretty cool, huh? That demonstrates WM_PAINT perfectly: it is called when the window needs to be redrawn. If you resize the window, multiple calls to WM_PAINT occur, each time with a different rectangle (returned by GetClientRect).

The last line of the paint message handler calls EndPaint to shut down the graphics system for that iteration of the message handler.

Advice

WM_PAINT is not called continuously, as in a real-time loop, but only when the window must be redrawn. Therefore, WM_PAINT is not a suitable place to insert the screen refresh code for a game. Instead, as you will learn in the next chapter, you must modify the loop in WinMain to have code run in a real-time loop.

What Is a Game Loop?

There's a lot more to Windows programming than we will cover in these pages but we're focusing on just the limited code needed to get DirectX fired up. A "real" Windows application would have a menu, a status bar, a tool bar, and dialogs— which is why your average Windows programming book tends to be so large. I want to focus on game creation rather than spending many pages on the logistics of the operating system. What I'd really like to do is get away from the Windows code and come up with just a simple, run-of-the-mill main function, which is standard in C++ programs (but which is missing from Windows programs, which use WinMain).

Advice

See Appendix B for recommended books on Windows programming.

One way to do this is to put all of the basic Windows code (including WinMain) inside one source code file (such as winmain.cpp) and then use another source code file (such as game.cpp) just for the game. Then, it would be a simple matter to call some sort of main function from within WinMain and your "game code" will start running right after the program window is created. This is actually a standard practice on many systems and libraries, abstracting away the operating system and presenting the programmer with a standard interface. One such library is Allegro, a cross-platform game library available for Windows, Linux, Mac, and Unix systems. If you write a program that uses Allegro, then your program can be compiled on any of these systems without modification! This brings "porting" down to a manageable level, because it requires little effort to re-compile a program for Linux after it has been developed for Windows (and vice versa). I don't really want to move in that direction here, but it is a good example of how beneficial it is to abstract your code as much as possible.

Advice

If you want to learn more about the Allegro game library, see Appendix B for information about a cutting-edge book on the subject!

The Old WinMain

Here's the version of WinMain that we have been using so far:

```
int WINAPI WinMain(HINSTANCE hInstance,
                   HINSTANCE hPrevInstance,
                   LPSTR     lpCmdLine,
                   int       nCmdShow)
{
    MSG msg;
    MyRegisterClass(hInstance);
    if (!InitInstance (hInstance, nCmdShow))
        return FALSE;

    while (GetMessage(&msg, NULL, 0, 0))
    {
        TranslateMessage(&msg);
        DispatchMessage(&msg);
    }
    return msg.wParam;
}
```

There's just one problem with this version of WinMain: it doesn't have a continuous loop, just a limited loop that processes any pending messages and then exits. (See the highlighted "while" line for reference.)

The Need for Continuity

When you have sprites or 3D models animating on the screen, with enemy characters moving around and with guns and explosions and thermonuclear detonations in the background, you need things to keep moving regardless of Windows messages! In short, listed above is a stodgy, inanimate version of WinMain that is totally unsuitable for a game. You need something that keeps on running regardless of whether there are event messages coming in. The key to creating a real-time loop that keeps running all of the time regardless of what Windows is doing is modifying the while loop in WinMain.

First of all, the while loop is conditional upon a message being present, while a game should keep running through the loop regardless of whether there's a message or not. This definitely needs to be changed! See Figure 2.3 for an illustration of the current WinMain.

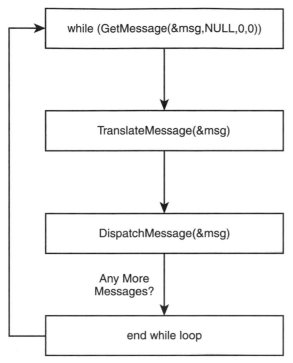

Figure 2.3
The standard `WinMain` is not friendly to a real-time game loop.

The Real-Time Terminator

Notice how the main loop terminates if there are no messages, but will keep on processing any messages that *are* present. What would happen if the main game loop were called from this version of `WinMain`? Well, once in a while the game loop would execute and things would be updated on the screen, but more often it would do nothing at all. Why is that? Because this is an event-driven `while` loop, and we need a common, run-of-the-mill *procedural* `while` loop that keeps going, and going, and going… regardless of what's happening. A real-time game loop has to keep running non-stop until the game ends. And in case you were wondering, I'll show you how to create a consistent, regular frame rate in the next chapter. Our goal at this point is to make things run as blindingly fast as possible, and then worry about timing later. Always work on getting something to work first, and then optimize or clean it up it later (if you have time).

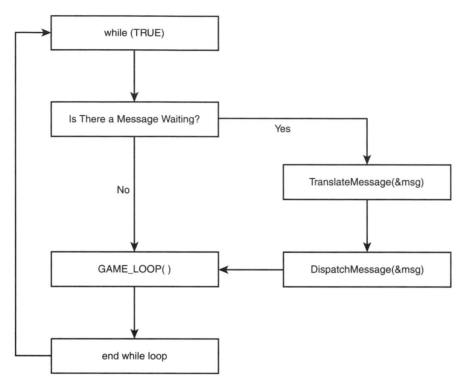

Figure 2.4
The newly modified WinMain is much more friendly to a real-time game loop.

Now, let's look at another illustration, in Figure 2.4, that shows a new version of WinMain, only this time it features a real-time game loop that doesn't just loop through the events but keeps on looping regardless of the events.

WinMain and Looping

The key to making a real-time loop is modifying the while loop in WinMain so that it runs indefinitely, and then check for messages *inside* the while loop. By indefinitely, I mean that the loop will keep running forever unless something interrupts the loop and causes it to exit (by calling exit or return inside the loop). In addition to using an endless loop, there's an alternative to calling the GetMessage function to detect event messages coming in. The alternate function is called PeekMessage. As the name implies, this function can look at incoming messages without necessarily retrieving them out of the message queue.

Now, as you don't want the message queue to just pile up (it will probably crash your program eventually), you want to use PeekMessage in place of GetMessage, regardless of whether there are messages or not. If there are messages, fine, go ahead and process them. Otherwise, just return control to the next line of code. As it turns out, GetMessage is not very polite, and doesn't let us keep the game loop going unless a message is actually sitting in the message queue to be processed. PeekMessage, on the other hand, is polite and will just pass control on to the next statement if no message is waiting.

Time to Take a Peek

Let's take a look at the format of the PeekMessage function:

```
BOOL PeekMessage(
    LPMSG lpMsg,              //pointer to message struct
    HWND hWnd,               //window handle
    UINT wMsgFilterMin,      //first message
    UINT wMsgFilterMax,      //last message
    UINT wRemoveMsg);        //removal flag
```

Now for a rundown on the parameters:

- **LPMSG lpMsg.** This parameter is a pointer to the message structure that describes the message (type, parameters, and so on).

- **HWND hWnd.** This is a handle to the window that is associated with the event.

- **UINT wMsgFilterMin.** This is the first message that has been received.

- **UINT wMsgFilterMax.** This is the last message that has been received.

- **UINT wRemoveMsg.** This is a flag that determines how the message will be handled after it has been read. This can be PM_NOREMOVE to leave the message in the message queue, or PM_REMOVE to remove the message from the queue after it has been read.

Plugging PeekMessage into WinMain

Okay, now let's make use of PeekMessage so that you can see how this all fits in with writing a game. Here's a new version of the main loop in WinMain with the new PeekMessage function in place (along with a few extra lines that I'll explain shortly).

```
bool gameover = false;
while (!gameover)
{
    if (PeekMessage(&msg, NULL, 0, 0, PM_REMOVE))
    {
```

```
        //handle any event messages
        TranslateMessage(&msg);
        DispatchMessage(&msg);
    }

    //process game loop
    Game_Run();
}
```

In this new version of the while loop you'll notice that PeekMessage is now called instead of GetMessage, and you'll recognize the PM_REMOVE parameter, which causes any event messages to be pulled out of the queue and processed. In actuality, there are really no messages coming in to a DirectX program (except perhaps WM_QUIT) because most of the processing takes place in the DirectX libraries.

Take a look at the if statement that looks for the WM_QUIT message. This is really the only case that causes the while loop to exit; otherwise, it keeps on running indefinitely.

So, suppose you now have a game loop. What can you do with it? I sneaked in an extra line of code that should have caught your eye, as it is called Game_Run. This function is not part of Windows; in fact, it doesn't even exist yet. You're going to write this function yourself shortly! It will also make more sense in the next chapter when you finally get a chance to start digging into DirectX code.

That said, let's take a look at the finished version of WinMain:

```
int WINAPI WinMain(HINSTANCE hInstance,
                   HINSTANCE hPrevInstance,
                   LPSTR     lpCmdLine,
                   int       nCmdShow)
{
    MyRegisterClass(hInstance);
    if (!InitInstance(hInstance, nCmdShow)) return 0;

    //initialize the game
    if (!Game_Init()) return 0;

    // main message loop
    bool gameover = false;
    while (!gameover)
    {
```

```
            MSG msg;
            if (PeekMessage(&msg, NULL, 0, 0, PM_REMOVE))
            {


                //decode and pass messages on to WndProc
                TranslateMessage(&msg);
                DispatchMessage(&msg);
            }

            //process game loop
            Game_Run();
        }
        //do cleanup
        Game_End();

        //end program
        return msg.wParam;
}
```

Okay, I admit it: I skipped ahead a little and sneaked a few new things in without warning. What I'm talking about are the new unknown functions called `Game_Init`, `Game_Run`, and `Game_End`. Now, don't get upset—I'm not going to make a habit of unceremoniously dropping new things on you without warning or explanation. But sometimes I think it's interesting to show how something works before explaining it fully in advance. In this case, what I'm doing is planning ahead a little.

State-Driven Games

This is actually one of those annoying sources of debate among die-hard game programmers. Some argue that a game should be state-driven from the start, and all function calls should be abstracted in the extreme so that code is portable to other platforms. For instance, some people write code wherein all the Windows code is hidden away, and they'll then have a similar Mac or Linux version, at which point it's possible to port much of the game to those platforms without too much difficulty.

I'm going to delve into this a *little* just because it's such a good habit to develop! Even while being stressed out over getting a game finished and pounding out code for 16 hours at a time, if you are a true professional, you'll manage that while also sparing some neurons for higher-level things like writing clean code. I've found that the cleanest code is that which will compile with more than one compiler.

For example, all—and I mean *all*—of the code in this book can be compiled with the freeware compiler Dev-C++ by Bloodshed Software using the DirectX Devpack. Using the GCC compiler used by Dev-C++ helps you to write better code since the code must conform to the C++ standard.

The GameLoop Project

In order to show you how this discussion of real-time programming applies, I'm going to have you create a new project that includes the new version of `WinMain` and all these new functions that I've added to the code listing.

Go ahead and create a new Win32 project like usual (see Appendix A if you need help with this). Name the new project GameLoop, as shown in Figure 2.5. Next, open the File menu, select New to bring up the New dialog. Select C++ Source File from the list of available files to add to the project. (Remember to ignore the C++ part and name your file with a .c extension.) Name the new file winmain.cpp and click OK to add the file to your new project, as shown in Figure 2.6. As an option, you can also load the GameLoop project from the CD-ROM.

Source Code for the GameLoop Program

The code I will present here will be the basis for all of the programs that will follow, with only very few changes to come. You might notice quite a few minor improvements from the similar code listing presented in the last chapter. Go ahead and open the winmain.cpp file in the GameLoop project and type in the following code listing. I'll go over it shortly.

Figure 2.5
Creating a new Win32 project called GameLoop.

Figure 2.6
Adding the winmain.cpp file to the project.

```cpp
/**
    Beginning Game Programming, Third Edition
    Chapter 2
    GameLoop project
**/

#include <windows.h>
#include <iostream>
#include <time.h>
using namespace std;

const string APPTITLE = "Game Loop";
HWND window;
HDC device;
bool gameover = false;

/**
 ** Loads and draws a bitmap from a file and then frees the memory
 **/
void DrawBitmap(char *filename, int x, int y)
{
    //load the bitmap image
```

```
    HBITMAP image = (HBITMAP)LoadImage(0,"c.bmp",IMAGE_BITMAP,0,0,
    LR_LOADFROMFILE);

    //read the bitmap's properties
    BITMAP bm;
    GetObject(image, sizeof(BITMAP), &bm);

    //create a device context for the bitmap
    HDC hdcImage = CreateCompatibleDC(device);
    SelectObject(hdcImage, image);

    //draw the bitmap to the window (bit block transfer)
    BitBlt(
        device,                     //destination device context
        x, y,                       //x,y location on destination
        bm.bmWidth, bm.bmHeight, //width,height of source bitmap
        hdcImage,                   //source bitmap device context
        0, 0,                       //start x,y on source bitmap
        SRCCOPY);                   //blit method

    //delete the device context and bitmap
    DeleteDC(hdcImage);
    DeleteObject((HBITMAP)image);
}

/**
 ** Startup and loading code goes here
 **/
bool Game_Init()
{
    //start up the random number generator
    srand(time(NULL));

    return 1;
}

/**
 ** Update function called from inside game loop
 **/
void Game_Run()
{
    if (gameover == true) return;
```

```
    //get the drawing surface
    RECT rect;
    GetClientRect(window, &rect);

    //draw bitmap at random location
    int x = rand() % (rect.right - rect.left);
    int y = rand() % (rect.bottom - rect.top);
    DrawBitmap("c.bmp", x, y);
}

/**
 ** Shutdown code
 **/
void Game_End()
{
    //free the device
    ReleaseDC(window, device);
}

/**
 ** Window callback function
 **/
LRESULT CALLBACK WinProc(HWND hWnd, UINT message, WPARAM wParam, LPARAM lParam)
{
    switch (message)
    {
        case WM_DESTROY:
            gameover = true;
            PostQuitMessage(0);
            break;
    }
    return DefWindowProc(hWnd, message, wParam, lParam);
}

/**
 ** MyRegiserClass function sets program window properties
 **/
ATOM MyRegisterClass(HINSTANCE hInstance)
{
    //create the window class structure
    WNDCLASSEX wc;
    wc.cbSize = sizeof(WNDCLASSEX);
```

```
    //fill the struct with info
    wc.style           = CS_HREDRAW | CS_VREDRAW;
    wc.lpfnWndProc     = (WNDPROC)WinProc;
    wc.cbClsExtra      = 0;
    wc.cbWndExtra      = 0;
    wc.hInstance       = hInstance;
    wc.hIcon           = NULL;
    wc.hCursor         = LoadCursor(NULL, IDC_ARROW);
    wc.hbrBackground   = (HBRUSH)GetStockObject(BLACK_BRUSH);
    wc.lpszMenuName    = NULL;
    wc.lpszClassName   = APPTITLE.c_str();
    wc.hIconSm         = NULL;

    //set up the window with the class info
    return RegisterClassEx(&wc);
}



/**
 ** Helper function to create the window and refresh it
 **/
BOOL InitInstance(HINSTANCE hInstance, int nCmdShow)
{
    //create a new window
    window = CreateWindow(
        APPTITLE.c_str(),                //window class
        APPTITLE.c_str(),                //title bar
        WS_OVERLAPPEDWINDOW,    //window style
        CW_USEDEFAULT,          //x position of window
        CW_USEDEFAULT,          //y position of window
        640,                    //width of the window
        480,                    //height of the window
        NULL,                   //parent window
        NULL,                   //menu
        hInstance,              //application instance
        NULL);                  //window parameters

    //was there an error creating the window?
    if (window == 0) return 0;

    //display the window
    ShowWindow(window, nCmdShow);
```

```
    UpdateWindow(window);

    //get device context for drawing
    device = GetDC(window);

    return 1;
}

/**
 ** Entry point function
 **/
int WINAPI WinMain(HINSTANCE hInstance, HINSTANCE hPrevInstance,
    LPSTR lpCmdLine, int nCmdShow)
{
    MSG msg;

    //create window
    MyRegisterClass(hInstance);
    if (!InitInstance (hInstance, nCmdShow)) return 0;

    //initialize the game
    if (!Game_Init()) return 0;

    // main message loop
    while (!gameover)
    {
        //process Windows events
        if (PeekMessage(&msg, NULL, 0, 0, PM_REMOVE))
        {
            TranslateMessage(&msg);
            DispatchMessage(&msg);
        }

        //process game loop
        Game_Run();
    }

    //free game resources
    Game_End();

    return msg.wParam;
}
```

Drawing Bitmaps with Windows

The DrawBitmap function in this demo draws a bitmap—rather slowly, I'll admit. This function is suitable for loading a full background image or a small bitmap where you only need to draw the image once, but I'm using (or rather, abusing) it by repeatedly loading and drawing the bitmap from a file. The function loads a bitmap file into memory, does some Windows fuddling with it, and then draws it at a random location on the window (using the window's device context).

Advice

Be sure to copy the c.bmp file into the project folder for this program if you have created it from the code listing in the book. You will find it in the \sources\chapter02\GameLoop folder. You can use any bitmap file you wish if you just change the filename in the code.

You would never want to do this in a real game, because it loads the darned bitmap file every single time it goes through the loop! That's insanely slow and wasteful, but it is okay for demonstration purposes because all of the bitmap-related code is located in this function rather than strewn about the rest of the listing. I want you to focus on the game loop and support functions rather than this antiquated bitmap code that we won't even use beyond this chapter.

```
void DrawBitmap(char *filename, int x, int y)
{
    //load the bitmap image
    HBITMAP image = (HBITMAP)LoadImage(0,"c.bmp",IMAGE_BITMAP,0,0,
    LR_LOADFROMFILE);

    //read the bitmap's properties
    BITMAP bm;
    GetObject(image, sizeof(BITMAP), &bm);

    //create a device context for the bitmap
    HDC hdcImage = CreateCompatibleDC(device);
    SelectObject(hdcImage, image);

    //draw the bitmap to the window (bit block transfer)
    BitBlt(
        device,                     //destination device context
        x, y,                       //x,y location on destination
        bm.bmWidth, bm.bmHeight,    //width,height of source bitmap
        hdcImage,                   //source bitmap device context
        0, 0,                       //start x,y on source bitmap
```

```
    SRCCOPY);                       //blit method

    //delete the device context and bitmap
    DeleteDC(hdcImage);
    DeleteObject((HBITMAP)image);
}
```

Advice

If this were a book about programming the Windows GDI (graphics device interface), I would certainly go over all of the GDI graphics functions with you in vast detail! But since it's a side note at best, we'll just ignore the GDI for the most part.

To draw the bitmap repeatedly, the Game_Run function passes the bitmap filename and a random x,y location (bound within the limits of the window's width and height) to the DrawBitmap function:

```
void Game_Run()
{
    if (gameover == true) return;

    //get the drawing surface
    RECT rect;
    GetClientRect(window, &rect);

    //draw bitmap at random location
    int x = rand() % (rect.right - rect.left);
    int y = rand() % (rect.bottom - rect.top);
    DrawBitmap("c.bmp", x, y);
}
```

Running the GameLoop Program

Alrighty, then! Go ahead and run the program now, and you should see a window appear with a bunch of freaking crazy C bitmaps being blasted onto the window, as shown in Figure 2.7.

The Windows GDI—which is the system that provides you with window handles and device contexts and allows you to draw on windows to build a user interface (or a game that does not use DirectX)—is a step backward, to be blunt. I want to keep moving forward, covering only the aspects of Windows coding necessary to provide a footing for DirectX, so kindly ignore this lapse in my own judgment. I was being nostalgic.

Figure 2.7
The GameLoop program window is filled with C bitmaps.

What You Have Learned

In this chapter, you have learned the basics of Windows programming in preparation for DirectX coding. Here are the key points:

- You learned even more Windows programming concepts.

- You wrote a simple program that draws bitmaps using the Windows GDI.

- You learned how to draw pixels in a window.

- You dissected a complete Windows program and learned how it works.

- You learned all about the PeekMessage function.

- You learned how to modify the main loop in WinMain.

- You added some new functions that will make it easier to write a game.

Review Questions

Here are some review questions that will help you to think outside the box and retain some of the information covered in this chapter. The answers to these questions can be found in Appendix C.

1. What does the WinMain function do?

2. What does the WinProc function do?

3. What is a program instance?

4. What function can you use to draw pixels in a window?

5. What function is used to draw text inside a program window?

6. What is a real-time game loop?

7. Why do you need to use a real-time loop in a game?

8. What is the main helper function used to create a real-time loop?

9. What Windows API function can you use to draw a bitmap onto the screen?

10. What does DC stand for?

On Your Own

These exercises will challenge you to learn more about the subjects presented in this chapter and will help you to push yourself to see what you are capable of doing on your own.

Exercise 1. The window in the WindowTest program has a white background (WHITE_ BRUSH). Modify the program so that it uses a black background.

Exercise 2. Modify the GameLoop program so that it draws just a single bitmap that moves around in the window. (Hint: You will need to make sure the bitmap doesn't "fly off" the boundaries of the window.)

CHAPTER 3

INITIALIZING DIRECT3D

This chapter will show you how to write a program that initializes DirectX and creates a Direct3D device. The Direct3D device gives you access to the video card's primary surface or frame buffer, and a back buffer (which produces smooth graphics). The following chapter takes you deeper into the depths of Direct3D's architecture by exploring bitmaps and surfaces. Before you start loading 3D objects and rendering animated characters on the screen, you need to know the basics of DirectX. Here are the specific topics:

- How to initialize the Direct3D object.

- How to create a device for accessing the video display.

- How to create a back buffer for flicker-free graphics.

- How to run a Direct3D program in windowed mode.

- How to run a Direct3D program in full-screen mode.

Getting Started with Direct3D

To use Direct3D or any other component of DirectX, you must be somewhat familiar with how to use headers and library files (standard fare in C programming), because DirectX function calls are stored in header files, and the pre-compiled DirectX functions are stored in libs. For instance, the Direct3D functions are stored in d3d9.lib, and the way your program "sees" Direct3D is by including the d3d9.h header file using the #include <d3d9.h> directive in your source code files.

I will assume that you have already installed the DirectX 9 Software Development Kit (SDK) for Visual C++ or the separate version of DX9 for Dev-C++. If you have not installed one of these yet, you should do that before reading any further. The DirectX 9 SDK is located on the CD-ROM that accompanies this book in the \DirectX folder, while the Dev-C++ version is located in \dev-cpp. When given the DirectX Runtime Support option, you want to install the debug version for development.

Okay, ready to go?

The Direct3D Interfaces

In order to write a program that uses Direct3D, you must create one variable for the Direct3D interface and another for the graphics device. The Direct3D interface is called LPDIRECT3D9 and the device object is called LPDIRECT3DDEVICE9. You can create the variables like this:

```
LPDIRECT3D9      d3d    = NULL;
LPDIRECT3DDEVICE9 d3ddev = NULL;
```

The LPDIRECT3D9 object is the big boss of the Direct3D library, the object that controls everything, while LPDIRECT3DDEVICE9 represents the video card. You can probably tell what those objects are by their names. LP means "long pointer," so LPDIRECT3D9 is a long pointer to the DIRECT3D9 object. These definitions are located in the d3d9.h header file, which you must #include in your source code file. Here is how LPDIRECT3D9 is defined:

```
typedef struct IDirect3D9 *LPDIRECT3D9;
```

This may be confusing if you aren't particularly adept with pointers; they can be confusing until you "get it." Pointers are certainly the biggest obstacle to most programmers' mastery of C. When I don't understand something, I prefer to let my subconscious work on it—because my conscious mind just gets in the way sometimes. Seriously—if you don't get it, just start using these pointers and objects and give yourself time. You'll slowly come to understand. One mistake programmers often make is to assume that they must know how something works in order to use it. Not so! Just go ahead and write Direct3D programs; you don't need to know anything about 3D modeling or rendering right away. Practice builds experience, which makes up for a lack of understanding.

IDirect3D9 is an interface; therefore, LPDIRECT3D9 is a long pointer to the Direct3D9 interface. The same goes for LPDIRECT3DDEVICE9, which is a long pointer to the IDirect3DDevice9 interface.

Creating the Direct3D Object

Let me now show you how to initialize the main Direct3D object:

```
d3d = Direct3DCreate9(D3D_SDK_VERSION);
```

This code initializes Direct3D, which means that it is ready to be used. First, you must create the device upon which Direct3D will display output. This is where the d3ddev variable will be used (note that d3d is used to call this function):

```
d3d->CreateDevice(
    D3DADAPTER_DEFAULT,                     //use default video card
    D3DDEVTYPE_HAL,                         //use the hardware renderer
    hWnd,                                   //window handle
    D3DCREATE_SOFTWARE_VERTEXPROCESSING,    //do not use T&L (for compatibility)
    &d3dpp,                                 //presentation parameters
    &d3ddev);                               //pointer to the new device
```

Hardware T&L

If you are a technophile (that is, someone who loves to tinker with gadgets), or rather, if you are a hardcore gamer who loves to argue about video card specifications, then the parameter `D3DCREATE_SOFTWARE_VERTEXPROCESSING` probably irritated you. If you don't know anything about video cards, then no harm done! But I suspect you make it a habit to keep up to date on all the latest computer technology, right? Well, we all know that "transform and lighting" was a big buzz-phrase years ago, and all video cards since then have come with T&L—while the most recent development has been with programmable shaders. What this really means is that much of the 3D setup work is handled by the video card itself, rather than your computer's central processor (CPU).

When 3Dfx came out with the world's first 3D accelerator card for the PC, it took the industry by storm and revolutionized gaming. It would have happened sooner or later anyway, but 3Dfx was first because the company had been building 3D hardware for arcade game machines for years. I remember the first time I saw *Quake* running with 3D acceleration; my jaw dropped.

Having the rendering pipeline reside in the 3D card rather than the CPU is a given at this point. Evolution takes over for a few years and video cards are bumping up the polygon counts and feature sets. Then nVidia ushered in the next revolution by adding the transform and lighting phase of the 3D rendering pipeline to the 3D chip itself, offloading that work from the CPU.

What is transform and lighting, anyway? A *transform* is the manipulation of polygons, while lighting is just like it sounds—adding lighting effects to those polygons. While 3D chips first enhanced games by rendering textured polygons in the hardware (vastly improving quality and speed), T&L added the final touch by having the 3D chip manipulate and light the scene as well. This frees up the CPU for other tasks, like artificial intelligence and game physics—which, in case you haven't noticed, have really taken off in recent years! This is not due to just faster CPUs, but primarily due to the GPU taking the load off.

The last two parameters of `CreateDevice` specify the device parameters (d3dpp) and the device object (d3ddev). d3dpp must be defined before use, so let's go over it now. There are a lot of options that you can specify for the device, which you can see in Table 3.1.

First, create a variable of the `D3DPRESENT_PARAMETERS` struct that is used to set up the device parameters:

```
D3DPRESENT_PARAMETERS d3dpp;
```

and then clear out the struct to zero all values before use:

```
ZeroMemory(&d3dpp, sizeof(d3dpp));
```

Let's take a look at all the possible Direct3D presentation parameters:

There are a lot of options in the d3dpp struct, and a lot of substructs within it as well. I'll go over options that you need in order to work through the topics in this chapter, but I may not cover every option (which would amount to information

Table 3.1 Direct3D Presentation Parameters

Variable	Type	Description
BackBufferWidth	UINT	Width of the back buffer.
BackBufferHeight	UINT	Height of the back buffer.
BackBufferFormat	D3DFORMAT	Format of the back buffer, D3DFORMAT. Pass D3DFMT_UNKNOWN to use desktop format in windowed mode.
BackBufferCount	UINT	Number of back buffers.
MultiSampleType	D3DMULTISAM-PLE_TYPE	Number of multi-sampling levels for full-screen anti-aliasing. Normally pass D3DMULTISAMPLE_NONE.
MultiSampleQuality	DWORD	Quality level of multi-sampling. Normally pass 0.
SwapEffect	D3DSWAPEFFECT	Swapping method for back buffer.
hDeviceWindow	HWND	Parent window for this device.
Windowed	BOOL	Set to TRUE for windowed mode, FALSE for full-screen mode
EnableAutoDepthStencil	BOOL	Allow D3D to control the depth buffers (normally set to TRUE)
AutoDepthStencilFormat	D3DFORMAT	Format of the depth buffers.
Flags	DWORD	Optional flags (normally set to 0).
FullScreen_RefreshRateInHz	UINT	Full-screen refresh rate (must be 0 for windowed).
PresentationInterval	UINT	Controls the buffer swap rate.

overload). Let's fill in the d3dpp struct with just a few values needed to get a windowed Direct3D program running:

```
d3dpp.Windowed = TRUE;
d3dpp.SwapEffect = D3DSWAPEFFECT_DISCARD;
d3dpp.BackBufferFormat = D3DFMT_UNKNOWN;
```

After these few values have been filled in, you can then call CreateDevice to create the primary Direct3D drawing surface.

Taking Direct3D for a Spin

Let's create a sample project to use in this section on Direct3D to get a feel for how a complete Direct3D program works. Create a new Win32 Project type of program and call it Direct3D_Windowed (or whatever name you want, although this is the name of the project on the CD-ROM). Add a new file, called winmain.cpp, to the empty project. Now let's configure the project for Direct3D.

Advice

Remember that this is all basically just C code (rather than C++), even though the filenames all have an extension of .cpp. Visual C++ may complain if the source files don't end with .cpp in some cases.

Linking with the Direct3D Library

There are two ways to add a library to the project so that it can be used by your program. For example, Direct3D is a library that is included with the DirectX SDK (software development kit). The Direct3D library file is called d3d9.lib, and the header file that describes it is called d3d9.h. There are other library and header files in the DirectX SDK too. You can either add d3d9.lib to the project's properties or add a #pragma line to cause the compiler (or, to be more precise, the linker) to add that library file to the final executable file that is created. I'll be using the #pragma method, but want to at least show you how to add Direct3D to the linker settings in Visual C++.

```
#pragma comment(lib, "d3d9.lib")
```

Open the Project menu and select Properties (the last option on the bottom of the menu). The Properties dialog is shown in Figure 3.1.

Figure 3.1
The Project Properties dialog for the d3d_windowed project in Microsoft Visual C++.

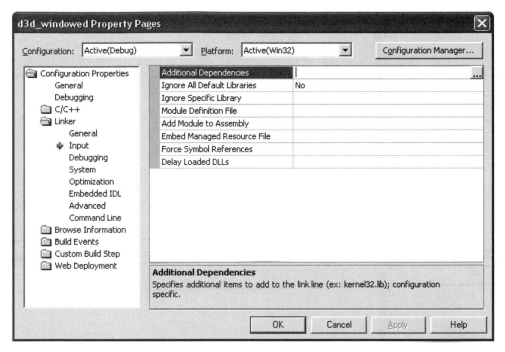

Figure 3.2
Opening the Link tab in the Project Properties dialog.

Now, click the Linker item on the list at the left to open up the linker options. You'll notice several subitems under the Linker tree item, such as General, Input, Debugging, and so on. Select the subitem called Input under the Linker tree menu, as shown in Figure 3.2.

Pay special attention to the field called Additional Dependencies. This field shows all of the library files that are linked to your program when all of the various source code files are compiled and linked together to form the executable file. If you have a winmain.cpp file in your project, then it is compiled to winmain.obj (which is an object file), which contains the binary instructions that will run on your computer. This is a very low-level binary file that is not readable, so don't even try to open it (you can see the various output files inside the Debug folder, as it is created inside your program's main folder when you compile the program).

Now, let's add the Direct3D library file to the list of libraries. Add "d3d9.lib" to the Additional Dependencies field, as shown in Figure 3.3, and then close the dialog.

Assuming your source code is correct, this is all you need to do to compile a Direct3D program. You have now configured your first DirectX project in Visual

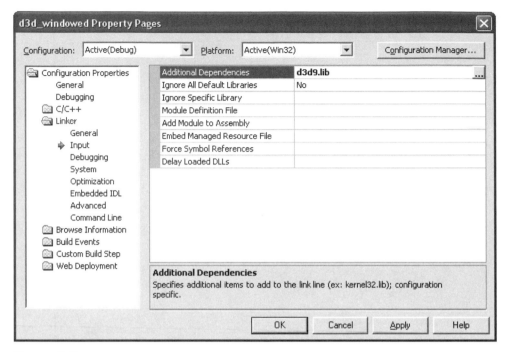

Figure 3.3
Adding d3d9.lib to the Additional Dependencies field.

C++! This is no easy thing to do, so you should feel like you're making some serious progress—especially if you are new to the C++ language!

Advice

Having any trouble compiling your project at this point? You may need to tell Visual C++ where the DirectX SDK is installed. For instructions on how to configure Visual C++ to support DirectX, refer to Appendix A.

Typing in the Source Code

Here is the standard Windows code needed to get the program rolling. I'll show you the Direct3D-specific code at the end of this listing.

```
/*
    Beginning Game Programming, Third Edition
    Chapter 3
    Direc3D_Windowed program
*/

#include <windows.h>
#include <d3d9.h>
```

```cpp
#include <time.h>
#include <iostream>
using namespace std;

#pragma comment(lib,"d3d9.lib")
#pragma comment(lib,"d3dx9.lib")

//program settings
const string APPTITLE = "Direct3D_Windowed";
const int SCREENW = 1024;
const int SCREENH = 768;

//Direct3D objects
LPDIRECT3D9 d3d = NULL;
LPDIRECT3DDEVICE9 d3ddev = NULL;

bool gameover = false;

//macro to detect key presses
#define KEY_DOWN(vk_code) ((GetAsyncKeyState(vk_code) & 0x8000) ? 1 : 0)

/**
 ** Game initialization function
 **/
bool Game_Init(HWND window)
{
    MessageBox(window, "Game_Init", "BREAKPOINT", 0);

    //initialize Direct3D
    d3d = Direct3DCreate9(D3D_SDK_VERSION);
    if (d3d == NULL)
    {
        MessageBox(window, "Error initializing Direct3D", "Error", MB_OK);
        return 0;
    }

    //set Direct3D presentation parameters
    D3DPRESENT_PARAMETERS d3dpp;
    ZeroMemory(&d3dpp, sizeof(d3dpp));
    d3dpp.Windowed = TRUE;
    d3dpp.SwapEffect = D3DSWAPEFFECT_DISCARD;
    d3dpp.BackBufferFormat = D3DFMT_X8R8G8B8;
    d3dpp.BackBufferCount = 1;
```

```
    d3dpp.BackBufferWidth = SCREENW;
    d3dpp.BackBufferHeight = SCREENH;
    d3dpp.hDeviceWindow = window;

    //create Direct3D device
    d3d->CreateDevice(
        D3DADAPTER_DEFAULT,
        D3DDEVTYPE_HAL,
        window,
        D3DCREATE_SOFTWARE_VERTEXPROCESSING,
        &d3dpp,
        &d3ddev);

    if (d3ddev == NULL)
    {
        MessageBox(window, "Error creating Direct3D device", "Error", MB_OK);
        return 0;
    }

    return true;
}

/**
 ** Game update function
 **/void Game_Run(HWND hwnd)
{
    //make sure the Direct3D device is valid
    if (!d3ddev) return;

    //clear the backbuffer to bright green
    d3ddev->Clear(0, NULL, D3DCLEAR_TARGET, D3DCOLOR_XRGB(0,255,0), 1.0f, 0);

    //start rendering
    if (d3ddev->BeginScene())
    {
        //do something?

        //stop rendering
        d3ddev->EndScene();

        //copy back buffer on the screen
        d3ddev->Present(NULL, NULL, NULL, NULL);
    }
```

```
    //check for escape key (to exit program)
    if (KEY_DOWN(VK_ESCAPE))
        PostMessage(hwnd, WM_DESTROY, 0, 0);
}

/**
 ** Game shutdown function
 **/void Game_End(HWND hwnd)
{
    //display close message
    MessageBox(hwnd, "Program is about to end", "Game_End", MB_OK);

    //free memory
    if (d3ddev) d3ddev->Release();
    if (d3d) d3d->Release();
}

/**
 ** Windows event handling function
 **/
LRESULT WINAPI WinProc( HWND hWnd, UINT msg, WPARAM wParam, LPARAM lParam )
{
    switch( msg )
    {
        case WM_DESTROY:
            gameover = true;
            PostQuitMessage(0);
            return 0;
    }
    return DefWindowProc( hWnd, msg, wParam, lParam );
}

/**
 ** Main Windows entry function
 **/
int WINAPI WinMain(HINSTANCE hInstance, HINSTANCE hPrevInstance,
    LPSTR lpCmdLine, int nCmdShow)
{
    //set the new window's properties
    //previously found in the MyRegisterClass function
    WNDCLASSEX wc;
    wc.cbSize = sizeof(WNDCLASSEX);
    wc.style         = CS_HREDRAW | CS_VREDRAW;
```

```cpp
    wc.lpfnWndProc    = (WNDPROC)WinProc;
    wc.cbClsExtra     = 0;
    wc.cbWndExtra     = 0;
    wc.hInstance      = hInstance;
    wc.hIcon          = NULL;
    wc.hCursor        = LoadCursor(NULL, IDC_ARROW);
    wc.hbrBackground  = (HBRUSH)GetStockObject(WHITE_BRUSH);
    wc.lpszMenuName   = NULL;
    wc.lpszClassName  = APPTITLE.c_str();
    wc.hIconSm        = NULL;
    RegisterClassEx(&wc);

    //create a new window
    //previously found in the InitInstance function
    HWND window = CreateWindow( APPTITLE.c_str(), APPTITLE.c_str(),
        WS_OVERLAPPEDWINDOW,
        CW_USEDEFAULT, CW_USEDEFAULT,
        SCREENW, SCREENH,
        NULL, NULL, hInstance, NULL);

    //was there an error creating the window?
    if (window == 0) return 0;

    //display the window
    ShowWindow(window, nCmdShow);
    UpdateWindow(window);

    //initialize the game
    if (!Game_Init(window)) return 0;

    // main message loop
    MSG message;
    while (!gameover)
    {
        if (PeekMessage(&message, NULL, 0, 0, PM_REMOVE))
        {
            TranslateMessage(&message);
            DispatchMessage(&message);
        }

        Game_Run(window);
    }
```

```
    Game_End(window);

    return message.wParam;
}
```

The first thing you might have noticed about this code is that the `MyRegisterClass` and `InitInstance` functions are missing! I just moved the code directly into `WinMain` because the Direct3D code needs access to the window handle and I would prefer to just keep the `CreateWindow` function right inside `WinMain`.

There are several more changes in this code listing that make it differ from the `GameLoop` program that you saw in the last chapter. For one thing, `Game_End` gets called when the `gameover` variable becomes true (either as a result of the `WM_DESTROY` message or from the Escape key being pressed). This function removes the Direct3D objects from memory before the program ends. If you want to see the program hang, just terminate the program without first releasing Direct3D—it will keep running in memory, even though the program window is gone! This is what you might call a *bad thing*. Oh, why beat around the bush? This is a *very bad thing*.

Now let's go over the code to initialize Direct3D. I have put the code you have learned about in this chapter so far inside `Game_Init`, which is called by `WinMain` just before the main loop starts running. The calls to `MessageBox` are for testing purposes, and can be removed once you understand how the program works.

```
int Game_Init(HWND hwnd)
{
    MessageBox(window, "Game_Init", "BREAKPOINT", 0);

    //initialize Direct3D
    d3d = Direct3DCreate9(D3D_SDK_VERSION);
    if (d3d == NULL)
    {
        MessageBox(window, "Error initializing Direct3D", "Error", MB_OK);
        return 0;
    }

    //set Direct3D presentation parameters
    D3DPRESENT_PARAMETERS d3dpp;
    ZeroMemory(&d3dpp, sizeof(d3dpp));
    d3dpp.Windowed = TRUE;
    d3dpp.SwapEffect = D3DSWAPEFFECT_DISCARD;
    d3dpp.BackBufferFormat = D3DFMT_X8R8G8B8;
    d3dpp.BackBufferCount = 1;
```

```
    d3dpp.BackBufferWidth = SCREENW;
    d3dpp.BackBufferHeight = SCREENH;
    d3dpp.hDeviceWindow = window;

    //create Direct3D device
    d3d->CreateDevice(
        D3DADAPTER_DEFAULT,
        D3DDEVTYPE_HAL,
        window,
        D3DCREATE_SOFTWARE_VERTEXPROCESSING,
        &d3dpp,
        &d3ddev);

    if (d3ddev == NULL)
    {
        MessageBox(window, "Error creating Direct3D device", "Error", MB_OK);
        return 0;
    }

    return true;
}
```

Did you see that first line that calls MessageBox to display a message? I inserted this to demonstrate how things work in the program, how the functions are called, and to demonstrate the ordering of events in a Windows program. If you want to really see how it all works, you may insert similar MessageBox function calls elsewhere in the program. You can insert them basically anywhere except for in the game loop, which you don't really want to interrupt with a message box, as that will mess everything up. Okay, let's take a look at Game_Run to see what happens to draw on the Direct3D display:

```
void Game_Run(HWND hwnd)
{
    //make sure the Direct3D device is valid
    if (!d3ddev) return;

    //clear the backbuffer to bright green
    d3ddev->Clear(0, NULL, D3DCLEAR_TARGET, D3DCOLOR_XRGB(0,255,0), 1.0f, 0);

    //start rendering
    if (d3ddev->BeginScene())
    {
        //do something?
```

```
        //stop rendering
        d3ddev->EndScene();
        //copy back buffer on the screen
        d3ddev->Present(NULL, NULL, NULL, NULL);
    }

    //check for escape key (to exit program)
    if (KEY_DOWN(VK_ESCAPE))
        PostMessage(hwnd, WM_DESTROY, 0, 0);
}
```

Advice

We will be spending a *lot* of time going over the Direct3D rendering code in Game_Run in later chapters. For now, while still learning Direct3D initialization, we'll put off that explanation until later.

First, this function makes sure that the d3ddev (Direct3D device) exists; otherwise, it returns an error. Next, the Clear function is called to clear the back buffer with the color green. This is not just a cosmetic function call to Clear. This literally blanks out the screen before each frame is rendered (and as you will learn later on, this function can also clear the z-buffer used to draw polygons). Imagine that you have a character walking on the screen. At each frame (here within Game_Run) you will change to the next frame of animation, so that over time the character really appears to be walking. Well, if you don't clear the screen first, then each frame of the animation is drawn over the last frame, resulting in a big mess on the screen. That is why Clear is called before the rendering begins: to wipe the slate clean and prepare it for the next frame.

Now for the last part of the program:

```
void Game_End(HWND hwnd)
{
    //display close message
    MessageBox(hwnd, "Game_End", "BREAKPOINT", MB_OK);

    //free memory
    if (d3ddev) d3ddev->Release();
    if (d3d) d3d->Release();
}
```

The Game_End function is called from within WinMain, as you'll recall, after a WM_DESTROY message comes in. This usually happens when you close the program

Figure 3.4
The Direct3D_Windowed program demonstrates how to initialize Direct3D.

window (clicking the small X icon at the top-right corner—duh, you knew that, right?).

Running the Program

If you run the program (F5 from Visual C++), you should see a blank window pop up, as shown in Figure 3.4. Hey, it doesn't do much, but you've learned a lot about initializing Direct3D—that baby is ready for some polygons!

Direct3D in Full-Screen Mode

The next step is to learn how to program Direct3D to run in full-screen mode, which is how most games run. This requires a change to the CreateWindow function and a few changes to the Direct3D presentation parameters. Using the Direct3D_Windowed program as a basis, you can just make the following few changes to make the program run in full-screen mode.

Tip

It's good to have your game run full-screen for production, but it's preferable to run the game in windowed mode while you are working on it because in full-screen mode Direct3D takes control over the screen, and you won't be able to see any error messages that pop up.

Modifying CreateWindow

Now, down in `WinMain`, I have made some changes to the `CreateWindow` function call that you should note (the changes appear in bold):

```
//create a new window
HWND window = CreateWindow( APPTITLE.c_str(), APPTITLE.c_str(),
    WS_EX_TOPMOST | WS_VISIBLE | WS_POPUP,
    CW_USEDEFAULT, CW_USEDEFAULT,
    SCREENW, SCREENH,
    NULL, NULL, hInstance, NULL);
```

The `CreateWindow` function includes the screen width and height values, but I also made some changes to the `WS_OVERLAPPED` window style. It now includes the `WS_EX_TOPMOST` value, which causes the window to take precedence over all other windows. The other two options are `WS_VISIBLE` and `WS_POPUP`, which ensure that the window has focus and no longer includes a border or title bar.

Changing the Direct3D Device Presentation Parameters

The next change involves the `D3DPRESENT_PARAMETERS` struct, which directly affects the appearance and capabilities of the Direct3D primary surface. You may recall that the last program set it up with the following three lines:

```
//set Direct3D presentation parameters
D3DPRESENT_PARAMETERS d3dpp;
ZeroMemory(&d3dpp, sizeof(d3dpp));
d3dpp.Windowed = FALSE;
d3dpp.SwapEffect = D3DSWAPEFFECT_DISCARD;
d3dpp.BackBufferFormat = D3DFMT_X8R8G8B8;
d3dpp.BackBufferCount = 1;
d3dpp.BackBufferWidth = SCREENW;
d3dpp.BackBufferHeight = SCREENH;
d3dpp.hDeviceWindow = window;
```

The output of the Direct3D_Fullscreen program is just a big blank window filled with a bright green color, like the windowed program, so there's no need for a screenshot. To exit the program, just press the Escape key.

What You Have Learned

In this chapter, you have learned how to initialize and run a Direct3D program in windowed and full-screen modes. Here are the key points:

- You learned about the Direct3D interface objects.

- You learned about the `CreateDevice` function.

- You learned about the Direct3D presentation parameters.

- You learned what settings to use to run Direct3D in windowed mode.

- You learned how to run Direct3D in full-screen mode.

Review Questions

Here are some review questions to challenge your impressive intellect and see if you have any weaknesses. You may check your answers by reviewing Appendix C.

1. What is Direct3D?

2. What is the Direct3D interface object called?

3. What is the Direct3D device called?

4. Which Direct3D function do you use to start rendering?

5. What function lets you read from the keyboard asynchronously?

6. What is the name of the main Windows function, known as the "entry point" of the program?

7. What is the common name for the event handling function in a Windows program?

8. Which Direct3D function refreshes the screen after rendering is complete, by copying the back buffer onto the frame buffer in video memory?

9. What version of DirectX are we using in this book?

10. What is the name of the Direct3D header file?

On Your Own

These exercises will challenge you to learn more about the subjects presented in this chapter and will help you to push yourself to see what you are capable of doing on your own.

Exercise 1. Modify the Direct3D_Windowed program so that it displays a different color in the background other than green.

Exercise 2. Modify the Direct3D_Fullscreen program so that it uses a different resolution other than 1024 × 768.

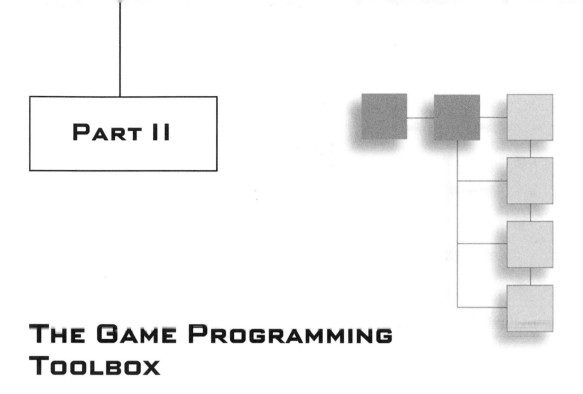

PART II

THE GAME PROGRAMMING TOOLBOX

The chapters in this second part explain many of the core concepts in game programming needed to get the simplest of games to work. Concepts like keyboard input, mouse input, sprites, animation, timing, collision detection and response, and other important key topics are explored here. As you go through these chapters you will begin to create your own game programming *toolbox*—a collection of reusable data types and functions that will make it much easier to program a game with C++ and DirectX. As we cover each new subject, we will add new data types and functions to a set of reusable source code files, which you will be able to simply add to any new game project and reuse—which is the first step toward creating your own game engine! Here are the chapters in Part II, which make up the bulk of the book:

- Chapter 4: Drawing Bitmaps

- Chapter 5: Getting Input with the Keyboard, Mouse, and Controller

- Chapter 6: Drawing and Animating Sprites

- Chapter 7: Transforming Sprites

- Chapter 8: Detecting Sprite Collisions

- Chapter 9: Printing Text

- Chapter 10: Scrolling the Background

- Chapter 11: Playing Audio

- Chapter 12: Learning the Basics of 3D Rendering

- Chapter 13: Rendering 3D Model Files

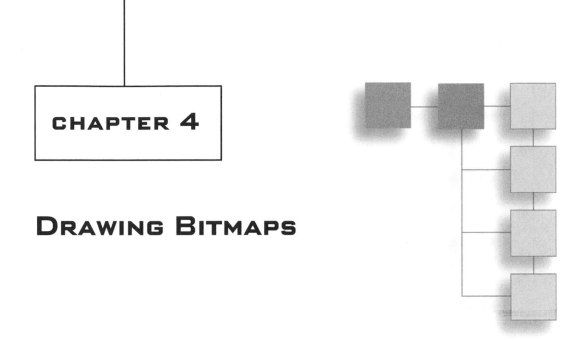

CHAPTER 4

DRAWING BITMAPS

Some of the best games ever made were 2D games that didn't even require an advanced 3D accelerated video card. It is important to learn about 2D graphics because they are the basis for all graphics that are displayed on your monitor—regardless of how those graphics are rendered, game graphics are all converted to an array of pixels on the screen. In this chapter, you will learn about surfaces, which are just regular bitmaps that can be drawn to the screen. So, think back on some of your all-time favorite games. Were they all 3D games? Very likely not—there have been more blockbuster 2D games than there have been of the 3D variety. Rather than compare and contrast 2D and 3D, it's better to just learn both and then use whichever one your game calls for. A game programmer should know everything in order to create the best games.

Here is what you will learn in this chapter:

- How to create a surface in memory.

- How to fill a surface with color.

- How to load a bitmap image file.

- How to draw a surface on the screen.

Surfaces and Bitmaps

We are beginning our study of Direct3D graphics programming with the simplest of techniques—loading and drawing a bitmap with a Direct3D *surface*. Surfaces are very easy to work with because surfaces are used internally by Direct3D to send graphics output to the frame buffer—that part of the video card that actually draws the pixels on the screen. Although Direct3D surfaces are easy to use, they do have some limitations, such as no support for transparency. We'll have to work around that limitation until we learn how to use *textures* and *sprites* beginning in Chapter 6, "Drawing and Animating Sprites." Direct3D surfaces do have longer-term uses as well, so we won't be abandoning surfaces after this chapter. In fact, we'll use a surface for scrolling in Chapter 10, "Scrolling the Background." Scrolling is one of my favorite subjects! Now let's get on with the details of working with Direct3D surfaces.

Direct3D uses surfaces for many things. The monitor (shown in Figure 4.1) displays what the video card sends to it, and the video card pulls the video display out of a frame buffer that is sent to the monitor one pixel at a time (they might be in single file, but they move insanely fast!).

The frame buffer is stored in the memory chips on the video card itself (shown in Figure 4.2), and these chips are usually very fast. There was a time when video memory (VRAM) was extremely expensive because it was so fast—much faster than standard system RAM. Now things are somewhat reversed, as the PC's main memory usually has the best technology and the video cards are a step or two behind. The reason for this is because it's difficult to redo the architecture of a video card, which is a very precise and complex circuit board.

Advice

Direct3D surfaces are not used for either sprites or textures in a game project, but are capable of being blitted, which is why we are covering them now. This is merely a step toward texture-based graphics.

Figure 4.1
A typical monitor.

Figure 4.2
The monitor displays the linear array of pixels sent to it by the video card.

The PC motherboard, on the other hand, is constantly in a state of flux, as semiconductor companies strive to outdo each other. Video card companies, no matter how competitive they may be, can't gamble on putting six months worth of effort into a memory technology that fails in the market and is replaced by other types of memory. (Remember Rambus memory, which Intel tried to support in the earliest versions of the Pentium III processor?) Also, while motherboards are built for a variety of industries and uses—and, thus, have been subject to much experimentation—video cards are built for one thing only: displaying graphics. Therefore, less experimentation goes on with the chips on a

Frame Buffer
(in video card)   **Monitor**

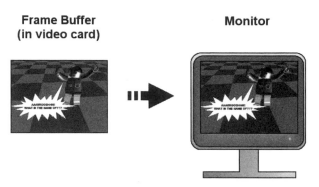

Figure 4.3
The frame buffer in video memory contains the image that is rendered on the monitor.

video card. After the PC market has decided on a memory standard, it tends to show up on video cards. You may recall when the first DDR (double data rate) memory was used on video cards; it was quite a while after DDR had been initially released.

Where was I? Oh, right! The frame buffer resides in video memory, and represents the image you see on the monitor (as shown in Figure 4.3). So it makes sense that the easiest way to create graphics is to just modify the frame buffer directly; the result is that you see the changes on the screen right away. This is how things work, basically, but I'm leaving out one small detail. You don't want to draw directly on the frame buffer because that causes flicker as your graphics are drawn, erased, moved, and redrawn while the screen is being refreshed. Instead, what you want to do is draw everything on an off-screen buffer and then blast that "double" or "back" buffer to the screen very quickly. This is called *double buffering*. There are other methods of creating a flicker-free display, such as page flipping, but I tend to prefer a back buffer because it is more straightforward (and a bit easier).

The Primary Surfaces

You might recall from the last chapter that you created a back buffer by setting the presentation parameters. Then, using the Clear function, you filled the back buffer with green and then used the Present function to refresh the screen. You were using a double/back buffer without even realizing it! That's one nice feature that Direct3D provides—a built-in back buffer. And it makes sense, because double buffering is as common today in games as bread and butter is to your kitchen.

The "frame buffer" that I mentioned earlier is also called the *front buffer*, which makes sense in that the back buffer is copied to it during each frame. Both the front and back buffers are created for you when you configure the presentation parameters and call `CreateDevice`. Isn't that great?

Secondary Off-Screen Surfaces

The other type of surface you can use is called a *secondary* or *off-screen* surface. This type of surface is really just an array in memory that looks like a bitmap (where it has a header and then data representing pixels). You can create as many off-screen surfaces as you need for your game; it is common to use hundreds of surfaces and textures while a game is running. The reason is because all of the graphics in a game are stored in surfaces or textures, and these images are copied to the screen in a process called *bit-block transfer*. The common way to refer to this term is "blitter"—you "blit" surfaces to the screen.

You might remember the GameLoop program from Chapter 2 that used a function called `BitBlt` (that I purposely neglected to explain at the time). `BitBlt` is a Windows GDI function for "blitting" bitmaps to device contexts, such as the main window of your program. A device context is sort of like a Direct3D surface, but is more difficult to use (due to the complexity of the Windows GDI). Direct3D surfaces are simple in comparison, as you'll see shortly. In fact, I might use the word *refreshing* to describe them after writing Windows code for so many years.

Creating a Surface

You create a Direct3D surface by first declaring a variable to point to the surface in memory. The surface object is called `LPDIRECT3DSURFACE9`, and you create a variable like so:

```
LPDIRECT3DSURFACE9 surface = NULL;
```

Once you have created a surface, you have a lot of freedom as to what you can do with the surface. You can use the blitter (`StretchRect`) to draw bitmaps to the surface (from other surfaces, of course), or you can fill the surface with a color, among other things. If you want to clear the surface prior to drawing on it, for instance, you would use the ColorFill function, which has this syntax:

```
HRESULT ColorFill(

    IDirect3DSurface9 *pSurface,
    CONST RECT *pRect,
    D3DCOLOR color
);
```

This usage causes the destination surface to be filled with the color red:

```
d3ddev->ColorFill(surface, NULL, D3DCOLOR_XRGB(255,0,0));
```

Drawing the Surface (Blitting)

Probably the most interesting function, of course, is the blitter. You can blit portions or all of one surface onto another surface (including the back buffer or the screen). The blitter is called StretchRect (strange name, huh?). Here is what it looks like:

```
HRESULT StretchRect(

    IDirect3DSurface9 *pSourceSurface,
    CONST RECT *pSourceRect,
    IDirect3DSurface9 *pDestSurface,
    CONST RECT *pDestRect,
    D3DTEXTUREFILTERTYPE Filter
);
```

Well, didn't I tell you that bitmaps were easier to deal with in Direct3D than they are with the Windows GDI? I wasn't kidding. This sweet little function only has five parameters, and it is really easy to use. Let me give you an example:

```
d3ddev->StretchRect(surface, NULL, backbuffer, NULL, D3DTEXF_NONE);
```

This is the easiest way to call the function, assuming that the two surfaces are the same size. If the source surface is smaller than the destination, then it is blitted to the upper-left corner of the destination surface. Of course, this isn't very interesting; when this function is really handy is when you specify the rectangles for the source and destination. The source rectangle can be just a small portion or the entire surface; the same goes for the destination, but you'll usually blit the source somewhere "on" the destination. Here's an example:

```
rect.left = 100;
rect.top = 90;
```

```
rect.right = 200;
rect.bottom = 180;
d3ddev->StretchRect(surface, NULL, backbuffer, &rect, D3DTEXF_NONE);
```

This code copies the source surface onto the destination, stretching it into the rectangle at (100, 90, 200, 180), which is 100 × 90 pixels in size. Regardless of the size of the source surface, as long as it isn't NULL, it will be "stuffed" into the dimensions specified by the destination rectangle.

I've been using backbuffer without first explaining where it came from. No, there is not a global variable called backbuffer that you can freely use! (Although that would be kind of cool.) But it's not a big deal—you can create this variable yourself. It is actually just a pointer to the real back buffer, and you can get this pointer by calling a special function called GetBackBuffer. Boy, was that a tough call, huh? Well, you can't argue with the straightforward approach (which is not Microsoft's usual approach).

```
HRESULT GetBackBuffer(

    UINT iSwapChain,
    UINT BackBuffer,
    D3DBACKBUFFER_TYPE Type,
    IDirect3DSurface9 **ppBackBuffer
);
```

Here is how you might call this function to retrieve a pointer to the back buffer. First, let's create the backbuffer variable (that is, pointer) and then have this fancy GetBackBuffer function "point it" to the real back buffer:

```
LPDIRECT3DSURFACE9 backbuffer = NULL;
d3ddev->GetBackBuffer(0, 0, D3DBACKBUFFER_TYPE_MONO, &backbuffer);
```

I'll bet you were worried that Direct3D was going to be hard. Well, it all depends on your point of view. You can either be the pessimist and complain about every unknown function in the DirectX SDK help file (which I refer to often), or you can just do what works, use what you learn, and get started writing a game. Granted, you have yet to draw a polygon, but we'll be there soon enough.

The Create_Surface Example

Let's turn this into a sample program so that you can see it all come together nicely. I have written a program called Create_Surface that demonstrates the functions ColorFill, StretchRect, and GetBackBuffer, and, more importantly, shows how to

Figure 4.4
The Create_Surface program copies random rectangles from an off-screen surface to the screen.

use surfaces! You can see sample output from the program in Figure 4.4. In case you're wondering why there's just one rectangle in the figure, it's because when the program is running, there is only one rectangle on the screen at a time, though it's running so fast there appear to be many on the screen at once.

Go ahead and create a new project called Create_Surface and add a new file to the project called winmain.cpp. Now, as before, go into the Project menu, click on Settings, click on the Linker/Input item, and add d3d9.lib to the Additional Dependencies field.

Ready? Okay, let's do it; here's the code for the program. I've highlighted important lines of code in bold so you can identify them if you're just modifying one of the example programs from the last chapter (from which this program was originally based).

Advice

You can load this project off the CD-ROM or just modify a program from the last chapter and make changes to it, as much of the Windows code remains unchanged.

```cpp
/*
    Beginning Game Programming, Third Edition
    Chapter 4
    Create_Surface program
*/

#include <windows.h>
#include <d3d9.h>
#include <time.h>
#include <iostream>
using namespace std;

//application title
const string APPTITLE = "Create Surface Program";

//macro to read the keyboard
#define KEY_DOWN(vk_code) ((GetAsyncKeyState(vk_code)&0x8000)?1:0)

//screen resolution
#define SCREENW 1024
#define SCREENH 768

//Direct3D objects
LPDIRECT3D9 d3d = NULL;
LPDIRECT3DDEVICE9 d3ddev = NULL;
LPDIRECT3DSURFACE9 backbuffer = NULL;
LPDIRECT3DSURFACE9 surface = NULL;

bool gameover = false;

/**
 ** Game initialization function
 **/
bool Game_Init(HWND hwnd)
{
    //initialize Direct3D
    d3d = Direct3DCreate9(D3D_SDK_VERSION);
    if (d3d == NULL)
```

```
    {
        MessageBox(hwnd, "Error initializing Direct3D", "Error", MB_OK);
        return false;
    }

    //set Direct3D presentation parameters
    D3DPRESENT_PARAMETERS d3dpp;
    ZeroMemory(&d3dpp, sizeof(d3dpp));
    d3dpp.Windowed = TRUE;
    d3dpp.SwapEffect = D3DSWAPEFFECT_DISCARD;
    d3dpp.BackBufferFormat = D3DFMT_X8R8G8B8;
    d3dpp.BackBufferCount = 1;
    d3dpp.BackBufferWidth = SCREENW;
    d3dpp.BackBufferHeight = SCREENH;
    d3dpp.hDeviceWindow = hwnd;

    //create Direct3D device
    d3d->CreateDevice( D3DADAPTER_DEFAULT, D3DDEVTYPE_HAL, hwnd,
        D3DCREATE_SOFTWARE_VERTEXPROCESSING, &d3dpp, &d3ddev);

    if (!d3ddev)
    {
        MessageBox(hwnd, "Error creating Direct3D device", "Error", MB_OK);
        return false;
    }

    //set random number seed
    srand(time(NULL));

    //clear the backbuffer to black
    d3ddev->Clear(0, NULL, D3DCLEAR_TARGET, D3DCOLOR_XRGB(0,0,0), 1.0f, 0);

    //create pointer to the back buffer
    d3ddev->GetBackBuffer(0, 0, D3DBACKBUFFER_TYPE_MONO, &backbuffer);

    //create surface
    HRESULT result = d3ddev->CreateOffscreenPlainSurface(
        100,                //width of the surface
        100,                //height of the surface
        D3DFMT_X8R8G8B8,    //surface format
        D3DPOOL_DEFAULT,    //memory pool to use
        &surface,           //pointer to the surface
        NULL);              //reserved (always NULL)
```

```
    if (!SUCCEEDED(result)) return false;

    return true;
}

/**
 ** Game update function
 **/
void Game_Run(HWND hwnd)
{
    //make sure the Direct3D device is valid
    if (!d3ddev) return;

    //start rendering
    if (d3ddev->BeginScene())
    {
        //fill the surface with random color
        int r = rand() % 255;
        int g = rand() % 255;
        int b = rand() % 255;
        d3ddev->ColorFill(surface, NULL, D3DCOLOR_XRGB(r,g,b));

        //copy the surface to the backbuffer
        RECT rect;
        rect.left = rand() % SCREENW/2;
        rect.right = rect.left + rand() % SCREENW/2;
        rect.top = rand() % SCREENH;
        rect.bottom = rect.top + rand() % SCREENH/2;
        d3ddev->StretchRect(surface, NULL, backbuffer, &rect, D3DTEXF_NONE);

        //stop rendering
        d3ddev->EndScene();

        //display the back buffer on the screen
        d3ddev->Present(NULL, NULL, NULL, NULL);
    }

    //check for escape key (to exit program)
    if (KEY_DOWN(VK_ESCAPE))
        PostMessage(hwnd, WM_DESTROY, 0, 0);

}
```

```
/**
 ** Game shutdown function
 **/
void Game_End(HWND hwnd)
{
    if (surface) surface->Release();
    if (d3ddev) d3ddev->Release();
    if (d3d) d3d->Release();
}



/**
 ** Windows event callback function
 **/

LRESULT WINAPI WinProc( HWND hWnd, UINT msg, WPARAM wParam, LPARAM lParam )
{
    switch( msg )
    {
        case WM_DESTROY:
            gameover = true;
            PostQuitMessage(0);
            return 0;
    }
    return DefWindowProc( hWnd, msg, wParam, lParam );
}

/**
 ** Windows entry point function
 **/
int WINAPI WinMain(HINSTANCE hInstance, HINSTANCE hPrevInstance,
    LPSTR lpCmdLine, int nCmdShow)
{
    //create the window class structure
    WNDCLASSEX wc;
    wc.cbSize = sizeof(WNDCLASSEX);
    wc.style        = CS_HREDRAW | CS_VREDRAW;
    wc.lpfnWndProc  = (WNDPROC)WinProc;
    wc.cbClsExtra    = 0;
    wc.cbWndExtra    = 0;
    wc.hInstance    = hInstance;
    wc.hIcon        = NULL;
    wc.hCursor       = LoadCursor(NULL, IDC_ARROW);
```

```
    wc.hbrBackground = (HBRUSH)GetStockObject(WHITE_BRUSH);
    wc.lpszMenuName  = NULL;
    wc.lpszClassName = APPTITLE.c_str();
    wc.hIconSm       = NULL;
    RegisterClassEx(&wc);

    //create a new window
    HWND window = CreateWindow(APPTITLE.c_str(), APPTITLE.c_str(),
        WS_OVERLAPPEDWINDOW, CW_USEDEFAULT, CW_USEDEFAULT,
        SCREENW, SCREENH, NULL, NULL, hInstance, NULL);

    //was there an error creating the window?
    if (window == 0) return 0;

    //display the window
    ShowWindow(window, nCmdShow);
    UpdateWindow(window);

    //initialize the game
    if (!Game_Init(window)) return 0;

    // main message loop
    MSG message;
    while (!gameover)
    {
        if (PeekMessage(&message, NULL, 0, 0, PM_REMOVE))
        {
            TranslateMessage(&message);
            DispatchMessage(&message);
        }

        Game_Run(window);
    }

    return message.wParam;
}
```

Loading Bitmaps from Disk

Now that you've seen how to draw a bitmap using the StretchRect function, you
should be ready for the next step—loading a bitmap from file into a surface
object and drawing it from there. Unfortunately, Direct3D does not have any

function for loading a bitmap file, so you'll have to write your own bitmap loader.

<Indeterminate pause>. Just kidding!

Actually, what I was thinking at this very moment was Balki Bartokamous from the TV show *Perfect Strangers*, and his famous quote: "Don't be reedeeculose!" Writing your own bitmap loader, for a program running on the Windows, the native platform for BMP files: yes, that *would be* ridiculous.

However, the truth is, Direct3D really doesn't know how to load a bitmap. Fortunately, there is a helper library called *D3DX* (which stands for *Direct3D Extensions*) that provides many helpful functions, including one to load a bitmap into a surface. The only stipulation is that you must add the #include <d3dx.h> include statement to your program, and you must also add d3dx9.lib to the project settings. No big whoop.

Advice

Why is it that whenever someone at Microsoft can't think of a good name for a new product, that they just call it "X" something? DirectX. Windows XP. XNA Game Studio. Xbox. Xbox 360. Office XP. The whole "X" thing was trendy in the '90s, but it's really overdone at this point. There was one software product called Microsoft Bob but it did not sell very well. Maybe that's a good thing, or we might be seeing a lot of "Bob" branded products from this company!

The function we're interested in is called D3DXLoadSurfaceFromFile, which has this syntax:

```
HRESULT D3DXLoadSurfaceFromFile(

    LPDIRECT3DSURFACE9 pDestSurface,
    CONST PALETTEENTRY* pDestPalette,
    CONST RECT* pDestRect,
    LPCTSTR pSrcFile,
    CONST RECT* pSrcRect,
    DWORD Filter,
    D3DCOLOR ColorKey,
    D3DXIMAGE_INFO* pSrcInfo
);
```

Okay, now for the good part. Not only can this great function load a standard Windows bitmap file, it can also load a bunch more formats! Table 4.1 has the list.

Table 4.1 Graphics File Formats

Extension	Format
.bmp	Windows Bitmap
.dds	DirectDraw Surface
.dib	Windows Device Independent Bitmap
.jpg	Joint Photographic Experts Group (JPEG)
.png	Portable Network Graphics
.tga	Truevision Targa

As usual, many of these parameters will be NULL, so it's not as difficult as it appears (although when I see any function with more than six parameters, my eyes tend to glaze over...).

The Load_Bitmap Program

Let's write a short program to demonstrate how to load a bitmap file into a surface and draw it on the screen. First of all, you don't need to type in all that code again; you can just make the noted changes to the Create_Surface program, so I'll just list the code that's necessary to make the changes. Second, I need to show you how to configure the project for D3DX. Open the Project Settings dialog, click the Link tab, and type in both d3d9.lib and d3dx9.lib into the Additional Dependencies field, as shown in Figure 4.5. Do you remember the other way to add a library file to a project?

The first thing you need to do is add the #include <d3dx9.h> to the code as shown:

```
/*
    Beginning Game Programming, Third Edition
    Chapter 4
    Load Bitmap program
*/
#include <windows.h>
#include <d3d9.h>
#include <d3dx9.h>
#include <time.h>
#include <iostream>
using namespace std;
```

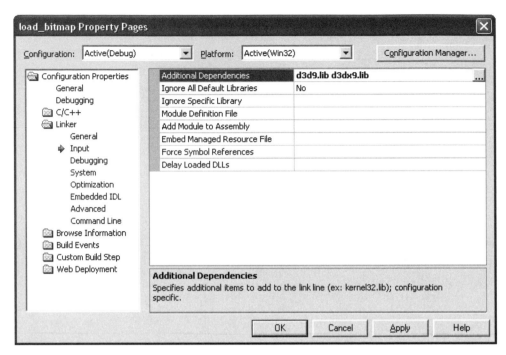

Figure 4.5
Adding support for the D3DX library to the project.

```
//program values
const string APPTITLE = "Load Bitmap Program";
const int SCREENW = 1024;
const int SCREENH = 768;
```

Now scroll on down to the Game_Init function and make the changes noted in bold (deleting any lines of code that no longer belong from the previous project). Most of the code remains unchanged.

```
/**
 ** Game initialization function
 **/
bool Game_Init(HWND window)
{
    //initialize Direct3D
    d3d = Direct3DCreate9(D3D_SDK_VERSION);
    if (!d3d)
    {
        MessageBox(window, "Error initializing Direct3D", "Error", MB_OK);
        return false;
    }
```

```
//set Direct3D presentation parameters
D3DPRESENT_PARAMETERS d3dpp;
ZeroMemory(&d3dpp, sizeof(d3dpp));
d3dpp.Windowed = TRUE;
d3dpp.SwapEffect = D3DSWAPEFFECT_DISCARD;
d3dpp.BackBufferFormat = D3DFMT_X8R8G8B8;
d3dpp.BackBufferCount = 1;
d3dpp.BackBufferWidth = SCREENW;
d3dpp.BackBufferHeight = SCREENH;
d3dpp.hDeviceWindow = window;

//create Direct3D device
d3d->CreateDevice( D3DADAPTER_DEFAULT, D3DDEVTYPE_HAL, window,
    D3DCREATE_SOFTWARE_VERTEXPROCESSING, &d3dpp, &d3ddev);

if (!d3ddev)
{
    MessageBox(window, "Error creating Direct3D device", "Error", MB_OK);
    return 0;
}

//clear the backbuffer to black
d3ddev->Clear(0, NULL, D3DCLEAR_TARGET, D3DCOLOR_XRGB(0,0,0), 1.0f, 0);

//create surface
HRESULT result = d3ddev->CreateOffscreenPlainSurface(
    SCREENW,                  //width of the surface
    SCREENH,                  //height of the surface
    D3DFMT_X8R8G8B8,        //surface format
    D3DPOOL_DEFAULT,        //memory pool to use
    &surface,                //pointer to the surface
    NULL);                   //reserved (always NULL)

if (!SUCCEEDED(result)) return false;

//load surface from file into newly created surface
result = D3DXLoadSurfaceFromFile(
    surface,                 //destination surface
    NULL,                    //destination palette
    NULL,                    //destination rectangle
    "legotron.bmp",        //source filename
    NULL,                    //source rectangle
    D3DX_DEFAULT,          //controls how image is filtered
```

```
            0,                  //for transparency (0 for none)
            NULL);              //source image info (usually NULL)

    //make sure file was loaded okay
    if (!SUCCEEDED(result)) return false;

    return true;
}
```

There are a few changes that need to be made to Game_Run, mainly involving the removal of some code because no screen updates will take place after the image has been drawn.

```
/**
 ** Game update function
 **/
void Game_Run(HWND hwnd)
{
    //make sure the Direct3D device is valid
    if (!d3ddev) return;

    //create pointer to the back buffer
    d3ddev->GetBackBuffer(0, 0, D3DBACKBUFFER_TYPE_MONO, &backbuffer);

    //start rendering
    if (d3ddev->BeginScene())
    {
        //draw surface to the backbuffer
        d3ddev->StretchRect(surface, NULL, backbuffer, NULL, D3DTEXF_NONE);

        //stop rendering
        d3ddev->EndScene();
        d3ddev->Present(NULL, NULL, NULL, NULL);
    }

    //check for escape key (to exit program)
    if (KEY_DOWN(VK_ESCAPE))
        PostMessage(hwnd, WM_DESTROY, 0, 0);
}
```

The complete source listing and project for the program are included on the CD-ROM in \sources\chapter04\Load Bitmap Demo. When you run the program, you should see the bitmap shown in Figure 4.6 fill the screen.

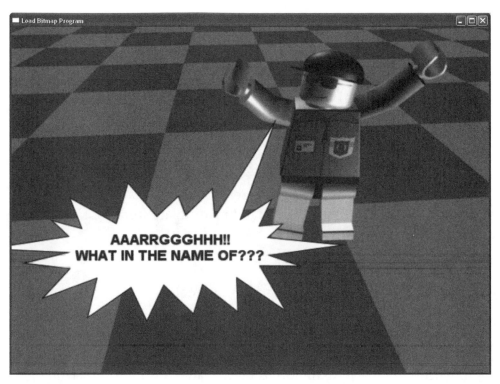

Figure 4.6
The Load Bitmap program loads a bitmap image into a Direct3D surface and then blits it to the screen.

Recycling Code

Have you noticed that the Windows code over the last two chapters hasn't changed one bit? WinProc and WinMain are the same from one program to the next. We're already seeing the benefit of recycling code in each new project. By moving the *inconsistent* portion of a program into the standard game functions (Game_Init, Game_Run, and Game_End), we have made it possible to recycle the calling functions so that WinProc and WinMain will not need to be included in every project. Of course you will *need* those functions to exist in your programs, and all of the examples on the CD-ROM are complete with these functions; we don't have to focus on them and repeat the code listings in every chapter. Less typing for you, which is good for your sanity, and less paper used to print this book, which is great for the environment! It's all good. Plus, that explains why such a phenomenally awesome book like this ended up being so small in print: because we write tight code!

What You Have Learned

In this chapter you learned how to create and manipulate surfaces. Here are the key points:

- You learned how to create a surface.

- You were able to fill the surface with random colors.

- You found out how to load a bitmap image from disk into a surface, with support for many graphics file formats.

- You learned how to draw whole and partial surfaces onto the screen.

Review Questions

Here are some review questions to dash your self-image and shatter your motivation. To see how badly you did on this quiz, refer to Appendix C, "Chapter Quiz Answers."

1. What is the name of the primary Direct3D object?

2. What is the Direct3D device called?

3. What is the name of the Direct3D surface object?

4. What function can you use to draw a Direct3D surface to the screen?

5. What is the term that describes copying images in memory?

6. What is the name of the struct used to handle a Direct3D surface?

7. What is the name of the long-pointer defined version of the same struct?

8. Which function returns a pointer to the Direct3D back buffer?

9. Which Direct3D device function fills a surface with a given color?

10. Which function is used to load a bitmap file into a Direct3D surface in memory?

On Your Own

These exercises will help to reinforce the material you have learned today. It may not stick, but it's worth a shot!

Exercise 1. The Load_Bitmap program loads a bitmap file and displays it on the screen. Use what you have learned about StretchRect to draw only a portion of the bitmap image to the screen.

Exercise 2. You have been recruited by the Star League to defend the frontiers against the Zurg. Using the knowledge you have learned in this chapter, write a simple game to demonstrate your worthiness to continue reading this book.

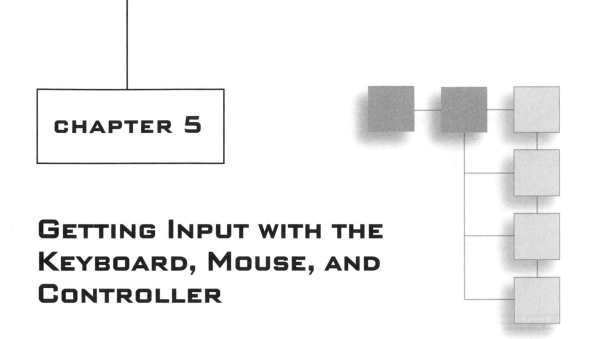

CHAPTER 5

GETTING INPUT WITH THE KEYBOARD, MOUSE, AND CONTROLLER

Welcome to the virtual interface chapter! In the coming pages, you will learn how to use DirectInput to program the keyboard and mouse to provide your games with support for the most common input devices. You will also learn how to program an Xbox 360 controller (if you have one—and I highly recommend it because the examples are a lot more fun with one!). We will be creating simple 2D images out of loaded bitmaps, each based on a Direct3D surface which you learned about in the previous chapter, and we will use this to make a game in this chapter called Bomb Catcher—so watch out for it! This game will help to illustrate how a keyboard, mouse, and even a controller can be used simultaneously in a game.

Here is what you will learn in this chapter:

- How to create DirectInput devices.

- How to get input from a keyboard.

- How to get input from a mouse.

- How to get input from an Xbox 360 controller.

- How to create and move a sprite.

- How to make your first game.

Keyboard Input

The keyboard is the standard input device for all games, even for those that don't specifically use the keyboard, so it is a given that your games will use the keyboard one way or another. If nothing else, you should allow the user to exit your game or at least bring up some sort of in-game menu by pressing the Escape key (that's the standard). Programming the keyboard using DirectInput is not difficult, but you do need to initialize DirectInput first.

The primary DirectInput object is called IDirectInput8; you can reference it directly or using the LPDIRECTINPUT8 pointer data type. Why is the number "8" attached to these interfaces? Because, like DirectSound, DirectInput has not changed in a long time. Kind of makes you wonder why we're at a full version upgrade to 9.0c already (and very likely beyond that by the time you read this).

The DirectInput library file is called dinput8.lib, so be sure to add this file to the linker options in the Project Settings dialog along with the other libs. I'll assume that you read the last chapter and learned how to set up the project to support DirectX and the game framework you've been building up to this point. If you have any question about how to set up the project at this point in the book, refer to the last chapter for a complete overview and tutorial. In this chapter, I'll have you add a new component to the framework for DirectInput using two new files (dxinput.h and dxinput.cpp).

DirectInput Object and Device

Okay, you are familiar with the drill of initializing the DirectX components, so let's learn how to scan the keyboard for button input. You will want to first define the primary DirectInput object used by your program along with the object for the device:

```
LPDIRECTINPUT8 dinput;
```

```
LPDIRECTINPUTDEVICE8 dinputdev;
```

After defining the variables, you can then call `DirectInputCreate8` to initialize DirectInput. The function has this format:

```
HRESULT WINAPI DirectInput8Create(
    HINSTANCE hinst,
    DWORD dwVersion,
    REFIID riidltf,
    LPVOID *ppvOut,
    LPUNKNOWN punkOuter
);
```

This function just creates the primary DirectInput object that you pass to it. The first parameter is the instance handle for the current program. A convenient way to get the current instance when it is not immediately available (normally this is only found in `WinMain`) is by using the `GetModuleHandle` function. The second parameter is the DirectInput version, which is always passed as `DIRECT-INPUT_VERSION`, defined in dinput.h. The third parameter is a reference identifier for the version of DirectInput that you want to use. At present, this value is `IID_IDirectInput8`. The fourth parameter is a pointer to the primary DirectInput object pointer (note the double pointer here), and the fifth parameter is always NULL. Here is an example of how you might call this function:

```
HRESULT result = DirectInput8Create(
    GetModuleHandle(NULL),
    DIRECTINPUT_VERSION,
    IID_IDirectInput8,
    (void**)&dinput,
    NULL);
```

After initializing the object, you can then use the object to create a new Direct-Input device by calling the `CreateDevice` function:

```
HRESULT CreateDevice(
    REFGUID rguid,
    LPDIRECTINPUTDEVICE *lplpDirectInputDevice,
    LPUNKNOWN pUnkOuter
);
```

The first parameter is a value that specifies the type of object you want to create (such as the keyboard or mouse). Here are the values you can use for this parameter:

- GUID_SysKeyboard

- GUID_SysMouse

The second parameter is your device pointer that receives the address of the DirectInput device handler. The third parameter is always NULL. Here is how you might call this function:

```
result = dinput->CreateDevice(GUID_SysKeyboard, &dikeyboard, NULL);
```

Initializing the Keyboard

Once you have the DirectInput object and device object for the keyboard, you can then initialize the keyboard handler to prepare it for input. The next step is to set the keyboard's data format, which instructs DirectInput how to pass the data back to your program. It is abstracted in this way because there are hundreds of input devices on the market with myriad features, so there has to be a uniform way to read them all.

Setting the Data Format

The SetDataFormat specifies how the data format is set.

```
HRESULT SetDataFormat(
     LPCDIDATAFORMAT lpdf
);
```

The single parameter to this function specifies the device type. For the keyboard, you want to pass the value of c_dfDIKeyboard as this parameter. The constant for a mouse would be c_dfDIMouse. Here, then, is a sample function call:

```
HRESULT result = dikeyboard->SetDataFormat(&c_dfDIKeyboard);
```

Note that you do not need to define c_dfDIKeyboard yourself, as it is defined in dinput.h.

Setting the Cooperative Level

The next step is to set the cooperative level, which determines how much of the keyboard DirectInput will give your program by way of priority. To set the cooperative level, you call the SetCooperativeLevel function:

```
HRESULT SetCooperativeLevel(
    HWND hwnd,
    DWORD dwFlags
);
```

The first parameter is the window handle. The second parameter is the interesting one, as it specifies the priority that your program will have over the keyboard or mouse. The most common values to pass when working with the keyboard are DISCL_NONEXCLUSIVE and DISCL_FOREGROUND. If you try to gain exclusive use of the keyboard, DirectInput will probably complain, so ask for non-exclusive access with priority as the foreground application in order to give your game the most control over the keyboard. So, then, here is how you might call the function:

```
HRESULT result = dikeyboard->SetCooperativeLevel(hwnd,
    DISCL_NONEXCLUSIVE | DISCL_FOREGROUND);
```

Acquiring the Device

The last step in initializing the keyboard is to acquire the keyboard device using the Acquire function:

```
HRESULT Acquire(VOID);
```

If the function returns a positive value (DI_OK) then you have successfully acquired the keyboard and are ready to start checking for key presses.

An important point that I should make here is that you *must* unacquire the keyboard before your game ends or it will leave DirectInput and the keyboard handler in an unknown state. Windows and DirectInput will probably take care of cleaning up after you, but it really depends on the version of Windows that the user is running. Believe it or not, there are still computers running Windows 98 and ME, despite these operating systems being quite out of date. Windows XP (and later versions) are much more stable, but you shouldn't leave anything to chance. It's best to unacquire the device before your game ends. Each DirectInput device has an Unacquire function with the following format:

```
HRESULT Unacquire(VOID);
```

Reading Key Presses

Somewhere in your game loop you need to poll the keyboard to update its key values. Speaking of keys, it is up to you to define the array of keys that are to be populated with the keyboard device status, like this:

```
char keys[256];
```

You must poll the keyboard to fill in this array of characters, and to do that you call the GetDeviceState function. This function is used for all devices regardless of type, so it is standard for all input devices:

```
HRESULT GetDeviceState(
    DWORD cbData,
    LPVOID lpvData
);
```

The first parameter is the size of the device state buffer to be filled with data. The second parameter is a pointer to the data. In the case of the keyboard, here is how you would call this function:

```
dikeyboard->GetDeviceState(sizeof(keys), (LPVOID)&keys);
```

After polling the keyboard, you can then check the keys array for values corresponding to the DirectInput key codes; these values are listed in Appendix B of this book.

Here is how you would check for the Escape key:

```
if (keys[DIK_ESCAPE] & 0x80)
{
    //ESCAPE key was pressed, so do something!
}
```

Mouse Input

Once you have written a handler for the keyboard, it is a piece of cake to support the mouse as well, because the code is very similar and it shares the DirectInput object and device pointers. So let's jump into it right now and learn about the mouse interface. First, define the mouse device:

```
LPDIRECTINPUTDEVICE8 dimouse;
```

Next, create the mouse device:

```
result = dinput->CreateDevice(GUID_SysMouse, &dimouse, NULL);
```

Initializing the Mouse

So, let's assume DirectInput is all squared away, and now you want to add a mouse handler. The next step is to set the data format for the mouse, which instructs DirectInput how to pass the data back to your program. It functions in exactly the same way for the mouse as it does for the keyboard.

Setting the Data Format

The SetDataFormat function looks like this:

```
HRESULT SetDataFormat(
    LPCDIDATAFORMAT lpdf
);
```

The single parameter to this function specifies the device type. The constant for your mouse is c_dfDIMouse. Here, then, is a sample function call:

```
HRESULT result = dimouse->SetDataFormat(&c_dfDIMouse);
```

Note, again, that you do not need to define c_dfDIMouse, as it is defined in dinput.h.

Setting the Cooperative Level

The next step is to set the cooperative level, which determines how much priority over the mouse DirectInput will give your program. To set the cooperative level, you call the SetCooperativeLevel function:

```
HRESULT SetCooperativeLevel(
    HWND hwnd,
    DWORD dwFlags
);
```

The first parameter is the window handle. The second parameter is the interesting one, as it specifies the priority that your program will have over the mouse. The most common values to pass when working with the mouse are DISCL_NONEXCLUSIVE and DISCL_FOREGROUND. Here is how to call this function:

```
HRESULT result = dimouse->SetCooperativeLevel(hwnd,
    DISCL_NONEXCLUSIVE | DISCL_FOREGROUND);
```

Acquiring the Device

The last step is to acquire the mouse device using the Acquire function. If the function returns DI_OK, then you have successfully acquired the mouse and are ready to start checking for movement and button presses.

As with the keyboard device, you must also unacquire the mouse device after you are done using it, or else you could leave DirectInput in an unstable state:

```
HRESULT Unacquire(VOID);
```

Reading the Mouse

Somewhere in your game loop you need to poll the mouse to update the mouse position and button status. You poll the mouse using the GetDeviceState function:

```
HRESULT GetDeviceState(
    DWORD cbData,
    LPVOID lpvData
);
```

The first parameter is the size of the device state buffer to be filled with data. The second parameter is a pointer to the data. There is a struct available for your use in polling the mouse:

```
DIMOUSESTATE mouse_state;
```

Here is how you would fill the DIMOUSESTATE struct by calling the GetDeviceState function:

```
dimouse->GetDeviceState(sizeof(mouse_state), (LPVOID)&mouse_state);
```

The struct looks like this:

```
typedef struct DIMOUSESTATE {
    LONG lX;
    LONG lY;
    LONG lZ;
    BYTE rgbButtons[4];
} DIMOUSESTATE;
```

There is an alternate struct available for your use when you want to support complex mouse devices with more than four buttons, in which case the button array is doubled in size but the struct is otherwise the same:

```
typedef struct DIMOUSESTATE2 {
    LONG lX;
    LONG lY;
    LONG lZ;
    BYTE rgbButtons[8];
} DIMOUSESTATE2;
```

After polling the mouse, you can then check the mouse_state struct for x and y motion and button presses. You can check for mouse movement, also called *mickeys*, using the lX and lY member variables. What are mickeys? *Mickeys* represent motion of the mouse rather than an absolute position, so you must keep track of the old position if you want to use these mouse-positioning values to draw your own pointer. Mickeys are a convenient way of handling mouse motion because you can continue to move in a single direction and the mouse will continue to report movement, even if the "pointer" would have reached the edge of the screen.

As you can see from the struct, the rgbButtons array holds the result of button presses. If you want to check for a specific button (starting with 0 for button 1), here is how you might do that:

```
button_1 = obj.rgbButtons[0] & 0x80;
```

A more convenient method of detecting button presses is by using a define:

```
#define BUTTON_DOWN(obj, button) (obj.rgbButtons[button] & 0x80)
```

By using the define, you can check for button presses like so:

```
button_1 = BUTTON_DOWN(mouse_state, 0);
```

Xbox 360 Controller Input

Most Windows users do not have an Xbox 360 controller plugged into their PC. It's just a fact that we must accept. Writing a DirectX game that requires a controller in order to function is a big mistake, because you will be leaving out most of your potential audience that way. It's a rare gamer (casual or hardcore) who is willing to jump through hoops to play your game. First, they would need to buy either a corded Xbox 360 controller or a wireless adapter for their PC to work with one of the more common wireless controllers. They both work equally well, but that is an extra cost beyond the user's existing keyboard and mouse, which they will be accustomed to using with their PC games—and might be more than a little irritated if you try to force a controller on them. For this reason, I will not be supporting *just* a controller in any game. However, there's no reason why we can't support an Xbox 360 controller (shown in Figure 5.1) *in addition* to the keyboard and mouse! And that's exactly what we'll be doing in this and all future chapters. Once you start using the familiar controller (if you're a console gamer—and who isn't?) it's difficult to go back to just the boring old keyboard and mouse.

Figure 5.1
Xbox 360 controller.

We can use the XInput library to gain access to the Xbox 360 controller. This library is comprised of an XInput.h header file and XInput.lib library file. You can add the header file to the project with:

```
#include <xinput.h>
```

and reference the library file in your game project with:

```
#pragma comment(lib,"xinput.lib")
```

Advice

The XInput library should have been installed with the DirectX SDK automatically, so you shouldn't need to do anything special to gain access to the XInput library. But if you have any problems getting it to work, refer to Appendix A for instructions on how to configure Visual C++ with DirectX.

Initializing XInput

If you don't have a controller plugged in to your PC when you run a program that uses it, nothing bad happens—no error messages will appear. But if a controller *is* available, then you can begin reading it's input data.

Here is one way to initialize the XInput library: by getting the capabilities of a controller and checking those values to see if a controller is actually plugged in (either via the wireless adapter or a wired controller plugged into a USB port):

```
XINPUT_CAPABILITIES caps;
ZeroMemory(&caps, sizeof(XINPUT_CAPABILITIES));
XInputGetCapabilities(0, XINPUT_FLAG_GAMEPAD, &caps);
if (caps.Type != 0) return false;
```

If you have any other Xbox 360 accessory plugged into your PC, then this code which only checks for a controller (e.g., "gamepad") will report a failure. If you do want to support one of those unusual devices, you'll need to look up its device type value in xinput.h.

Advice

Although DirectInput supports joysticks, gamepads, driving wheels, and other accessories made by other companies (such as Logitech), the XInput library only works with Xbox 360 accessories—which currently includes the Xbox 360 controller, driving wheel, arcade stick, flight stick, dance pad, guitar, and even the drum kit!

Reading the Controller State

You can read an Xbox 360 controller using XInput's controller status struct and function. The struct is called XINPUT_STATE, while the supporting function is called XInputGetState. We want to first create a new struct variable and clear it out:

```
XINPUT_STATE state;
ZeroMemory( &state, sizeof(XINPUT_STATE) );
```

and then read the controller state by calling the XInputGetState function:

```
DWORD result = XInputGetState( 0, &state );
```

If result is zero, then a controller was found and the XINPUT_STATE struct was filled with data. Otherwise, if the result is not zero, that means no controller could be found.

After checking the result of XInputGetState, we can then look at the properties in the XINPUT_STATE variable with code such as this:

```
if (state.Gamepad.bLeftTrigger)
    MessageBox(0, "Left Trigger", "Controller", 0);
```

The XINPUT_STATE struct contains these properties:

- DWORD   dwPacketNumber;

- XINPUT_GAMEPAD Gamepad;

which is further broken down into the XINPUT_GAMEPAD struct where the real important properties are to be found:

- WORD wButtons;

- BYTE bLeftTrigger;

- BYTE bRightTrigger;

- SHORT   sThumbLX;

- SHORT   sThumbLY;

- SHORT   sThumbRX;

- SHORT   sThumbRY;

The analog trigger buttons (bLeftTrigger and bRightTrigger) produce an 8-bit number in the range of 0 to 255.

The analog "thumb" sticks produce a 16-bit number for each axis (x and y) in the range of –32,768 (all the way left) to +32,767 (all the way right). The "dead space" at the center of each stick is usually around +/– 1,500 units. So, if you just want to use the analog stick as a directional button of sorts, it's best to compare it with a value of around +/– 5,000 (e.g., if (sThumbLX < –5000) ...).

The wButtons property is a single number containing a bit-mask with the button states all combined.

- XINPUT_GAMEPAD_DPAD_UP

- XINPUT_GAMEPAD_DPAD_DOWN

- XINPUT_GAMEPAD_DPAD_LEFT

- XINPUT_GAMEPAD_DPAD_RIGHT

- XINPUT_GAMEPAD_START

- XINPUT_GAMEPAD_BACK

- XINPUT_GAMEPAD_LEFT_THUMB

- XINPUT_GAMEPAD_RIGHT_THUMB

- XINPUT_GAMEPAD_LEFT_SHOULDER

- XINPUT_GAMEPAD_RIGHT_SHOULDER

- XINPUT_GAMEPAD_A

- XINPUT_GAMEPAD_B

- XINPUT_GAMEPAD_X

- XINPUT_GAMEPAD_Y

When you want to check for a certain button, you must use a bitwise AND (&) to compare wButtons with the defined button to see if that particular button has been pressed, like so:

```
if (state.wButtons & XINPUT_GAMEPAD_DPAD_LEFT)  ...
```

You can include multiple button checks for combo moves (such as A + B to perform a special attack or special move) but it's usually easier to just handle each button press individually or nest the if statements.

Controller Vibration

As a matter of fact, we can even tell the controller to vibrate with a very simple function call! To use vibration (also called "force feedback"), we use the XINPUT_VIBRATION struct, which has two properties: wLeftMotorSpeed and wRightMotorSpeed, which can be set to a value between 0 and 65,535 (where 0 is off and 65,535 is full vibration—and watch out, it will cause the controller to vibrate right off your desk!).

```
XINPUT_VIBRATION vibration;
ZeroMemory( &vibration, sizeof(XINPUT_VIBRATION) );
vibration.wLeftMotorSpeed = left;
vibration.wRightMotorSpeed = right;
XInputSetState( 0, &vibration );
```

Testing XInput

I have a very short example program to share with you, called Xinput Test. This program includes three helpful functions that you can use to support an

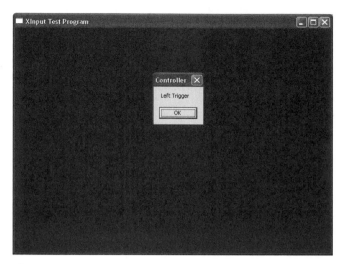

Figure 5.2
The XInput Test program reports controller input events via `MessageBox`.

Xbox 360 controller in your own DirectX games. Actually, you know, you can use XInput even without DirectX, because it's an independent library that does not require the DirectX object to function. The only time you would need to link up with DirectX is if you wanted to use the voice chat headset that plugs into the controller (in which case XInput works with DirectSound). So if you want to add controller input support to a database application at work, without telling your boss, go for it! (I recommend using the buttons to perform database queries.) Figure 5.2 shows the simple XInput Test program, which is just showing a message box with the name of the button that was pressed.

The source code for the XInput Test program will be the last time the full source code for a program will actually be listed in its entirety. Since we're duplicating a lot of the Windows code in every program, we will be breaking this program into smaller parts for the Bomb Catcher game coming up next. The important new code is highlighted in bold.

Advice

The XInput Test program uses button A to start vibration, button B to stop vibration, and the Back button to end the program. You may still use the Escape key to exit as well. This will be a trend in all of our future programs.

```
/*
    Beginning Game Programming, Third Edition
    Chapter 5
    XInput_Test Program
*/

#include <windows.h>
#include <d3d9.h>
#include <d3dx9.h>
#include <xinput.h>
#include <iostream>
using namespace std;

#pragma comment(lib,"d3d9.lib")
#pragma comment(lib,"d3dx9.lib")
#pragma comment(lib,"xinput.lib")

//application title
const string APPTITLE = "XInput Test Program";

//macro to read the keyboard
#define KEY_DOWN(vk_code) ((GetAsyncKeyState(vk_code) & 0x8000) ? 1 : 0)

//screen resolution
const int SCREENW = 640;
const int SCREENH = 480;

//Direct3D objects
LPDIRECT3D9 d3d = NULL;
LPDIRECT3DDEVICE9 d3ddev = NULL;

bool gameover = false;

/**
 ** Initializes XInput and any connected controllers
 **/
bool XInput_Init(int contNum = 0)
{
    XINPUT_CAPABILITIES caps;
    ZeroMemory(&caps, sizeof(XINPUT_CAPABILITIES));
    XInputGetCapabilities(contNum, XINPUT_FLAG_GAMEPAD, &caps);
    if (caps.Type != XINPUT_DEVTYPE_GAMEPAD) return false;

    return true;
}
```

```cpp
/**
 ** Causes the controller to vibrate
 **/
void XInput_Vibrate(int contNum = 0, int left = 65535, int right = 65535)
{
    XINPUT_VIBRATION vibration;
    ZeroMemory( &vibration, sizeof(XINPUT_VIBRATION) );
    vibration.wLeftMotorSpeed = left;
    vibration.wRightMotorSpeed = right;
    XInputSetState( contNum, &vibation );
}


/**
 ** Checks the state of the controller
 **/
void XInput_Update()
{
    for (int i=0; i< 4; i++ )
    {
        XINPUT_STATE state;
        ZeroMemory( &state, sizeof(XINPUT_STATE) );

        //get the state of the controller
         DWORD result = XInputGetState( i, &state );

         if( result == 0 )
         {
             // controller is connected
             if (state.Gamepad.bLeftTrigger)
                 MessageBox(0, "Left Trigger", "Controller", 0);

             else if (state.Gamepad.bRightTrigger)
                 MessageBox(0, "Right Trigger", "Controller", 0);

             else if (state.Gamepad.sThumbLX < -10000 ||
                 state.Gamepad.sThumbLX > 10000)
                 MessageBox(0, "Left Thumb Stick", "Controller", 0);

             else if (state.Gamepad.sThumbRX < -10000 ||
                 state.Gamepad.sThumbRX > 10000)
                 MessageBox(0, "Right Thumb Stick", "Controller", 0);

             else if (state.Gamepad.wButtons & XINPUT_GAMEPAD_DPAD_UP)
                 MessageBox(0, "DPAD Up", "Controller", 0);
```

```
else if (state.Gamepad.wButtons & XINPUT_GAMEPAD_DPAD_DOWN)
    MessageBox(0, "DPAD Down", "Controller", 0);

else if (state.Gamepad.wButtons & XINPUT_GAMEPAD_DPAD_LEFT)
    MessageBox(0, "DPAD Left", "Controller", 0);

else if (state.Gamepad.wButtons & XINPUT_GAMEPAD_DPAD_RIGHT)
    MessageBox(0, "DPAD Right", "Controller", 0);

else if (state.Gamepad.wButtons & XINPUT_GAMEPAD_START)
    MessageBox(0, "Start", "Controller", 0);

else if (state.Gamepad.wButtons & XINPUT_GAMEPAD_LEFT_THUMB)
    MessageBox(0, "Left Thumb", "Controller", 0);

else if (state.Gamepad.wButtons & XINPUT_GAMEPAD_RIGHT_THUMB)
    MessageBox(0, "Right Thumb", "Controller", 0);

else if (state.Gamepad.wButtons & XINPUT_GAMEPAD_LEFT_SHOULDER)
    MessageBox(0, "Left Shoulder", "Controller", 0);

else if (state.Gamepad.wButtons & XINPUT_GAMEPAD_RIGHT_SHOULDER)
    MessageBox(0, "Right Shoulder", "Controller", 0);

else if (state.Gamepad.wButtons & XINPUT_GAMEPAD_A)
{
    XInput_Vibrate(0, 65535, 65535);
    MessageBox(0, "A", "Controller", 0);
}

else if (state.Gamepad.wButtons & XINPUT_GAMEPAD_B)
{
    XInput_Vibrate(0, 0, 0);
    MessageBox(0, "B", "Controller", 0);
}

else if (state.Gamepad.wButtons & XINPUT_GAMEPAD_X)
    MessageBox(0, "X", "Controller", 0);

else if (state.Gamepad.wButtons & XINPUT_GAMEPAD_Y)
    MessageBox(0, "Y", "Controller", 0);

else if (state.Gamepad.wButtons & XINPUT_GAMEPAD_BACK)
    gameover = true;
```

```
        }
        else {
            // controller is not connected
        }
    }
}

/**
 ** Game initialization
 **/
bool Game_Init(HWND hwnd)
{
    //initialize Direct3D
    d3d = Direct3DCreate9(D3D_SDK_VERSION);
    if (d3d == NULL)
    {
        MessageBox(hwnd, "Error initializing Direct3D", "Error", MB_OK);
        return false;
    }

    //set Direct3D presentation parameters
    D3DPRESENT_PARAMETERS d3dpp;
    ZeroMemory(&d3dpp, sizeof(d3dpp));
    d3dpp.Windowed = TRUE;
    d3dpp.SwapEffect = D3DSWAPEFFECT_DISCARD;
    d3dpp.BackBufferFormat = D3DFMT_X8R8G8B8;
    d3dpp.BackBufferCount = 1;
    d3dpp.BackBufferWidth = SCREENW;
    d3dpp.BackBufferHeight = SCREENH;
    d3dpp.hDeviceWindow = hwnd;

    //create Direct3D device
    d3d->CreateDevice( D3DADAPTER_DEFAULT, D3DDEVTYPE_HAL, hwnd,
        D3DCREATE_SOFTWARE_VERTEXPROCESSING, &d3dpp, &d3ddev );

    if (!d3ddev)
    {
        MessageBox(hwnd, "Error creating Direct3D device", "Error", MB_OK);
        return false;
    }

    //initialize XInput
    XInput_Init();
```

```
        return true;
}

/**
 ** Game update
 **/
void Game_Run(HWND hwnd)
{
        //make sure the Direct3D device is valid
        if (!d3ddev) return;

        //clear the backbuffer to black
        d3ddev->Clear(0, NULL, D3DCLEAR_TARGET, D3DCOLOR_XRGB(0,0,150), 1.0f, 0);

        //start rendering
        if (d3ddev->BeginScene())
        {
            d3ddev->EndScene();
            d3ddev->Present(NULL, NULL, NULL, NULL);
        }

        //check for escape key (to exit program)
        if (KEY_DOWN(VK_ESCAPE))
            PostMessage(hwnd, WM_DESTROY, 0, 0);

    //check for controller input
    XInput_Update();
}

/**
 ** Game shutdown
 **/
void Game_End(HWND hwnd)
{
        if (d3ddev) d3ddev->Release();
        if (d3d) d3d->Release();
}

/**
 ** Windows event handler
 **/
LRESULT WINAPI WinProc( HWND hWnd, UINT msg, WPARAM wParam, LPARAM lParam )
```

```cpp
{
    switch( msg )
    {
        case WM_DESTROY:
            gameover = true;
            PostQuitMessage(0);
            return 0;
    }
    return DefWindowProc( hWnd, msg, wParam, lParam );
}


/**
 ** Windows entry point
 **/
int WINAPI WinMain(HINSTANCE hInstance, HINSTANCE hPrevInstance,
    LPSTR lpCmdLine, int nCmdShow)
{
    //create the window class structure
    WNDCLASSEX wc;
    wc.cbSize = sizeof(WNDCLASSEX);
    wc.style        = CS_HREDRAW | CS_VREDRAW;
    wc.lpfnWndProc  = (WNDPROC)WinProc;
    wc.cbClsExtra    = 0;
    wc.cbWndExtra    = 0;
    wc.hInstance    = hInstance;
    wc.hIcon        = NULL;
    wc.hCursor      = LoadCursor(NULL, IDC_ARROW);
    wc.hbrBackground = (HBRUSH)GetStockObject(WHITE_BRUSH);
    wc.lpszMenuName  = NULL;
    wc.lpszClassName = APPTITLE.c_str();
    wc.hIconSm      = NULL;
    RegisterClassEx(&wc);

    //create a new window
    HWND window = CreateWindow(APPTITLE.c_str(), APPTITLE.c_str(),
        WS_OVERLAPPEDWINDOW, CW_USEDEFAULT, CW_USEDEFAULT,
        SCREENW, SCREENH, NULL, NULL, hInstance, NULL);

    //was there an error creating the window?
    if (window == 0) return 0;

    //display the window
    ShowWindow(window, nCmdShow);
```

```
UpdateWindow(window);

//initialize the game
if (!Game_Init(window)) return 0;

// main message loop
MSG message;
while (!gameover)
{
    if (PeekMessage(&message, NULL, 0, 0, PM_REMOVE))
    {
        TranslateMessage(&message);
        DispatchMessage(&message);
    }
    Game_Run(window);
}
Game_End();
return message.wParam;
}
```

A Brief Introduction to Sprite Programming

There are two ways to draw a sprite with Direct3D. Both methods require that you keep track of the sprite's position, size, speed, and other properties on your own, so the logistics are not relevant. The simpler of the two methods is to load a sprite image into a D3D surface (which you learned about in the last chapter) and then draw the sprite using StretchRect. The more difficult—but more powerful—method is to use a special object called D3DXSprite to handle sprites in Direct3D. D3DXSprite uses textures rather than surfaces to hold the sprite image, so using it requires a slightly different approach than what you learned in the last chapter. However, loading a bitmap image into a texture is no more difficult than loading an image into a surface. I will cover the simple method of drawing sprites in this chapter, and then go over D3DXSprite in the next chapter.

A *sprite* is a small bitmapped image that is drawn on the screen and represents a character or object in a game. Sprites can be used for inanimate objects like trees and rocks, or animated game characters like a hero/heroine in a role-playing game. One thing is certain in the modern world of game development: Sprites are reserved exclusively for the 2D realm. You will not find a sprite in a 3D game, unless that sprite is being drawn "over" the 3D rendered game scene, as with a

Figure 5.3
A bitmapped font used to print text on the screen in a game.

Figure 5.4
A tank sprite with animated treads, courtesy of Ari Feldman (www.flyingyogi.com).

heads-up display or bitmapped font. For instance, in a multi-player game with a chat feature, the text messages appearing on the screen from other players are usually drawn as individual letters, each treated as a sprite. Figure 5.3 shows an example of a bitmapped font stored in a bitmap file.

A sprite is typically stored in a bitmap file as a series of tiles, each tile representing a single frame of that sprite's animation sequence. An animation might look less like movement than a change of direction, as in the case of an airplane or spaceship in a shoot-'em-up game. Figure 5.4 shows a tank sprite that faces in a single direction but includes animated treads for movement.

Now what if you wanted that tank to face other directions as well as animate? As you can imagine, the number of frames can increase exponentially as you add a new frame of animation for each direction of travel. Figure 5.5 shows a non-animated tank that has been rotated in 32 directions for a very smooth turning rate. Unfortunately, when you add the moving tank treads, those 32 frames suddenly become 32 * 8 = 256 frames! It would be difficult to program a tank with so many frames, and how would you store them in the bitmap file? Linearly, most likely, in rows and columns. A better solution is usually to reduce the number of frames until you get the game finished, and then perhaps (if you are so inclined) add more precision and detail to the animation. But, this is all conjecture, because in the next chapter we will learn how to just rotate a sprite in code!

Figure 5.5
A 32-frame rotation of the tank sprite (not animated), courtesy of Ari Feldman.

MechCommander (MicroProse, FASA Studios) was one of the most highly animated video games ever made, and were it not for the terrible AI in this game and unrealistic difficulty level, I would have considering it among my all-time favorite games. The fascinating thing about *MechCommander* is that it is a highly detailed 2D sprite-based game. Every single mech in the game is a 2D sprite stored in a series of bitmap files. The traditional 2D nature of this game becomes amazing when you consider that the game featured about 100,000 frames! Imagine the amount of time it took to first model the mechs with a 3D modeler (like *3ds max*), and then render out 100,000 snapshots of various angles and positions, and then resize and add the final touches to each sprite.

Note

In August of 2006, Microsoft released the source code to *MechCommander 2*, along with all of the game's resources (artwork, etc). You can download the complete code for the game (which is powered by DirectX) from here: http://www.microsoft.com/downloads/details.aspx?familyid= 6D790CDE-C3E5-46BE-B3A5-729581269A9C&displaylang=en. I found this link by Googling for "mechcommander 2 source code".

Another common type of sprite is the platformer game sprite, shown in Figure 5.6. Programming a platform game is more difficult than programming a shoot-'em-up, but the results are usually worth the extra work.

Figure 5.6
An animated platform game character, courtesy of Ari Feldman.

A Useful Sprite Struct

The key to this program is the SPRITE struct:

```
//sprite structure
struct SPRITE {
    float x,y;
    int width,height;
    float velx,vely;
}
```

The obvious members of this struct are x, y, width, and height. What may not be so obvious is velx and vely. These member variables are used to update the x and y position of the sprite during each frame update.

Here is an example of how you could create a sprite with this new struct:

```
SPRITE spaceship;
spaceship.x = 100;
spaceship.y = 150;
spaceship.width = 96;
spaceship.height = 96;
spaceship.velx = 8.0f;
spaceship.vely = 0.0f;
```

Loading a Sprite Image

This struct, along with a Direct3D surface for the image, is all you need to make simple sprites. For review, let's take a look again at the surface loading and drawing code. First, we'll see again how to load a bitmap file and store it in a surface in memory (this was covered in the previous chapter):

```
//get width and height from bitmap file
D3DXIMAGE_INFO info;
HRESULT result = D3DXGetImageInfoFromFile(filename, &info);

//create surface
LPDIRECT3DSURFACE9 image = NULL;
result = d3ddev->CreateOffscreenPlainSurface(
    info.Width,            //width of the surface
    info.Height,           //height of the surface
    D3DFMT_X8R8G8B8,       //surface format
    D3DPOOL_DEFAULT,       //memory pool to use
    &image,                //pointer to the surface
    NULL);                 //reserved (always NULL)

//load surface from file into newly created surface
result = D3DXLoadSurfaceFromFile(
    image,                 //destination surface
    NULL,                  //destination palette
    NULL,                  //destination rectangle
    filename,              //source filename
    NULL,                  //source rectangle
    D3DX_DEFAULT,          //controls how image is filtered
    transcolor,            //for transparency (0 for none)
    NULL);                 //source image info (usually NULL)
```

Drawing a Sprite Image

When you have successfully loaded a bitmap file into a Direct3D surface in memory, then you can draw the image using the StretchRect function. Assuming you have already created a pointer to the back buffer, here is how you might draw an image:

```
//draw surface to the backbuffer
d3ddev->StretchRect(image, NULL, backbuffer, NULL, D3DTEXF_NONE);
```

The two NULL parameters here are the source and destination rectangles that allow you to specify the dimensions exactly where an image should come from, and exactly where it should be drawn to. Normally you would want to pass actual rectangles to make the sprite show up exactly the way you want it. Here is a helpful function that accomplished just that. This function uses D3DSURFACE_DESC and the GetDesc() function to retrieve the width and height of the source bitmap in order to draw it correctly onto the destination surface.

```
void DrawSurface( LPDIRECT3DSURFACE9 dest, float x, float y,
    LPDIRECT3DSURFACE9 source)
{
    //get width/height from source surface
    D3DSURFACE_DESC desc;
    source->GetDesc(&desc);

    //create rects for drawing
    RECT source_rect = {0, 0, (long)desc.Width, (long)desc.Height };
    RECT dest_rect = { (long)x, (long)y, (long)x+desc.Width,
                                        (long)y+desc.Height};

    //draw the source surface onto the dest
    d3ddev->StretchRect(source, &source_rect, dest, &dest_rect,
    D3DTEXF_NONE);
}
```

Advice

We will replace this surface-based sprite code in the next two chapters with texture-based sprites, which have much better capabilities—such as rotation and scaling!

Bomb Catcher Game

That about sums up the code needed to program the input devices. Are you ready to put it into practice with your first DirectX game? We're going to create a pseudo-game called Bomb Catcher to demonstrate everything you've learned so far. This game will let you move a bucket on the bottom of the screen in order to catch random bombs falling down from the top. See how many bombs you can catch—but if one hits the bottom of the screen, watch out! Let's go over the list of skills you've accumulated so far:

- Initializing Direct3D

- Loading a bitmap file into memory

- Drawing a bitmap

- Keyboard input

- Mouse input

- Xbox 360 controller input

That's a sizable list of skills in a very short amount of time—we're still only in Chapter 5! But these are the minimum things we need in order to make the simplest of games (which will not have any sound effects yet). And, admittedly, we don't absolutely *have* to support controller input, but it's very easy to do so we might as well while we're on the subject.

Figure 5.7 shows the Bomb Catcher game in action. The game supports keyboard, mouse, and controller input, and is ready for your own enhancements! More importantly, this is the first program that separates the Windows, DirectX, and game source code into separate files:

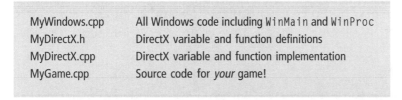

MyWindows.cpp	All Windows code including `WinMain` and `WinProc`
MyDirectX.h	DirectX variable and function definitions
MyDirectX.cpp	DirectX variable and function implementation
MyGame.cpp	Source code for *your* game!

Figure 5.7
The Bomb Catcher game demonstrates mouse, keyboard, and controller input.

Code re-use is the key to becoming a professional programmer. You simply cannot rewrite code again and again and expect to have any time to get real work done. The source code files you have created thus far provide a game framework that greatly reduces the amount of work you must do to write a Windows/ DirectX game. And we're talking about a full-blown Direct3D game, at that! What? We haven't even gone into 3D yet?

I've been holding off on 3D for a reason: it's a little more complicated. I wanted to have this basis of code (the framework) ready to go before diving headfirst into the 3D code because otherwise we'd be swimming in reams of code right now. The 3D chapters that follow (starting with Chapter 12, "Learning the Basics of 3D Rendering") will be easy to understand and grasp because I'm not getting into any 3D math, but there is a lot of code involved when you're working with Direct3D.

Go ahead and create the new Bomb Catcher project now and add these new source code files to the project. We'll go over the source code in each file separately.

MyWindows.cpp

Add a new source code file to your new Win32 project and call it MyWindows.cpp. This source code file contains all of the standard Windows code in the WinProc and

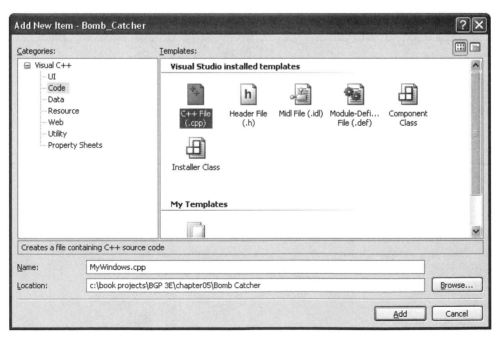

Figure 5.8
Adding the MyWindows.cpp file to the project.

WinMain functions. Since this is about the fifth time we've produced this listing in the book, it will be the last—so hang on to this source code file because we won't be duplicating it again.

```cpp
/*
    Beginning Game Programming, Third Edition
    MyWindows.cpp
*/

#include "MyDirectX.h"
using namespace std;
bool gameover = false;

/**
 ** Windows event handler
 **/
LRESULT WINAPI WinProc( HWND hWnd, UINT msg, WPARAM wParam, LPARAM lParam )
{
    switch( msg )
    {
        case WM_DESTROY:
            gameover = true;
            PostQuitMessage(0);
            return 0;
    }
    return DefWindowProc( hWnd, msg, wParam, lParam );
}

/**
 ** Windows entry point
 **/
int WINAPI WinMain(HINSTANCE hInstance, HINSTANCE hPrevInstance,
    LPSTR lpCmdLine, int nCmdShow)
{
    //initialize window settings
    WNDCLASSEX wc;
    wc.cbSize = sizeof(WNDCLASSEX);
    wc.style         = CS_HREDRAW | CS_VREDRAW;
    wc.lpfnWndProc   = (WNDPROC)WinProc;
    wc.cbClsExtra    = 0;
    wc.cbWndExtra    = 0;
    wc.hInstance     = hInstance;
    wc.hIcon         = NULL;
```

```
    wc.hCursor         = LoadCursor(NULL, IDC_ARROW);
    wc.hbrBackground = (HBRUSH)GetStockObject(WHITE_BRUSH);
    wc.lpszMenuName  = NULL;
    wc.lpszClassName = APPTITLE.c_str();
    wc.hIconSm        = NULL;
    RegisterClassEx(&wc);

    //create a new window
    HWND window = CreateWindow( APPTITLE.c_str(), APPTITLE.c_str(),
        WS_OVERLAPPEDWINDOW, CW_USEDEFAULT, CW_USEDEFAULT,
        SCREENW, SCREENH, NULL, NULL, hInstance, NULL);
    if (window == 0) return 0;

    //display the window
    ShowWindow(window, nCmdShow);
    UpdateWindow(window);

    //initialize the game
    if (!Game_Init(window)) return 0;

    // main message loop
    MSG message;
    while (!gameover)
    {
        if (PeekMessage(&message, NULL, 0, 0, PM_REMOVE))
        {
            TranslateMessage(&message);
            DispatchMessage(&message);
        }

        //process game loop
        Game_Run(window);
    }

    //shutdown
    Game_End();
    return message.wParam;
}
```

MyDirectX.h

Add a new source code file to your new Win32 project and call it MyDirectX.h.
This file contains all of the function prototypes, header files, library files, and

Figure 5.9
Adding the MyDirectX.h file to the project.

global variables needed to make a DirectX game! We will be adding to this file
when we add new features (such as texture loading in the next chapter).

```
/*
    Beginning Game Programming, Third Edition
    MyDirectX.h
*/

#pragma once

//header files
#define WIN32_EXTRA_LEAN
#define DIRECTINPUT_VERSION 0x0800
#include <windows.h>
#include <d3d9.h>
#include <d3dx9.h>
#include <dinput.h>
#include <xinput.h>
#include <ctime>
#include <iostream>
#include <iomanip>
using namespace std;

//libraries
#pragma comment(lib,"winmm.lib")
```

```cpp
#pragma comment(lib,"user32.lib")
#pragma comment(lib,"gdi32.lib")
#pragma comment(lib,"dxguid.lib")
#pragma comment(lib,"d3d9.lib")
#pragma comment(lib,"d3dx9.lib")
#pragma comment(lib,"dinput8.lib")
#pragma comment(lib,"xinput.lib")

//program values
extern const string APPTITLE;
extern const int SCREENW;
extern const int SCREENH;
extern bool gameover;

//Direct3D objects
extern LPDIRECT3D9 d3d;
extern LPDIRECT3DDEVICE9 d3ddev;
extern LPDIRECT3DSURFACE9 backbuffer;

//Direct3D functions
bool Direct3D_Init(HWND hwnd, int width, int height, bool fullscreen);
void Direct3D_Shutdown();
LPDIRECT3DSURFACE9 LoadSurface(string filename);
void DrawSurface(LPDIRECT3DSURFACE9 dest, float x, float y,
    LPDIRECT3DSURFACE9 source);

//DirectInput objects, devices, and states
extern LPDIRECTINPUT8 dinput;
extern LPDIRECTINPUTDEVICE8 dimouse;
extern LPDIRECTINPUTDEVICE8 dikeyboard;
extern DIMOUSESTATE mouse_state;
extern XINPUT_GAMEPAD controllers[4];

//DirectInput functions
bool DirectInput_Init(HWND);
void DirectInput_Update();
void DirectInput_Shutdown();
int Key_Down(int);
int Mouse_Button(int);
int Mouse_X();
int Mouse_Y();
void XInput_Vibrate(int contNum = 0, int amount = 65535);
bool XInput_Controller_Found();
```

```
//game functions
bool Game_Init(HWND window);
void Game_Run(HWND window);
void Game_End();
```

MyDirectX.cpp

Add a new source code file to your new Win32 project and call it MyDirectX.cpp. This file contains the DirectX implementation for our game projects. All of the DirectX code will be contained here, including Direct3D and DirectInput—yes, in the same source file to keep things simple. We will add to this file as we add new skills to our game programming tool set in each new chapter.

```
/*
    Beginning Game Programming, Third Edition
    MyDirectX.cpp
*/

#include "MyDirectX.h"
#include <iostream>
using namespace std;

//Direct3D variables
LPDIRECT3D9 d3d = NULL;
```

Figure 5.10
Adding the MyDirectX.cpp file to the project.

```
LPDIRECT3DDEVICE9 d3ddev = NULL;
LPDIRECT3DSURFACE9 backbuffer = NULL;

//DirectInput variables
LPDIRECTINPUT8 dinput = NULL;
LPDIRECTINPUTDEVICE8 dimouse = NULL;
LPDIRECTINPUTDEVICE8 dikeyboard = NULL;
DIMOUSESTATE mouse_state;
char keys[256];
XINPUT_GAMEPAD controllers[4];

/**
 ** Direct3D initialization
 **/
bool Direct3D_Init(HWND window, int width, int height, bool fullscreen)
{
    //initialize Direct3D
    d3d = Direct3DCreate9(D3D_SDK_VERSION);
    if (!d3d) return false;

    //set Direct3D presentation parameters
    D3DPRESENT_PARAMETERS d3dpp;
    ZeroMemory(&d3dpp, sizeof(d3dpp));
    d3dpp.Windowed = (!fullscreen);
    d3dpp.SwapEffect = D3DSWAPEFFECT_COPY;
    d3dpp.BackBufferFormat = D3DFMT_X8R8G8B8;
    d3dpp.BackBufferCount = 1;
    d3dpp.BackBufferWidth = width;
    d3dpp.BackBufferHeight = height;
    d3dpp.hDeviceWindow = window;

    //create Direct3D device
    d3d->CreateDevice( D3DADAPTER_DEFAULT, D3DDEVTYPE_HAL, window,
        D3DCREATE_SOFTWARE_VERTEXPROCESSING, &d3dpp, &d3ddev);
    if (!d3ddev) return false;

    //get a pointer to the back buffer surface
    d3ddev->GetBackBuffer(0, 0, D3DBACKBUFFER_TYPE_MONO, &backbuffer);

    return true;
}

/**
 ** Direct3D shutdown
```

```
**/
void Direct3D_Shutdown()
{
    if (d3ddev) d3ddev->Release();
    if (d3d) d3d->Release();
}


/**
 ** Draws a surface to the screen using StretchRect
 **/
void DrawSurface(LPDIRECT3DSURFACE9 dest,
    float x, float y,
    LPDIRECT3DSURFACE9 source)
{

    //get width/height from source surface
    D3DSURFACE_DESC desc;
    source->GetDesc(&desc);

    //create rects for drawing
    RECT source_rect = {0, 0,
        (long)desc.Width, (long)desc.Height };
    RECT dest_rect = { (long)x, (long)y,
        (long)x+desc.Width, (long)y+desc.Height};

    //draw the source surface onto the dest
    d3ddev->StretchRect(source, &source_rect, dest,
        &dest_rect, D3DTEXF_NONE);
}


/**
 ** Loads a bitmap file into a surface
 **/
LPDIRECT3DSURFACE9 LoadSurface(string filename)
{
    LPDIRECT3DSURFACE9 image = NULL;

    //get width and height from bitmap file
    D3DXIMAGE_INFO info;
    HRESULT result = D3DXGetImageInfoFromFile(filename.c_str(), &info);
    if (result != D3D_OK) return NULL;

    //create surface
    result = d3ddev->CreateOffscreenPlainSurface(
```

```
            info.Width,         //width of the surface
            info.Height,        //height of the surface
            D3DFMT_X8R8G8B8,    //surface format
            D3DPOOL_DEFAULT,    //memory pool to use
            &image,             //pointer to the surface
            NULL);              //reserved (always NULL)

        if (result != D3D_OK) return NULL;

        //load surface from file into newly created surface
        result = D3DXLoadSurfaceFromFile(
            image,              //destination surface
            NULL,               //destination palette
            NULL,               //destination rectangle
            filename.c_str(),   //source filename
            NULL,               //source rectangle
            D3DX_DEFAULT,       //controls how image is filtered
            D3DCOLOR_XRGB(0,0,0),  //for transparency (0 for none)
            NULL);              //source image info (usually NULL)

        //make sure file was loaded okay
        if (result != D3D_OK) return NULL;

        return image;
    }


    /**
     ** DirectInput initialization
     **/
    bool DirectInput_Init(HWND hwnd)
    {
        //initialize DirectInput object
        HRESULT result = DirectInput8Create(
            GetModuleHandle(NULL),
            DIRECTINPUT_VERSION,
            IID_IDirectInput8,
            (void**)&dinput,
            NULL);

        //initialize the keyboard
        dinput->CreateDevice(GUID_SysKeyboard, &dikeyboard, NULL);
        dikeyboard->SetDataFormat(&c_dfDIKeyboard);
        dikeyboard->SetCooperativeLevel(hwnd, DISCL_NONEXCLUSIVE |
                                DISCL_FOREGROUND);
```

```
        dikeyboard->Acquire();

        //initialize the mouse
        dinput->CreateDevice(GUID_SysMouse, &dimouse, NULL);
        dimouse->SetDataFormat(&c_dfDIMouse);
        dimouse->SetCooperativeLevel(hwnd, DISCL_NONEXCLUSIVE |
                                     DISCL_FOREGROUND);
        dimouse->Acquire();
        d3ddev->ShowCursor(false);

        return true;
}

/**
 ** DirectInput update
 **/
void DirectInput_Update()
{
        //update mouse
        dimouse->GetDeviceState(sizeof(mouse_state), (LPVOID)&mouse_state);

        //update keyboard
        dikeyboard->GetDeviceState(sizeof(keys), (LPVOID)&keys);

        //update controllers
        for (int i=0; i< 4; i++ )
        {
            ZeroMemory( &controllers[i], sizeof(XINPUT_STATE) );

            //get the state of the controller
            XINPUT_STATE state;
            DWORD result = XInputGetState( i, &state );

            //store state in global controllers array
            if (result == 0) controllers[i] = state.Gamepad;
        }
}

/**
 ** Return mouse x movement
 **/
int Mouse_X()
{
```

```
        return mouse_state.lX;
}

/**
 ** Return mouse y movement
 **/
int Mouse_Y()
{
        return mouse_state.lY;
}

/**
 ** Return mouse button state
 **/
int Mouse_Button(int button)
{
        return mouse_state.rgbButtons[button] & 0x80;
}

/**
 ** Return key press state
 **/
int Key_Down(int key)
{
        return (keys[key] & 0x80);
}

/**
 ** DirectInput shutdown
 **/
void DirectInput_Shutdown()
{
        if (dikeyboard)
        {
            dikeyboard->Unacquire();
            dikeyboard->Release();
            dikeyboard = NULL;
        }
        if (dimouse)
        {
            dimouse->Unacquire();
            dimouse->Release();
            dimouse = NULL;
```

```
    }
}

/**
 ** Returns true if controller is plugged in
 **/
bool XInput_Controller_Found()
{
    XINPUT_CAPABILITIES caps;
    ZeroMemory(&caps, sizeof(XINPUT_CAPABILITIES));
    XInputGetCapabilities(0, XINPUT_FLAG_GAMEPAD, &caps);
    if (caps.Type != 0) return false;

    return true;
}

/**
 ** Vibrates the controller
 **/
void XInput_Vibrate(int contNum, int amount)
{
    XINPUT_VIBRATION vibration;
    ZeroMemory( &vibration, sizeof(XINPUT_VIBRATION) );
    vibration.wLeftMotorSpeed = amount;
    vibration.wRightMotorSpeed = amount;
    XInputSetState( contNum, &vibration );
}
```

MyGame.cpp

Add a new source code file to your new Win32 project and call it MyGame.cpp. This is the main source code file for the Bomb Catcher game, and it is the same file you will edit in future example programs. As we add support for new DirectX features, they will mainly go into the MyDirectX.h and MyDirectX.cpp files, while our main file here (MyGame.cpp) will primarily contain game logic—the important stuff. Even though we've divided up the program into several files, this one is still rather large. That is due mainly to the over-zealous support for controller input. You can literally use any pair of buttons on the controller to move the bucket in the game (to catch bombs). This is not normal for a game, but I wanted to demonstrate how to use those buttons in the context of a real game.

Figure 5.11
Adding the MyGame.cpp file to the project.

```cpp
/*
    Beginning Game Programming, Third Edition
    MyGame.cpp
*/

#include "MyDirectX.h"
using namespace std;

const string APPTITLE = "Bomb Catcher Game";
const int SCREENW = 1024;
const int SCREENH = 768;

LPDIRECT3DSURFACE9 bomb_surf = NULL;
LPDIRECT3DSURFACE9 bucket_surf = NULL;

struct BOMB
{
    float x,y;

    void reset()
    {
        x = (float)(rand() % (SCREENW-128));
        y = 0;
    }
};
```

```
BOMB bomb;

struct BUCKET
{
     float x,y;
};

BUCKET bucket;

int score = 0;
int vibrating = 0;

/**
 ** Game initialization
 **/
bool Game_Init(HWND window)
{
     Direct3D_Init(window, SCREENW, SCREENH, false);

     DirectInput_Init(window);

     bomb_surf = LoadSurface("bomb.bmp");
     if (!bomb_surf) {
         MessageBox(window, "Error loading bomb","Error",0);
         return false;
     }

     bucket_surf = LoadSurface("bucket.bmp");
     if (!bucket_surf) {
         MessageBox(window, "Error loading bucket","Error",0);
         return false;
     }

     //get the back buffer surface
     d3ddev->GetBackBuffer(0, 0, D3DBACKBUFFER_TYPE_MONO, &backbuffer);

     //position the bomb
     srand( (unsigned int)time(NULL) );
     bomb.reset();

     //position the bucket
     bucket.x = 500;
     bucket.y = 630;
```

```
        return true;
}

/**
 ** Game update
 **/
void Game_Run(HWND window)
{
        //make sure the Direct3D device is valid
        if (!d3ddev) return;

        //update input devices
        DirectInput_Update();

        //move the bomb down the screen
        bomb.y += 2.0f;

        //see if bomb hit the floor
        if (bomb.y > SCREENH)
        {
            MessageBox(0,"Oh no, the bomb exploded!!","YOU STINK",0);
            gameover = true;
        }

        //move the bucket with the mouse
        int mx = Mouse_X();
        if (mx < 0) bucket.x -= 6.0f;
        else if (mx > 0) bucket.x += 6.0f;

        //move the bucket with the keyboard
        if (Key_Down(DIK_LEFT)) bucket.x -= 6.0f;
        else if (Key_Down(DIK_RIGHT)) bucket.x += 6.0f;

        //move the bucket with the controller
        if (XInput_Controller_Found())
        {
            //left analog thumb stick
            if (controllers[0].sThumbLX < -5000)
                bucket.x -= 6.0f;
            else if (controllers[0].sThumbLX > 5000)
                bucket.x += 6.0f;

            //left and right triggers
```

```
        if (controllers[0].bLeftTrigger > 128)
            bucket.x -= 6.0f;
        else if (controllers[0].bRightTrigger > 128)
            bucket.x += 6.0f;


        //left and right D-PAD
        if (controllers[0].wButtons & XINPUT_GAMEPAD_LEFT_SHOULDER)
            bucket.x -= 6.0f;
        else if (controllers[0].wButtons & XINPUT_GAMEPAD_RIGHT_SHOULDER)
            bucket.x += 6.0f;


        //left and right shoulders
        if (controllers[0].wButtons & XINPUT_GAMEPAD_DPAD_LEFT)
            bucket.x -= 6.0f;
        else if (controllers[0].wButtons & XINPUT_GAMEPAD_DPAD_RIGHT)
            bucket.x += 6.0f;
    }

    //update vibration
    if (vibrating > 0)
    {
        vibrating++;
        if (vibrating > 20)
        {
            XInput_Vibrate(0, 0);
            vibrating = 0;
        }
    }

    //keep bucket inside the screen
    if (bucket.x < 0) bucket.x = 0;
    if (bucket.x > SCREENW-128) bucket.x = SCREENW-128;

    //see if bucket caught the bomb
    int cx = bomb.x + 64;
    int cy = bomb.y + 64;
    if (cx > bucket.x && cx < bucket.x+128 &&
        cy > bucket.y && cy < bucket.y+128)
    {
        //update and display score
        score++;
        char s[255];
```

```
        sprintf(s, "%s [SCORE %d]", APPTITLE.c_str(), score);
        SetWindowText(window, s);

        //vibrate the controller
        XInput_Vibrate(0, 65000);
        vibrating = 1;

        //restart bomb
        bomb.reset();
    }

    //clear the backbuffer
    d3ddev->ColorFill(backbuffer, NULL, D3DCOLOR_XRGB(0,0,0));

    //start rendering
    if (d3ddev->BeginScene())
    {
        //draw the bomb
        DrawSurface(backbuffer, bomb.x, bomb.y, bomb_surf);

        //draw the bucket
        DrawSurface(backbuffer, bucket.x, bucket.y, bucket_surf);

        //stop rendering
        d3ddev->EndScene();
        d3ddev->Present(NULL, NULL, NULL, NULL);
    }

    //escape key exits
    if (Key_Down(DIK_ESCAPE))
        gameover = true;

    //controller Back button also exits
    if (controllers[0].wButtons & XINPUT_GAMEPAD_BACK)
        gameover = true;
}

/**
 ** Game shutdown
 **/
void Game_End()
{
```

```
    if (bomb_surf) bomb_surf->Release();
    if (bucket_surf) bucket_surf->Release();
    DirectInput_Shutdown();
    Direct3D_Shutdown();
}
```

What You Have Learned

In this chapter you have forged ahead in learning how to program the keyboard, mouse, and controller with DirectInput, and how to program 2D surfaces and sprites in Direct3D! Take heart if you are not entirely confident of all this new information, though, because learning it is no simple feat! If you have any doubts, I recommend reading this chapter again before forging ahead to the next one, which deals with advanced sprite programming. Don't balk at all the 2D graphics discussions here; I encourage you to keep learning because this is the foundation for the 3D chapters to come! Here are the key points:

- You learned how to initialize DirectInput.

- You learned how to create a keyboard handler.

- You learned how to create a mouse handler.

- Your learned how to program an Xbox 360 controller.

- You wrote an example game called Bomb Catcher.

- You learned a little bit about sprite collision.

- You learned how to create a 2D surface that is rendered by Direct3D.

Review Questions

These questions will challenge you to study this chapter further, if necessary.

1. What is the name of the primary DirectInput object?

2. What is the function that creates a DirectInput device?

3. What is the name of the struct that contains mouse input data?

4. What function do you call to poll the keyboard or mouse?

5. What is the name of the function that helps check for sprite collisions?

6. What is the benefit of having concept drawings for a game?

7. What is the name of the surface object in Direct3D?

8. What function should you use to draw a surface on the screen?

9. What D3DX helper function do you use to load a bitmap image into a surface?

10. Where can you find a good collection of free sprites on the Web?

On Your Own

The following exercises will help you to think outside the box and push the limits of your understanding of this material.

Exercise 1. The Bomb Catcher project does not pretend to be a complete game as it is only an input demo, but it fills the role well enough for a simple demo. The very nature of this simple demo makes it a good candidate for a game project because you would not need to start from scratch. See if you can add scoring, lives, and other gameplay features to make it feel less like a demo, more like a game. You might need to read a few more chapters to learn some new techniques and then return here to improve the game.

Exercise 2. Whether you enhance the Bomb Catcher project is yet to be seen, but one thing we *can* do in the short term is this: See if you can add another bomb to the demo so the player has to catch *two* bombs instead of just one!

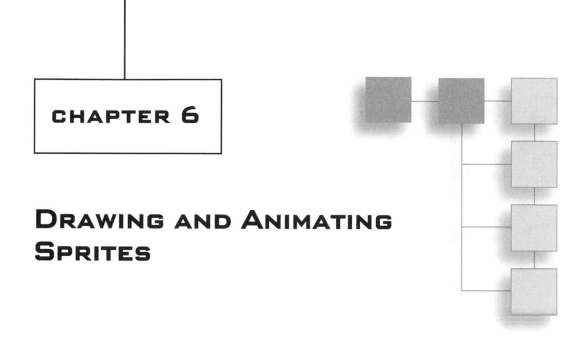

CHAPTER 6

DRAWING AND ANIMATING SPRITES

This chapter takes the subject of sprite programming to the next level. By utilizing a texture rather than a surface for our sprite image, it is possible to draw a sprite with transparency (where only the object's pixels show up and not its background—which happened in the Bomb Catcher game). Other special effects are also possible when we switch to this new way of drawing sprites, such as rotation and scaling. These things are called "transforms" by computer graphics experts, and you will learn to do these special effects over the next two chapters. You will develop a robust, reusable set of sprite functions that will be useful in future game projects. Following the basics, this chapter is rounded out with a discussion of sprite animation.

Here is what you will learn in this chapter:

- What a sprite is.

- How to load a texture.

- How to draw a transparent sprite.

- How to animate a sprite.

What Is a Sprite?

A *sprite* is a 2D representation of a game entity that usually must interact with the player in some way. A tree or rock might be rendered in 2D and interact with the player by simply getting in the way, stopping the player by way of collision physics. In the previous chapter we worked with Direct3D surfaces as a means of drawing sprites. But the biggest problem with a surface, aside from drawing quite slowly, is the complete lack of support for any kind of transparency (which is why our bomb and bucket sprites had black outlines around them).

We must also deal with game characters that directly or indirectly interact with the player's character (which might be a spaceship, an Italian plumber, or a spiky-haired hedgehog). The types of sprites that interact with the player might be an enemy ship or a laser in a space combat game—I could go on and on with examples.

There are two ways to render 2D objects in Direct3D. First, you can create a quad (or rectangle) comprised of two triangles with a texture representing the 2D image you wish to draw. This technique works and even supports transparency, responds to lighting, and can be moved in the Z direction. The second method available in Direct3D for rendering 2D objects is with sprites—and this is the method we will focus on in this chapter.

Loading the Sprite's Image

The first thing that you should be aware of is that ID3DXSprite uses a texture rather than a surface to store the sprite image. So, while the LPDIRECT3DSURFACE9 object was used in the last chapter for sprites, in this chapter you will use the LPDIRECT3DTEXTURE9 object instead. If I were creating a tile-based scrolling arcade game like *Super Mario World* or *R-Type* or *Mars Matrix*, I might use a surface to draw (and scroll) the background, but I would use a texture for the foreground sprites that represent the game characters/spaceships/enemies, as the case may be. There really is no performance benefit to using a surface over a texture, because your expensive video card (with an advanced 3D chip) will render your sprites on the screen using a hardware texture-mapping system that is light-years faster than anything you could do with software. Gone are the days when a 2D sprite blitter was written in assembly language! Today, we let Direct3D draw our sprites. And this is the reason why we will be using textures from now on.

The first thing you must do to create a game sprite is to create a texture object into which the sprite's bitmap image is loaded:

```
LPDIRECT3DTEXTURE9 texture = NULL;
```

The next thing you need to do is grab the resolution out of the bitmap file (assuming you have the sprite bitmap ready to go) using the D3DXGetImageInfoFromFile function:

```
D3DXIMAGE_INFO info;
result = D3DXGetImageInfoFromFile("image.bmp", &info);
```

If the file exists, then you will have the Width and Height, which are useful for the next step. This information is really handy to have, especially when you begin working on a game. So, we can write a reusable function that returns the size of an image as a D3DXVECTOR2 (which has an X and Y property that can contain the width and height of the image). You may add this function to the MyDirectX.h and MyDirectX.cpp files if you want to use it.

```
D3DXVECTOR2 GetBitmapSize(string filename)
{
    D3DXIMAGE_INFO info;
    D3DXVECTOR2 size = D3DXVECTOR2(0.0f,0.0f);

    HRESULT result = D3DXGetImageInfoFromFile(filename.c_str(), & info);
```

```
    if (result == D3D_OK)
        size = D3DXVECTOR2( (float)info.Width, (float)info.Height);
    else
        size = D3DXVECTOR2( (float)info.Width, (float)info.Height);

    return size;
}
```

Next, you load the sprite's image from a bitmap file directly into a texture in a single step using the D3DXCreateTextureFromFileEx function:

```
HRESULT WINAPI D3DXCreateTextureFromFileEx(

    LPDIRECT3DDEVICE9 pDevice,
    LPCTSTR pSrcFile,
    UINT Width,
    UINT Height,
    UINT MipLevels,
    DWORD Usage,
    D3DFORMAT Format,
    D3DPOOL Pool,
    DWORD Filter,
    DWORD MipFilter,
    D3DCOLOR ColorKey,
    D3DXIMAGE_INFO *pSrcInfo,
    PALETTEENTRY *pPalette,
    LPDIRECT3DTEXTURE9 *ppTexture
);
```

Don't worry too much about all these parameters, as most of them are filled in with default values and NULLs. The only thing left to do, then, is to write a little function that puts all of this information together and returns a texture for you. Here is that function, which I have called LoadTexture (creative, don't you think?):

```
LPDIRECT3DTEXTURE9 LoadTexture(string filename, D3DCOLOR transcolor)
{
    LPDIRECT3DTEXTURE9 texture = NULL;

    //get width and height from bitmap file
    D3DXIMAGE_INFO info;
    HRESULT result = D3DXGetImageInfoFromFile(filename.c_str(), &info);
    if (result != D3D_OK) return NULL;
```

```
    //create the new texture by loading a bitmap image file
    D3DXCreateTextureFromFileEx(
        d3ddev,                    //Direct3D device object
        filename.c_str(),          //bitmap filename
        info.Width,                //bitmap image width
        info.Height,               //bitmap image height
        1,                         //mip-map levels (1 for no chain)
        D3DPOOL_DEFAULT,           //the type of surface (standard)
        D3DFMT_UNKNOWN,            //surface format (default)
        D3DPOOL_DEFAULT,           //memory class for the texture
        D3DX_DEFAULT,              //image filter
        D3DX_DEFAULT,              //mip filter
        transcolor,                //color key for transparency
        &info,                     //bitmap file info (from loaded file)
        NULL,                      //color palette
        &texture );                //destination texture

    //make sure the bitmap texture was loaded correctly
    if (result != D3D_OK) return NULL;

    return texture;
}
```

Transparent Sprites

The ID3DXSprite object is really a wonderful surprise for any programmer planning to write a 2D game using Direct3D. One of the benefits of doing so is that you have a full 3D renderer at your disposal while using 2D functions that are every bit as fast as previous implementations (i.e., the old DirectDraw). By treating a sprite as a texture and rendering the sprite as a rectangle (comprised of two triangles, as is the case with all 3D rectangles), you have the ability to transform the sprite!

By *transform* I mean you can move the sprite with full 3D hardware acceleration. You can draw the sprite transparently by specifying an alpha color in the source bitmap that represents transparent pixels. Black (0,0,0) is a common color to use for transparency, but it is not a very good color to use. Why? Because it's hard to tell which pixels are transparent and which are simply dark in color. A better color to use is pink (255,0,255) because it is seldom used in game graphics and shows up brightly in the source image. You can instantly spot the transparent pixels in such an image.

Obviously, the ID3DXSprite method is the way to go, but I'm going to cover the simpler method as well because it may be helpful in some circumstances to use non-transparent images—for instance, to draw a tiled background. In the next chapter, which goes into more advanced sprite features, you will learn how to transform (that is, rotate, scale, and translate) a sprite using a Direct3D matrix! Do you realize what this means?! We can conceivably transform our sprites using a vertex shader that runs in the GPU (graphics processing unit) on the video card! I wonder how many sprites a high-end GPU can handle?

Initializing the Sprite Renderer

The ID3DXSprite object is just a sprite handler that includes a function to draw sprites from a texture (with various transformations). D3DX defines a pointer version of the class as LPD3DXSPRITE, which is more convenient for our purposes. Here is how you might declare it:

```
LPD3DXSPRITE spriteobj = NULL;
```

Advice

Always—*always*—set your new objects to NULL when you define them. If you don't, the object will be undefined, and a test for NULL will not even work. In other words, if (spriteobj == NULL) could crash the program instead of properly giving you a false result if the object is undefined.

You can then initialize the object by calling the D3DXCreateSprite function. What this does, basically, is attach the sprite handler to your Direct3D device so that it knows how to draw sprites on the back buffer.

```
HRESULT WINAPI D3DXCreateSprite(

    LPDIRECT3DDEVICE9 pDevice,
    LPD3DXSPRITE *ppSprite
);
```

And here is an example of how you might invoke this function:

```
result = D3DXCreateSprite(d3ddev, &spriteobj);
```

Starting the Sprite Renderer

I'll go over loading a sprite image shortly, but for the time being, let me show you how to use ID3DXSprite. When you have called BeginScene from your primary Direct3D device, you can start drawing sprites. The first thing you must do is lock the surface so that the sprites can be drawn. You do this by calling the ID3DXSprite.Begin function, which has this format:

```
HRESULT Begin(
    DWORD Flags
);
```

The flags parameter is required and will usually be D3DXSPRITE_ALPHABLEND, which draws sprites with transparency support. Here is an example:

```
spriteobj->Begin(D3DXSPRITE_ALPHABLEND);
```

Drawing a Sprite

Drawing a sprite is a little more complicated than simply blitting the image using a source and destination rectangle, as was the case with surfaces in the last chapter. However, D3DXSprite just uses a single function, Draw, for all of the transformation options, so once you understand how this function works you can perform transparency, scaling, and rotation by just altering the parameters. Here is the declaration for the Draw function:

```
HRESULT Draw(

    LPDIRECT3DTEXTURE9 pTexture,
    CONST RECT *pSrcRect,
    CONST D3DXVECTOR3 *pCenter,
    CONST D3DXVECTOR3 *pPosition,
    D3DCOLOR Color
);
```

The first parameter is the most important one, as it specifies the texture to use for the source image of the sprite. The second parameter is also important, as you can use it to grab "tiles" out of the source image and thus store all of your sprite's animation frames in a single bitmap file (more on that later in this chapter). The third parameter specifies the center point from which rotation takes place. The fourth parameter specifies the position of the sprite, and this is typically where you set the x and y value. The last parameter specifies the color alterations to be made on the sprite image as it is drawn (and doesn't affect transparency).

Advice

Note: We will learn how to apply matrix transforms to rotate, scale, and translate a sprite in the next chapter. I find it helpful to start with simple rendering first before getting into something as complex as a transform. By the time you get to the next chapter, you should have a good understanding of ID3DXSprite.

The D3DXVECTOR3 is a DirectX data type with three member variables: x, y, and z.

```
typedef struct D3DXVECTOR3 {
    FLOAT x;
    FLOAT y;
    FLOAT z;
} D3DXVECTOR3;
```

The first two, x and y, are the only ones you'll need to move the sprite on the 2D surface of the screen. I will show you an example of how to use Draw in a sample program shortly.

Stopping the Sprite Renderer

After you have finished drawing sprites, but before you have called EndScene, you must call ID3DXSprite.End to unlock the surface for other processes to use. Here is the syntax:

```
HRESULT End(VOID);
```

Usage is fairly obvious because the function is so short:

```
spriteobj->End();
```

Drawing Transparent Sprites

D3DXSprite doesn't care whether your sprites' source images use a color key or an alpha channel for transparency—it just renders the image as requested. If you have an image with an alpha channel—for instance, a 32-bit targa—then it will be rendered with alpha, including translucent blending with the background if your image has partial alpha ranges defined. But if your image has no alpha because you are using a background color key for transparency—for instance, a 24-bit bitmap—then it will be drawn without the color-keyed pixels. You can even draw an image with transparency using an alpha channel *and* a color key.

You can make an entire game using just color-keyed transparency, but there is a limitation on the quality when using this technique because you must have discrete pixels in such an image unless some sort of render-time blending is performed. Although it is possible to do alpha blending at runtime, it's not a good way to develop a game—it's best to prepare your artwork in advance.

The preferred method for rendering with transparency (especially among artists) is using an alpha channel. One great advantage to alpha-blended images is support for partial transparency—that is, translucent blending. Rather than using a black border around a color-keyed sprite (the old school way of highlighting a sprite), an artist will blend a border around a sprite's edges using an alpha level for partial translucency (which looks fantastic in comparison!). To do that, you must use a file format that supports 32-bit RGBA images. Targa is a good choice, and PNG files work well, too. Let's take a look at the spaceship sprite again—this time with an alpha channel rather than a color-keyed background. Note the checkerboard pattern in the background; this is a common way of showing the alpha channel in graphic editors.

Now that you understand how D3DXSprite works with Direct3D textures to draw a transparent sprite (at least, that's the theory!), let's write a short program to show how to pull it all together. You can load the project off the CD-ROM if you wish, or you can modify the Anim_Sprite project from the previous chapter. After all, that's the best way to learn.

Creating the Transparent Sprite Program

First of all, fire up Visual C++ and create a new Win32 Project, and give it the name Trans_Sprite. You will need to copy the source code files from the previous project (back in Chapter 5) over to this new project. The source code files are:

- MyGame.cpp

- MyDirectX.h

- MyDirectX.cpp

- MyWindows.cpp

Then you can just begin editing the MyGame.cpp file and go from there to create a new project. There is another option that you may use, and this is what I actually recommend you do from here on out. On the CD, under the folder for this chapter, is a project called "DirectX_Project." This is a template project for the chapter, and you will find a project with the same name in each new chapter folder on the CD, with all of the latest functions and variables needed for that chapter.

You may use this project as a template for your own work while following along in the book, rather than opening the completed project (in this case, Trans_Sprite, also on the CD). Opening an existing project, ready to run, is not a good learning experience! By starting with DirectX_Project each time, you can complete the code as listed and learn more in the process. Whichever method you use, I'll assume you have a working Trans_Sprite project that is ready to run, but that doesn't do anything useful yet.

Modifying MyDirectX.h

Now we need to add support for loading of textures to the framework file called MyDirectX.h. This file is already in your project, so you can simply open it and add the new line of code that will make the LoadTexture function visible throughout the project. We'll also add the GetBitmapSize function here for good measure.

Add the following highlighted code to MyDirectX.h in the Direct3D function prototypes section:

```
LPDIRECT3DTEXTURE9 LoadTexture(string filename,
    D3DCOLOR transcolor = D3DCOLOR_XRGB(0,0,0));
```

After you have added the line, the list of Direct3D functions should look like this:

```
//Direct3D functions
bool Direct3D_Init(HWND hwnd, int width, int height, bool fullscreen);
void Direct3D_Shutdown();
LPDIRECT3DSURFACE9 LoadSurface(string filename);
void DrawSurface(LPDIRECT3DSURFACE9 dest, float x, float y,
    LPDIRECT3DSURFACE9 source);

D3DXVECTOR2 GetBitmapSize(string filename);

LPDIRECT3DTEXTURE9 LoadTexture(string filename,
    D3DCOLOR transcolor = D3DCOLOR_XRGB(0,0,0));
```

We also need to add the sprite rendering object to the MyDirectX.h file. This definition can be added wherever you want in the file:

```
extern LPD3DXSPRITE spriteobj;
```

This new object is defined as "extern" because the real definition takes place in MyDirectX.cpp. This just tells the compiler not to freak out when it comes across spriteobj in the code, and reassures it that the object does exist. Later on in the compilation process, the linker will find the function in MyDirectX.cpp.

Modifying MyDirectX.cpp

Now that you have defined the new LoadTexture function so the rest of the program can use it, you'll need to open the MyDirectX.cpp file and add the actual function implementation to this file. We'll also add the GetBitmapSize function now as well.

```
LPDIRECT3DTEXTURE9 LoadTexture(std::string filename, D3DCOLOR transcolor)
{
    LPDIRECT3DTEXTURE9 texture = NULL;

    //get width and height from bitmap file
    D3DXIMAGE_INFO info;
    HRESULT result = D3DXGetImageInfoFromFile(filename.c_str(), &info);
    if (result != D3D_OK) return NULL;

    //create the new texture by loading a bitmap image file
    D3DXCreateTextureFromFileEx(
        d3ddev,                 //Direct3D device object
        filename.c_str(),       //bitmap filename
        info.Width,             //bitmap image width
        info.Height,            //bitmap image height
        1,                      //mip-map levels (1 for no chain)
        D3DPOOL_DEFAULT,        //the type of surface (standard)
        D3DFMT_UNKNOWN,         //surface format (default)
        D3DPOOL_DEFAULT,        //memory class for the texture
        D3DX_DEFAULT,           //image filter
        D3DX_DEFAULT,           //mip filter
        transcolor,             //color key for transparency
        &info,                  //bitmap file info (from loaded file)
        NULL,                   //color palette
        &texture );             //destination texture

    //make sure the bitmap textre was loaded correctly
    if (result != D3D_OK) return NULL;

    return texture;
}


D3DXVECTOR2 GetBitmapSize(string filename)
{
    D3DXIMAGE_INFO info;
    D3DXVECTOR2 size = D3DXVECTOR2(0.0f,0.0f);
    HRESULT result = D3DXGetImageInfoFromFile(filename.c_str(), &info);
    if (result == D3D_OK)
        size = D3DXVECTOR2( (float)info.Width, (float)info.Height);
```

```
    else
        size = D3DXVECTOR2( (float)info.Width, (float)info.Height);

    return size;
}
```

Now we need to make a change to `Direct3D_Init` and `Direct3D_Shutdown` in order to create and destroy the sprite object automatically when these functions are called. I will highlight the changes in bold text.

```
bool Direct3D_Init(HWND window, int width, int height, bool fullscreen)
{
    //initialize Direct3D
    d3d = Direct3DCreate9(D3D_SDK_VERSION);
    if (!d3d) return false;

    //set Direct3D presentation parameters
    D3DPRESENT_PARAMETERS d3dpp;
    ZeroMemory(&d3dpp, sizeof(d3dpp));
    d3dpp.hDeviceWindow = window;
    d3dpp.Windowed = (!fullscreen);
    d3dpp.SwapEffect = D3DSWAPEFFECT_DISCARD;
    d3dpp.EnableAutoDepthStencil = 1;
    d3dpp.AutoDepthStencilFormat = D3DFMT_D24S8;
    d3dpp.Flags = D3DPRESENTFLAG_DISCARD_DEPTHSTENCIL;
    d3dpp.PresentationInterval = D3DPRESENT_INTERVAL_IMMEDIATE;
    d3dpp.BackBufferFormat = D3DFMT_X8R8G8B8;
    d3dpp.BackBufferCount = 1;
    d3dpp.BackBufferWidth = width;
    d3dpp.BackBufferHeight = height;

    //create Direct3D device
    d3d->CreateDevice( D3DADAPTER_DEFAULT, D3DDEVTYPE_HAL, window,
        D3DCREATE_SOFTWARE_VERTEXPROCESSING, &d3dpp, &d3ddev);
    if (!d3ddev) return false;


    //get a pointer to the back buffer surface
    d3ddev->GetBackBuffer(0, 0, D3DBACKBUFFER_TYPE_MONO, &backbuffer);

    //create sprite object
    D3DXCreateSprite(d3ddev, &spriteobj);

    return 1;
```

```
}

void Direct3D_Shutdown()
{
    if (spriteobj) spriteobj->Release();
    if (d3ddev) d3ddev->Release();
    if (d3d) d3d->Release();
}
```

Modifying MyGame.cpp

Now that the new texture and sprite functionality has been added to the support files, we can demonstrate how to draw sprites with transparency. I'll highlight the texture- and sprite-specific lines in bold text so you will see how this program differs from the previous project you worked on back in Chapter 5. Isn't it great how much simpler the code is now that the supporting framework code (WinMain, Direct3D_Init, etc) has been moved out of the main source code file for the game or demo?

```
/*
    Beginning Game Programming, Third Edition
    MyGame.cpp
*/

#include "MyDirectX.h"
using namespace std;

const string APPTITLE = "Transparent Sprite Demo";
const int SCREENW = 1024;
const int SCREENH = 768;

LPDIRECT3DTEXTURE9 image_colorkey = NULL;
LPDIRECT3DTEXTURE9 image_alpha = NULL;
LPDIRECT3DTEXTURE9 image_notrans = NULL;


/**
 ** Game initialization
 **/
bool Game_Init(HWND window)
{
    //initialize Direct3D
```

```
    if (!Direct3D_Init(window, SCREENW, SCREENH, false))
    {
        MessageBox(0, "Error initializing Direct3D","ERROR",0);
        return false;
    }

    //initialize DirectInput
    if (!DirectInput_Init(window))
    {
        MessageBox(0, "Error initializing DirectInput","ERROR",0);
        return false;
    }

    //load non-transparent image
    image_notrans = LoadTexture("shuttle_notrans.bmp");
    if (!image_notrans) return false;

    //load color-keyed transparent image
    image_colorkey = LoadTexture("shuttle_colorkey.bmp", D3DCO-
LOR_XRGB(255,0,255));
    if (!image_colorkey) return false;

    //load alpha transparent image
    image_alpha = LoadTexture("shuttle_alpha.tga");
    if (!image_alpha) return false;

    return true;
}

/**
 ** Game update
 **/
void Game_Run(HWND window)
{
    //make sure the Direct3D device is valid
    if (!d3ddev) return;

    //update input devices
    DirectInput_Update();

    //clear the scene
    d3ddev->Clear(0, NULL, D3DCLEAR_TARGET | D3DCLEAR_ZBUFFER,
        D3DCOLOR_XRGB(0,0,100), 1.0f, 0);
```

```cpp
    //start rendering
    if (d3ddev->BeginScene())
    {
        //start drawing
        spriteobj->Begin(D3DXSPRITE_ALPHABLEND);

        //draw the sprite
        D3DXVECTOR3 pos1( 10, 10, 0);
        spriteobj->Draw( image_notrans, NULL, NULL, &pos1,
            D3DCOLOR_XRGB(255,255,255));

        D3DXVECTOR3 pos2( 350, 10, 0);
        spriteobj->Draw( image_colorkey, NULL, NULL, &pos2,
            D3DCOLOR_XRGB(255,255,255));

        D3DXVECTOR3 pos3( 700, 10, 0);
        spriteobj->Draw( image_alpha, NULL, NULL, &pos3,
            D3DCOLOR_XRGB(255,255,255));

        //stop drawing
        spriteobj->End();

        //stop rendering
        d3ddev->EndScene();
        d3ddev->Present(NULL, NULL, NULL, NULL);
    }

    //Escape key ends program
    if (KEY_DOWN(VK_ESCAPE)) gameover = true;

    //controller Back button also ends
    if (controllers[0].wButtons & XINPUT_GAMEPAD_BACK)
        gameover = true;
}

/**
 ** Game shutdown
 **/
void Game_End()
{
    //free memory and shut down
    image_notrans->Release();
    image_colorkey->Release();
```

```
    image_alpha->Release();

    DirectInput_Shutdown();
    Direct3D_Shutdown();
}
```

Running the Trans_Sprite Program

Figure 6.1 shows the Trans_Sprite program running. Now, the reason why there are three of the same image drawn in this program is because each demonstrates a different type of transparency.

The first image on the left is being drawn with essentially no transparency, because the source bitmap does not contain an alpha channel or an appropriate transparent color key. Our ID3DXSprite::Draw code uses black by default for the color key. Black in DirectX is created with this macro: D3DCOLOR_XRGB(0,0,0).

Figure 6.1
The Trans_Sprite program demonstrates how to draw transparent sprites with Direct3D.

However, there's a problem with this. If you look closely at the first image of the space shuttle, you might be able to discern that the black portions of the image (at the nose and leading edges of the wings) are being drawn with the background color. I'll assume you're running the Trans_Sprite program yourself, since the blue and black colors will look the same on the printed page, and you won't be able to discern the difference. If you run the program, sure enough, you can see right through the space shuttle at the blue background behind.

Why is this happening? Didn't we attempt to draw this image *without* transparency? Indeed we did! As you can see, most of the background is white in the source image. However, if we used white as the transparency color key, then most of the space shuttle (which is white) would have become transparent as well!

The key here is in the strategic use of color in your artwork. We can't use black as the color key when there are black pixels in the image itself. Instead, we'll have to use a different color or change the color key definition when loading the texture.

Next, take a look at the second image in the screen shot. This one looks correct, by golly! We have transparency around the edges of the sprite, and the interior black portions are being rendered—and they are *not* transparent! This is exactly what we wanted it to look like.

But, the third image in the screen shot draws our attention to the same transparent pixel problem we faced in the first sprite, even though the outer portion of the background is transparent. This exposes the way ID3DXSprite::Draw works with textures. If you specify a transparent color key when loading the texture, then ID3DXSprite::Draw will use that color key even if there is also an alpha channel in the image (which is actually the preferred way to handle transparent pixels).

Drawing an Animated Sprite

Up to this point, you have been learning about creating, manipulating, and drawing sprites using just a single bitmap image. This is a good starting point when learning sprite programming, but it is not very efficient. For one thing, if you need to do animation with this technique, your game will have to keep track of many textures (one per frame), which is slow and tedious. A much better way to handle animation is by arranging the frames of animation on a single tiled bitmap image. I hinted about this in the last chapter, when I showed you some tiled images of a tank sprite and a running caveman character, shown in Figure 6.2.

Figure 6.2
An animated caveman sprite (courtesy of Ari Feldman).

Working with Sprite Sheets

The trick to drawing animation efficiently is understanding that a source image can be made up of rows and columns of tiles—and in the context of a sprite, we call this tiled image a *sprite sheet*. What you want to do is figure out the upper-left corner of where the tile is located in the bitmap image and then copy from that source a rectangle based on the width and height of the sprite. Fortunately, the ID3DXSprite::Draw function lets us define the source rectangle for the image. This allows us to specify a small portion, or tile, or frame, if you will, in a larger image. Figure out how to do this and, presto, you have a very fast and efficient way to draw animation!

Figure 6.3 shows an illustration of an explosion sprite with the rows and columns identified. Use this figure while reading the animation algorithm below to help you understand how animation frames are copied out of the source image when the animation is being rendered (one frame at a time).

First, you need to figure out the left, or x, position of the tile. You do that by using the modulus operator, %. Modulus returns the remainder of a division. So, for instance, if the current frame is 20, and there are only five columns in the bitmap, then modulus will give you the horizontal starting position of the tile (when you multiply it by the width of the sprite). Calculating the top edge of the tile is then simply a matter of dividing the current frame by the number of columns, and multiplying the result by the sprite height. If there are five columns across, then tile 20 will be in row 4, column 5. Here is the pseudo-code:

```
left = (current frame % number of columns) * sprite width
top  = (current frame / number of columns) * sprite height
```

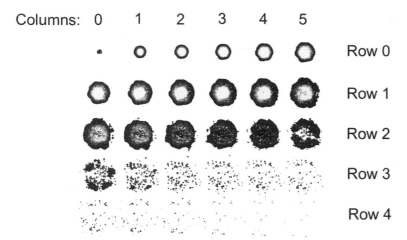

Columns: 0   1   2   3   4   5

Row 0

Row 1

Row 2

Row 3

Row 4

Figure 6.3
The frames of animation are arranged In columns and rows.

Here is an example. Note the use of the sprite width and height in the calculation for the left and top as well as for then calculating the right and bottom edges of the source rectangle.

```
left = (curframe % columns) * width;
top = (curframe / columns) * height;
right = left + width;
bottom = top + height;
```

Let's assume for this example that our sprite sheet has six columns (across) and five rows (down) of frame images in this explosion animation, and each frame is 128 × 128 pixels in size, and we want to draw frame number 10. Remember, the rows and columns are numbered beginning with zero (0); arrays and sequences in C++ are almost always zero-based. So, when I want to draw frame number 10, what I'm looking for, in the sprite sheet, is frame position number 9 (since we begin counting at 0).

```
left = ( 9 % 6) * 128;   // = 3 * 128 (use remainder)
top = ( 9 / 6) * 128;    // = 1 * 128 (use quotient)
right = left + 128;
bottom = top + 128;
```

See Figure 6.4 for the answer (but see if you can figure it out yourself first!). To check your work, begin counting at the upper left, then go from left to right, top to bottom, until you reach "number 10," and just remember that it's logically treated as #9.

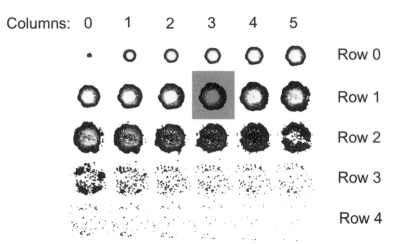

Figure 6.4
Animation frame 10 is highlighted in this sprite sheet.

Using this new technique for drawing a single frame, we can write a function that will draw *any frame* of a sprite sheet! To make this function as reusable as possible, you will have to pass all the properties to it that describe the sprite you want to draw, including the source texture, x and y position, frame number, frame dimensions, and number of columns. Let's take a look:

```
void Sprite_Draw_Frame(LPDIRECT3DTEXTURE9 texture, int destx, int desty,
    int framenum, int framew, int frameh, int columns)
{
    D3DXVECTOR3 position( (float)destx, (float)desty, 0 );
    D3DCOLOR white = D3DCOLOR_XRGB(255,255,255);

    RECT rect;
     rect.left = (framenum % columns) * framew;
    rect.top = (framenum / columns) * frameh;
    rect.right = rect.left + framew;
    rect.bottom = rect.top + frameh;

    spriteobj->Draw( texture, &rect, NULL, &position, white);
}
```

The color passed as the last parameter to ID3DXSprite::Draw can be any color you want, although white is the most common color used. When you use a different color, it will cause the sprite to be drawn with that shade of color. You can even pass an alpha component to cause a sprite to fade with an alpha blend!

To make this work, you should replace D3DCOLOR_XRGB with a different macro: D3DCOLOR_RGBA, which accepts four parameters (red, green, blue, and alpha). We might use this little trick for some special effects later on.

Furthermore, with the creative use of a timer, we can also devise a way to animate at any desired frame rate with another function. The GetTickCount() function (provided by the Windows API) returns a millisecond value that we can use for timing. By passing a frame variable, and a starting time variable, both by reference, the function will be able to modify those variables that will be returned by reference. Thus, each time you call the function, the frame number and timer will be updated. Used together, Sprite_Animate and Sprite_Draw_Frame provide all we need for high-quality sprite animation and rendering.

```
void Sprite_Animate(int &frame, int startframe, int endframe,
    int direction, int &starttime, int delay)
{
    if ((int)GetTickCount() > starttime + delay)
    {
        starttime = GetTickCount();

        frame += direction;
        if (frame > endframe) frame = startframe;
        if (frame < startframe) frame = endframe;
    }
}
```

The Animate Sprite Demo

We definitely need an example to properly demonstrate sprite animation. After all that theory, I don't know about you but I need to write some code. Let's get started by adding the new helper functions to the framework. I'll assume that you are now able to create a new project on your own, or use the DirectX_Project template project as a starting point when creating a new program. If you aren't sure how to create and configure a project, then I refer you to Appendix A for a thorough explanation of the process.

Updating MyDirectX.h

This process of updating the framework files when a new feature is added to our game programming toolbox will soon become second nature to you, because we've been doing it so often. Soon I will only need to give you a new function and you will be able to add it to the framework files yourself. Once you are in the habit of doing this, it will be natural for you to begin adding your *own* reusable functions, and soon you will have a fully-featured game library.

Let's begin with the two new sprite animation functions we created earlier. The prototype definitions for the functions need to be added to the MyDirectX.h header file. Here they are:

```
//new prototype functions added to MyDirectX.h file
void Sprite_Draw_Frame(LPDIRECT3DTEXTURE9 texture, int destx, int desty,
    int framenum, int framew, int frameh, int columns);
void Sprite_Animate(int &frame, int startframe, int endframe,
    int direction, int &starttime, int delay);
```

Advice

Please note: The new changes presented in this chapter are not included in the "DirectX_Project" template project. It will retain the code introduced in the previous chapter but not new code. This is intended to be a workspace where you can implement the new code presented in each new chapter. If you want to use the fully completed version of this project, then jump ahead to the next chapter for a version that includes all of the code from this chapter. The final version will be included on the CD-ROM in the \sources\DirectX_Project folder.

Updating MyDirectX.cpp

The complete implementation of the two functions must be added to the MyDirectX.cpp file. It doesn't really matter where in the file you add these functions, but I recommend adding them below the LoadSurface function.

```
void Sprite_Draw_Frame(LPDIRECT3DTEXTURE9 texture, int destx, int desty,
    int framenum, int framew, int frameh, int columns)
{
    D3DXVECTOR3 position( (float)destx, (float)desty, 0 );
    D3DCOLOR white = D3DCOLOR_XRGB(255,255,255);

    RECT rect;
    rect.left = (framenum % columns) * framew;
    rect.top = (framenum / columns) * frameh;
    rect.right = rect.left + framew;
    rect.bottom = rect.top + frameh;

    spriteobj->Draw( texture, &rect, NULL, &position, white);
}

void Sprite_Animate(int &frame, int startframe, int endframe,
```

```
   int direction, int &starttime, int delay)
{
   if ((int)GetTickCount() > starttime + delay)
   {
      starttime = GetTickCount();

      frame += direction;
      if (frame > endframe) frame = startframe;
      if (frame < startframe) frame = endframe;
   }
}
```

The Animate Sprite Source Code

The source code for the actual demo, which I am calling Animate_Sprite, goes into the MyGame.cpp source code file, like usual. Since you have seen very similar code to this several times now, I'm going to begin cutting down on the number of comments in the listing, since you should be familiar with the code by now.

Figure 6.5
The Animate Sprite program demonstrates animation.

```cpp
#include "MyDirectX.h"
using namespace std;

const string APPTITLE = "Animate Sprite Demo";
const int SCREENW = 800;
const int SCREENH = 600;

LPDIRECT3DTEXTURE9 explosion = NULL;
int frame = 0;
int starttime = 0;

bool Game_Init(HWND window)
{
    if (!Direct3D_Init(window, SCREENW, SCREENH, false))
    {
        MessageBox(0, "Error initializing Direct3D","ERROR",0);
        return false;
    }
    if (!DirectInput_Init(window))
    {
        MessageBox(0, "Error initializing DirectInput","ERROR",0);
        return false;
    }

    //load explosion sprite
    explosion = LoadTexture("explosion_30_128.tga");
    if (!explosion) return false;
    return true;
}

void Game_Run(HWND window)
{
    if (!d3ddev) return;

    DirectInput_Update();

    d3ddev->Clear(0, NULL, D3DCLEAR_TARGET | D3DCLEAR_ZBUFFER,
        D3DCOLOR_XRGB(0,0,100), 1.0f, 0);

    if (d3ddev->BeginScene())
    {
        //start drawing
        spriteobj->Begin(D3DXSPRITE_ALPHABLEND);
```

```
        //animate and draw the sprite
        Sprite_Animate(frame, 0, 29, 1, starttime, 30);
        Sprite_Draw_Frame(explosion, 200, 200, frame, 128, 128, 6);

        //stop drawing
        spriteobj->End();

        d3ddev->EndScene();
        d3ddev->Present(NULL, NULL, NULL, NULL);
    }

    //exit with Escape key or controller Back button
    if (KEY_DOWN(VK_ESCAPE)) gameover = true;
    if (controllers[0].wButtons & XINPUT_GAMEPAD_BACK)
        gameover = true;
}

void Game_End()
{
    explosion->Release();

    DirectInput_Shutdown();
    Direct3D_Shutdown();
}
```

What You Have Learned

In this chapter, you have learned how to use D3DXSprite to draw transparent sprites in Direct3D. Here are the key points:

- You learned how to create the D3DXSprite object.

- You learned how to load a texture from a bitmap file.

- You learned how to draw a transparent sprite.

- You learned how to grab sprite animation frames out of a single bitmap.

Review Questions

Here are some review questions to see how much you have retained from this chapter.

1. What is the name of the DirectX object used to handle sprites?

2. What function is used to load a bitmap image into a texture object?

3. What function do you use to create the sprite object?

4. What is the name of the D3DX function that draws a sprite?

5. What is the D3DX texture object called?

6. Which function returns the size of an image contained in a bitmap file?

7. Which Windows API function provides a clock tick value used for timing?

8. What is the name of the function that must be called before drawing any sprites?

9. What is the name of the function called when sprite drawing is finished?

10. What is the data type used to specify the source rectangle in the sprite drawing function?

On Your Own

The following exercises will help to challenge your grasp of the information presented in this chapter.

Exercise 1. The Animate Sprite project in this chapter does show how animation works, but it's kind of a boring demo. Modify the program so that it generates more than one explosion sprite at a time.

Exercise 2. Building on the previous exercise, now modify the project so that each explosion is animated at a random animation rate.

CHAPTER 7

TRANSFORMING SPRITES

This chapter continues our study of sprite programming that was begun in the previous chapter. We will add to our game programming toolbox the ability to not only draw a sprite, with or without animation, but also to transform that sprite, giving us the ability to rotate, scale, and translate sprites using a Direct3D matrix and an extremely handy D3DX helper function. While working on these sprite functions, you might be tempted to combine features into one large sprite drawing function, or perhaps a sprite class. Although I would encourage you to create a C++ class to handle sprites, I do recommend against the temptation to consolidate several functions into one larger function. Remember, we can *overload* functions of the same name with different sets of parameters, *and* we can set default values to parameters. Let's take advantage of these great features of the C++ language, along with the creative use of custom data types, to enable us to handle sprites effectively.

Here is what you will learn in this chapter:

- How to rotate a sprite.

- How to scale a sprite.

- How to translate a sprite.

- How to transform a matrix for 2D graphics.

- How to draw a transformed sprite with animation.

Sprite Rotation and Scaling

We can rotate and scale a sprite with relative ease thanks to the D3DX library. If we want to draw a single-frame sprite a single cell from a sprite sheet, or do full-blown animation, we can use the same multi-purpose ID3DXSprite::Draw() function. But, in order to add these special features, an additional step is needed. Recall from the previous chapter, our Sprite_Draw_Frame() function looked like this:

```
void Sprite_Draw_Frame(LPDIRECT3DTEXTURE9 texture, int destx, int desty,
    int framenum, int framew, int frameh, int columns)
{
    D3DXVECTOR3 position( (float)destx, (float)desty, 0 );
    D3DCOLOR white = D3DCOLOR_XRGB(255,255,255);
    RECT rect;
    rect.left = (framenum % columns) * framew;
    rect.top = (framenum / columns) * frameh;
    rect.right = rect.left + framew;
    rect.bottom = rect.top + frameh;
    spriteobj->Draw( texture, &rect, NULL, &position, white);
}
```

This function can handle animation just fine, and this is a good general-purpose function for doing sprite animation when you don't care about any special effects (such as rotation or scaling). But we do care about special effects! When you define the function prototype with default parameter values, then the function can be used to draw simple non-animated sprites very easily. Note the function definition here:

```
void Sprite_Draw_Frame(
    LPDIRECT3DTEXTURE9 texture,
    int destx,
    int desty,
```

```
    int framenum,
    int framew,
    int frameh,
    int columns
);
```

If we were to rearrange the function's parameters a bit, we could eliminate the framenum and columns parameters with default values—for the situation when you need to draw a single frame sprite (i.e., without animation frames):

```
void Sprite_Draw_Frame(
    LPDIRECT3DTEXTURE9 texture = NULL,
    int destx = 0,
    int desty = 0,
    int framew = 64,
    int frameh = 64,
    int framenum = 0,
    int columns = 1
);
```

With this function definition, the function's implementation would need to change to match it. Note that the parameters in the function's implementation do *not* have the default values included: those are only specified in the function prototype (which would be defined in the MyDirectX.h header). When you call the function, any parameter that has a default can be skipped; however, when you omit a parameter you must omit all parameters that follow it as well. For this reason, you will want to put the most variant parameters at the end of the parameter list, while the most essential or non-optional parameters at the front of the parameter list. In the function below, for instance, the texture parameter is absolutely essential because without it nothing can be drawn. The destx and desty parameters are also essential, but it's feasible that the image could be drawn at the default location of (0,0). The frame width and height parameters are also essential, but I've defaulted them to (64,64) since that is a very common size used in game sprites. Finally, the last two parameters are the *most* optional, especially for a nonanimated sprite (such as a single image in a bitmap file): defaulting to 0 and 1, respectively, will result in that single frame image being rendered.

One additional detail: since texture has been defaulted to NULL if no parameter is provided (however unlikely that seems), you must perform a check on NULL before attempting to draw the image. This is a good practice anyway that I encourage you to adopt any time you're working with pointers such as a LPDIRECT3DTEXTURE9 or any other pointer which, if null, will cause a crash.

```
void Sprite_Draw_Frame(
    LPDIRECT3DTEXTURE9 texture,
    int destx,
    int desty,
    int framew,
    int frameh,
    int framenum,
    int columns)
{
    //perform check for NULL
    if (!texture) return;

    D3DXVECTOR3 position( (float)destx, (float)desty, 0 );
    D3DCOLOR white = D3DCOLOR_XRGB(255,255,255);
    RECT rect;
    rect.left = (framenum % columns) * framew;
    rect.top = (framenum / columns) * frameh;
    rect.right = rect.left + framew;
    rect.bottom = rect.top + frameh;
    spriteobj->Draw( texture, &rect, NULL, &position, white);
}
```

I will leave the version of Sprite_Draw_Frame as it was originally in MyDirectX.h and MyDirectX.cpp, but encourage you to make these changes if you find them useful.

2D Transforms

The fascinating thing about ID3DXSprite is that it can handle a transformed matrix, just like the Direct3D device! Although we haven't delved into 3D yet, we'll get there soon enough, and you'll learn how to create a view matrix, a projection matrix, and a transform matrix (usually called the "world matrix") in order to render objects in a 3D scene. The great thing about ID3DXSprite is that we can do some of the very same things with our sprites, but just without the extra dimension (the Z axis, to be more precise).

Advice

A matrix is a 4 × 4 array with 4 rows and 4 columns, and is used to transform objects for rendering using very fast *matrix math* calculations rather than much slower sine and cosine calculations (which is how 3D graphics were transformed and rendered "in the old days" of computing). The DirectX name for a matrix is D3DXMATRIX.

Now I'd like to introduce you to the transform function that makes this possible. It's called D3DXMatrixTransformation2D and has this definition:

```
D3DXMATRIX * D3DXMatrixTransformation2D(
    D3DXMATRIX * pOut,
    CONST D3DXVECTOR2 * pScalingCenter,
    FLOAT pScalingRotation,
    CONST D3DXVECTOR2 * pScaling,
    CONST D3DXVECTOR2 * pRotationCenter,
    FLOAT Rotation,
    CONST D3DXVECTOR2 * pTranslation
);
```

First of all, this function produces a matrix (the first parameter) that is actually passed by reference, and thus, returned back to you filled with matrix values. That single 4 × 4 matrix contains all of the combined transforms: rotation, scaling, and translation (i.e., "position"). You will learn more about these transforms later; for now, just focus on grasping how a transform can be used to manipulate a sprite.

Advice

> A 3D vector can represent either a position (x,y,z) or a direction (also an x,y,z set) in 3D space. Since only the x and y values are used for sprite rendering, we can use a simpler 2D vector for sprite programming. The DirectX name for a sprite vector is D3DXVECTOR2.

The Transformed 2D Matrix

First, let's take a look at the parameter we'll pass which will be filled with the matrix data:

```
3DXMATRIX mat;
```

Here, D3DXMATRIX is the name of a struct in the D3DX extension library that is made up of 16 floats arranged in four rows and four columns. A matrix is not unique to Direct3D, nor to 3D computer graphics either; it is a mathematical construct that you might have learned about in a first-year algebra class.

As with any relatively advanced topic, don't try to assimilate it all at once, but give yourself time to gradually learn a new concept by *using it* in *practice*. You do not need to wrap your brain around every concept and function in 3D graphics in order to *use them* effectively. This is a fairly common mistake that beginners make—trying to understand *everything* up front, and then becoming frustrated and overwhelmed by information overload. That is simply not how the human mind learns. I like to think of learning this way—you have to sort of *prove* to your brain that you *need* the information for your *survival*. Strange as that may seem, it is the way we function. In similar fashion, you must *convince* your muscles that they need to increase by working out if you want to be in good shape. If your brain, like your body's muscles, does not need to retain something (whether it's a fact or increase of muscle tone, respectively) then it will not retain it. Our minds, like our bodies, can and do adapt to our environment. But advanced conceptual thinking, involving computer programming, is so wildly abstract that you have to work at it. That is why this field is at the same time difficult and rewarding.

Sprite Scaling

Next, we need to create a vector to represent the horizontal and vertical scaling values for the sprite's transform. We do this with a D3DXVECTOR2 variable that can be declared like so:

```
D3DXVECTOR2 scale( 2.0f, 2.0f );
```

In this case, the scale factor will cause the sprite to be drawn at twice its normal size. Next, we need to define another vector to represent the center of the sprite. This will become the pivot point in the sprite that is needed for rotation. If you don't set the pivot point to the center of the sprite, then when you try to rotate the sprite, it will sort of revolve around the upper-left corner (0,0) rather than rotating around its center.

```
D3DXVECTOR2 center( (width*scaling) / 2.0f, (height*scaling) / 2.0f );
```

In this example, you can see that the width and height is being multiplied by the scaling factor before being divided by two (to, presumably, give us the center point). If you do not change the scale of the sprite at all, then you may leave out the scaling. But, to be thorough, I've included it here so that if you do want to scale a sprite smaller or larger, as well as rotate it, then it will look correct. Otherwise, without this scale factor, the rotation will be distorted.

You may scale the sprite differently in the horizontal and vertical axes if you wish by using a different scale value for the width and height. Since this is seldom done, I have just coded the scaling to use the same scale factor for both width and height.

Sprite Rotation

Rotation is a fairly straightforward float value rather than a vector, as is the case with scaling and translation. There is one important issue to remember when rotating a sprite: is the angle supposed to be in *degrees* or *radians*?

The function we will use in a moment to create our fully transformed sprite matrix will expect a *radian* angle instead of a *degree* angle. We are most familiar with degrees with a range of 0 to 359 degrees making up a circle (for instance, a compass reads in degrees). But most rotations used in graphics programming require a radian angle, which has a range of 0.0 to 2.0 * PI * Radius—since the circumference of a circle is two times pie times the radius. The radius can be dropped when all you want is a *vector* or *direction*.

A simpler way of viewing this formula is to take the *diameter* of a circle (which is 2.0 * Radius) multiplied by PI, which is approximately 3.1415926535. Two times PI is approximately 6.28.

But I digress. We don't need the circumference of a circle—that is just an example for using radians. What we do need is a function to convert between degrees and radians. Most of the time we'll be working with degrees in our code, and then just convert the degree angle to a radian angle at the last instant when transforming the sprite. To convert from degrees to radians, we multiply the degree angle by PI, and then divide by 180:

```
radian angle = degree angle * PI / 180
```

Let's test the formula with a value we can easily discern. If a complete circle is 2*PI radians, then 180 degrees will be half that value, or just simply PI (instead of 2*PI), which is simply PI itself. A half circle in radians, therefore, is 3.14.

```
radian angle = 180 * 3.14 / 180
radian angle = 3.14
```

Let's encode this formula into a reusable function:

```
double toRadians(double degrees)
{
    return degrees * 3.1415926535 / 180.0;
}
```

There's just one problem with this code. Can you spot the inefficiency in this function? "PI" never changes, and the "180.0" also never changes. If we need to do this *a lot* in a game, which is likely since objects do move around and rotate quite a bit in a typical game, then this code will be (rather stupidly) calculating those values over and over again, senselessly. We need to optimize it. The best way to do that is to pre-calculate these values like so:

```
const double PI = 3.1415926535;
```

```
const double PI_under_180 = 180.0f / PI;
const double PI_over_180 = PI / 180.0f;
```

Now for the optimized function:

```
double toRadians(double degrees)
{
    return degrees * PI_over_180;
}
```

Converting from radians to degrees is not often needed, but for completeness sake, here is that function as well:

```
double toDegrees(double radians)
{
    return radians * PI_under_180;
}
```

Sprite Translation

The last parameter we need to create is the translation vector.

```
D3DXVECTOR2 trans( x, y );
```

With the translation vector set to the desired x,y location of the sprite, it will be encoded into the matrix when we call on the D3DXMatrixTransformation2D function to build the matrix with all of these parameters. While we're on the subject, let's just go ahead and do that now.

```
D3DXMatrixTransformation2D(
    &mat,      //the resulting matrix
    NULL,      //scaling center point (not used)
    0,         //scaling rotation value (not used)
    &scale,    //scaling vector
    &center,   //rotation center/pivot vector
    rotation,  //rotation angle
    &trans     //translation vector
);
```

Note that some of the parameters are passed by reference, which is why they have the ampersand in front of their names. The first one, in particular, is returned by the function with its 16 matrix values filled in. These values represent the rotation, scaling, and translation transformations for a sprite. After we have this matrix, we can tell the sprite object (ID3DXSprite) to use this as the current transform:

```
spriteobj->SetTransform( &mat );
```

Creating the Sprite Matrix

The D3DX library does it all for us with that single function call, D3DXMatrix-Transformation2D, which builds the matrix, and ID3DXSprite::SetTransform, which uses that matrix when rendering the next sprite. All together, we can see that the parameters and function calls look like this:

```
//create a scale vector
D3DXVECTOR2 scale( scaling, scaling );

//create a translate vector
D3DXVECTOR2 trans( x, y );

//set center by dividing width and height by two
D3DXVECTOR2 center( (float)( width * scaling )/2, (float)( height * scaling )/2);

//create 2D transformation matrix
D3DXMATRIX mat;
D3DXMatrixTransformation2D( &mat, NULL, 0, &scale, &center, rotation, &trans );

//tell sprite object to use the transform
spriteobj->SetTransform( &mat );
```

Drawing a Transformed Sprite

All that's left to do is draw the sprite! But, unlike the previous chapter, our call to ID3DXSprite::Draw must not use the position parameter, and instead just pass NULL to that. We'll have the same animation code as before:

```
int fx = (frame % columns) * width;
int fy = (frame / columns) * height;
RECT srcRect = {fx, fy, fx + width, fy + height};
```

but the Draw function call will have a slight change since the new transform matrix handles positioning of the sprite:

```
spriteobj->Draw( image, &srcRect, NULL, NULL, color );
```

Now that you have all the code for transforming and drawing an advanced sprite, we can put this code into a reusable function inside the MyDirectX.cpp file (and with the function prototype name in the MyDirectX.h header). Here is the prototype to be added to MyDirectX.h (note that some of the parameters have default values, which means they will use those defaults if you don't specify those parameters yourself):

```
void Sprite_Transform_Draw(
    LPDIRECT3DTEXTURE9 image,
    int x,
    int y,
    int width,
    int height,
    int frame = 0,
    int columns = 1,
    float rotation = 0.0f,
    float scaling = 1.0f,
    D3DCOLOR color = D3DCOLOR_XRGB(255,255,255)
);
```

This is the new function that must be added to MyDirectX.cpp (note the function implementation does not include the default parameter values, which should only be located in the prototype):

```
void Sprite_Transform_Draw(LPDIRECT3DTEXTURE9 image, int x, int y,
    int width, int height, nt frame, int columns,
    float rotation, float scaling, D3DCOLOR color)
{
    //create a scale vector
    D3DXVECTOR2 scale( scaling, scaling );

    //create a translate vector
    D3DXVECTOR2 trans( x, y );

    //set center by dividing width and height by two
    D3DXVECTOR2 center( (float)( width * scaling )/2, (float)( height * scaling )/2);

    //create 2D transformation matrix
    D3DXMATRIX mat;
    D3DXMatrixTransformation2D( &mat, NULL, 0, &scale, &center, rotation, &trans );

    //tell sprite object to use the transform
    spriteobj->SetTransform( &mat );

    //calculate frame location in source image
```

```
    int fx = (frame % columns) * width;
    int fy = (frame / columns) * height;
    RECT srcRect = {fx, fy, fx + width, fy + height};

    //draw the sprite frame
    spriteobj->Draw( image, &srcRect, NULL, NULL, color );
}
```

The Rotate_Scale_Demo Program

Let me show you what you can do with this new reusable function. Following is an example called Rotate_Scale_Demo, and a screen shot is shown in Figure 7.1.

```
/*
    Beginning Game Programming, Third Edition
    MyGame.cpp
*/
```

Figure 7.1
The Rotate_Scale_Demo program draws a sprite with transforms.

```cpp
#include "MyDirectX.h"
using namespace std;

const string APPTITLE = "Sprite Rotation and Scaling Demo";
const int SCREENW = 1024;
const int SCREENH = 768;

LPDIRECT3DTEXTURE9 sunflower;
D3DCOLOR color;
int frame=0, columns, width, height;
int startframe, endframe, starttime=0, delay;

bool Game_Init(HWND window)
{
    //initialize Direct3D
    Direct3D_Init(window, SCREENW, SCREENH, false);

    //initialize DirectInput
    DirectInput_Init(window);

    //load the sprite image
    sunflower = LoadTexture("sunflower.bmp");

    return true;
}

void Game_Run(HWND window)
{
    static float scale = 0.001f;
    static float r = 0;
    static float s = 1.0f;

    //make sure the Direct3D device is valid
    if (!d3ddev) return;

    //update input devices
    DirectInput_Update();

    //clear the scene
    d3ddev->Clear(0, NULL, D3DCLEAR_TARGET | D3DCLEAR_ZBUFFER,
        D3DCOLOR_XRGB(0,0,100), 1.0f, 0);

    //start rendering
```

```
    if (d3ddev->BeginScene())
    {
        //begin sprite rendering
        spriteobj->Begin(D3DXSPRITE_ALPHABLEND);

        //set rotation and scaling
        r = timeGetTime() / 600.0f;
        s += scale;
        if (s < 0.1 || s > 1.25f) scale *= -1;

        //draw sprite
        width = height = 512;
        frame = 0;
        columns = 1;
        color = D3DCOLOR_XRGB(255,255,255);
        Sprite_Transform_Draw( sunflower, 300, 150, width, height,
            frame, columns, r, s, color );

        //end sprite rendering
        spriteobj->End();

        //stop rendering
        d3ddev->EndScene();
        d3ddev->Present(NULL, NULL, NULL, NULL);
    }

    //exit when escape key is pressed
    if (KEY_DOWN(VK_ESCAPE)) gameover = true;

    //controller Back button also ends
    if (controllers[0].wButtons & XINPUT_GAMEPAD_BACK)
        gameover = true;

}

void Game_End()
{
    //free memory and shut down
    sunflower->Release();

    DirectInput_Shutdown();
    Direct3D_Shutdown();
}
```

The `Sprite_Transform_Draw()` function has several default parameters, and we can take advantage of this fact in order to simplify our code any time we don't need to use those advanced features. For instance, if you just need to draw a simple (non-animated) sprite, then you can call the function without the frame number, column count, rotate, scaling, or color parameters, like so:

```
Sprite_Transform_Draw( spaceship, 100, 100, 64, 64 );
```

This call to the function will draw a simple sprite image at x,y location 100,100, and it specifies that the dimensions of the sprite are 64 × 64 pixels. We might go a step further and pull the width and height of the image inside the `Sprite_Transform_Draw` function, but that would complicate the function, not to mention slow it down.

Animation with Transforms

Rotation and other transforms are great, but what if we want to also do animation? After all, a sprite is kind of useless if it doesn't support animation stored in a sprite sheet! Fortunately, we can apply this new transform functionality to animation as well. Since `ID3DXSprite` is used to draw single- or multi-frame sprites, you can use the same transformation to rotate and scale a sprite regardless of whether it's animated or not. Figure 7.2 shows a sprite sheet containing frames from an animated game character.

The great thing about the `Sprite_Transform_Draw()` function that we just added is that it is completely self contained and fully featured! Let's see what this one function can do:

- Draw a simple (non-animated) sprite at any x,y location.

- Rotate a simple sprite.

- Scale a simple sprite.

- Rotate *and* scale *and* translate a simple sprite.

- Draw an animated sprite at any x,y location.

- Rotate an animated sprite.

- Scale an animated sprite.

- Rotate *and* scale *and* translate an animated sprite.

Figure 7.2
An animated character with 64 frames of animation.

About the only thing this awesome function does *not* do is your dishes for you!

So, let's see how it works when animation is involved. I have a new program for you called Rotate_Animate_Demo. This program uses the same transforms that were applied to the "sunflower" sprite in the previous example; the difference now is that we're dealing with an animated sprite. What's the difference? As far as Direct3D is concerned, there is none. Our Sprite_Translate_Draw() function handles simple sprites as well as animated sprites with all transforms enabled.

Let's give animation with full transforms a try. Figure 7.3 shows the output from the Rotate_Animate_Demo program, with the code listing to follow.

Figure 7.3
The Rotate_Animate_Demo program draws a transformed and animated sprite.

```
/*
    Beginning Game Programming, Third Edition
    MyGame.cpp
*/

#include "MyDirectX.h"
using namespace std;

const string APPTITLE = "Sprite Rotation and Animation Demo";
const int SCREENW = 1024;
const int SCREENH = 768;

LPDIRECT3DTEXTURE9 paladin = NULL;
D3DCOLOR color = D3DCOLOR_XRGB(255,255,255);
float scale = 0.004f;
float r = 0;
```

```
float s = 1.0f;
int frame=0, columns, width, height;
int startframe, endframe, starttime=0, delay;

bool Game_Init(HWND window)
{
    //initialize Direct3D
    Direct3D_Init(window, SCREENW, SCREENH, false);

    //initialize DirectInput
    DirectInput_Init(window);

    //load the sprite sheet
    paladin = LoadTexture("paladin_walk.png");
    if (!paladin) {
        MessageBox(window, "Error loading sprite", "Error", 0);
        return false;
    }

    return true;
}

void Game_Run(HWND window)
{
    //make sure the Direct3D device is valid
    if (!d3ddev) return;

    //update input devices
    DirectInput_Update();

    //clear the scene
    d3ddev->Clear(0, NULL, D3DCLEAR_TARGET | D3DCLEAR_ZBUFFER,
        D3DCOLOR_XRGB(0,0,100), 1.0f, 0);

    //start rendering
    if (d3ddev->BeginScene())
    {
        //begin sprite rendering
        spriteobj->Begin(D3DXSPRITE_ALPHABLEND);

        //scale the sprite from tiny to huge over time
        s += scale;
```

```
            if (s < 0.5f || s > 6.0f) scale *= -1;

            //set animation properties
            columns = 8;
            width = height = 96;
            startframe = 24;
            endframe = 31;
            delay = 90;
            Sprite_Animate(frame,startframe,endframe,1,starttime,delay );

            //transform and draw sprite
            Sprite_Transform_Draw( paladin, 300, 200, width, height,
                frame, columns, 0, s, color );


            //end sprite rendering
            spriteobj->End();

            //stop rendering
            d3ddev->EndScene();
            d3ddev->Present(NULL, NULL, NULL, NULL);
        }

        //exit when escape key is pressed
        if (KEY_DOWN(VK_ESCAPE)) gameover = true;

        //controller Back button also ends
        if (controllers[0].wButtons & XINPUT_GAMEPAD_BACK)
            gameover = true;

}

void Game_End()
{
    //free memory and shut down
    paladin->Release();

    DirectInput_Shutdown();
    Direct3D_Shutdown();
}
```

What You Have Learned

In this chapter, you have learned how to render 2D sprites with full matrix-based transforms with support for animation, rotation, scaling, movement, and alpha blending all in a single function, `Sprite_Transform_Draw`. This function will now be the workhorse of any future 2D demos and games we write. In the next chapter, we will create a new sprite structure and learn two techniques for detecting sprite collisions.

In summary, you learned how to:

- Perform matrix-based sprite scaling.

- Perform matrix-based sprite rotation.

- Perform matrix-based sprite translation (or movement).

- Animate a sprite using a "sprite sheet" image.

- Use timing to set the speed of animation.

Review Questions

Here are some review questions to see how much you have retained from this chapter. The answers to these review questions are located in Appendix C.

1. What type of Direct3D object must we use for the source image of a sprite?

2. Which function creates a matrix for transforming a 2D sprite based on rotation, scaling, and translation vectors passed to it?

3. How are angles encoded when rotating a sprite, with degrees or radians?

4. What data type is used to hold a vector for sprite scaling?

5. What data type is used to hold a vector for sprite movement?

6. What data type is used to hold a value for sprite rotation?

7. Which ID3DXSprite function is used to apply a matrix to the sprite's transform?

8. What parameter is always passed to the ID3DXSprite::Begin function?

9. Besides width, height, and frame number, what other value is needed for animation?

10. Which macro is used to encode a D3DCOLOR with an alpha color component?

On Your Own

The following exercises will help to challenge your grasp of the information presented in this chapter.

Exercise 1. Modify the Rotate Animate demo by replacing the walking character with an animated sprite that you have acquired on your own—perhaps using SpriteLib.

Exercise 2. Modify the Rotate Scale demo so that the flower sprite remains in the center of the screen while the scale changes.

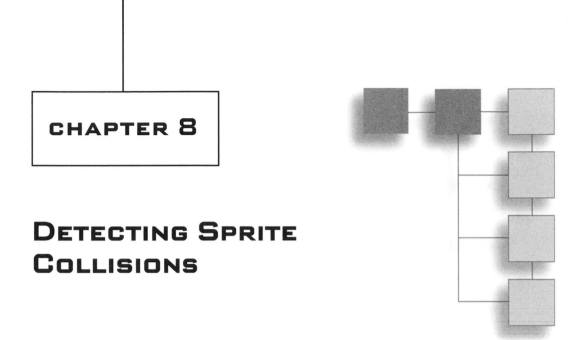

CHAPTER 8

DETECTING SPRITE COLLISIONS

So far you have learned how to draw sprites onto the screen, but it takes much more than this to make a game with simply the ability to draw. That is really only the beginning, like starting the engine of a car; once started, then you can drive. A real game has sprites (or 3D meshes—which we'll get to soon) that interact, where bullets and rockets hit enemy ships and cause them to explode, and sprites that must navigate a maze without going through walls, and sprites that can run and jump over crates and land on top of enemy characters (such as how Mario jumps onto turtles in *Super Mario World* to knock them out). All of these situations require the ability to detect when two sprites have collided, or touched each other. Collision detection is the simplest (and most important) type of *physics* that you can incorporate into a game. Sprite collision really opens up the world of game programming and makes it possible for you to build a real game!

Here is what you will learn in this chapter:

- Bounding box collision detection.

- Distance based collision detection.

Bounding Box Collision Detection

There are two primary algorithms (or methods) used to detect sprite collisions—the bounding rectangle (also referred to as "bounding box") and distance-based collision detection. What really makes a game stand out in the crowd is how well you program *responses* to collisions. We will learn very simply how to detect collision with these two methods, but it's the way you program sprites (and later, meshes) to respond in a collision event that really matters.

So, let's begin by studying bounding box collision detection. The key to this type of collision testing is to identify where two sprites are on the screen, and then compare their *bounding boxes* (or rectangles) to see if there is an overlap. That is why this type of collision testing is called bounding box collision detection—because each sprite is treated as a logical box, or rectangle.

If you know the location of two sprites and you know the width and height of each, then it is possible to determine whether the two sprites are intersecting. Bounding rectangle collision detection describes the use of a sprite's boundary for collision testing. You can get the upper-left corner of a sprite by merely looking at its X and Y values. To get the lower-right corner, add the width and height to the X and Y values. Collectively, these values may be represented as *left*, *top*, *right*, and *bottom*.

Working with Rectangles

We will use a RECT to represent each bounding box. A RECT has four properties: left, top, right, and bottom. Here is an example:

```
int x = 10, y = 10;
int width = 64, height = 64;
RECT rect;
rect.left = x;
rect.top = y;
rect.right = x + width;
rect.bottom = y + height;
```

You can also create a RECT with this simpler format:

```
RECT rect = { x, y, x + width, y + height };
```

The result of this statement is a RECT with these values:

```
left = 10
top = 10
right = 74
bottom = 74
```

When creating a rectangle to represent a sprite's bounding box, the rectangle's left and top properties are set to the sprite's x and y values, while the bottom-right corner is set with the sprite's position plus dimensions. The end result is a rectangle which logically wraps around (or bounds) a sprite on the screen.

To actually put this code to use, we'll call on a Windows API function. The function is extremely helpful, because it performs the collision test for us with a single call! The function is called IntersectRect. It accepts two RECT variables and simply returns 0 for false, or 1 for true (which indicates that the sprites are colliding). This function also returns the union of the two sprites—the portions that overlapped—although we aren't interested in this information (a simple yes or no will suffice!).

But wait a minute! We have been working with sprites using nothing but global variables—for the texture, the position, the dimensions, the rotation, the scaling, and so on. We can't possibly pass all these variables to a collision function. So, what's needed is a sprite structure to contain all of these properties. Maybe something like the BOMB structure back in Chapter 5:

```
struct BOMB
{
    float x,y;

    void reset()
    {
```

```
        x = (float)(rand() % (SCREENW-128));
        y = 0;
    }
};
```

I liked how well this improved the program, making it possible to easily keep track of a bomb's position, and also to randomly move it with the reset() function. We need to come up with a similar structure for a more generic sprite, and then just add new features to it whenever we want. So, for starters, let's code the basic struct with just the sprite properties needed to test for a collision:

```
struct SPRITE
{
    float x,y;
    int width, height;
};
```

Writing the Collision Function

Now we'll look at a function that creates two rectangles based on these sprite properties, and then calls IntersectRect to see if they have collided. This function is called Collision, and is very reusable (even if we change the SPRITE struct):

```
int Collision(SPRITE sprite1, SPRITE sprite2)
{
    RECT rect1;
    rect1.left = sprite1.x;
    rect1.top = sprite1.y;
    rect1.right = sprite1.x + sprite1.width;
    rect1.bottom = sprite1.y + sprite1.height;

    RECT rect2;
    rect2.left = sprite2.x;
    rect2.top = sprite2.y;
    rect2.right = sprite2.x + sprite2.width;
    rect2.bottom = sprite2.y + sprite2.height;

    RECT dest; //ignored
    return IntersectRect(&dest, &rect1, &rect2);
}
```

Advice

You will notice some compiler warnings within the `Collision` function because the `SPRITE.x` and `SPRITE.y` properties are floats, while the `RECT` properties are long integers. To get rid of the warnings, you can typecast the sprite properties with (long).

A New Sprite Structure

We need to add more features to the `SPRITE` struct so that it can handle at least all of the features presented in the previous chapter, at bare minimum. We can add to it after this initial definition as the need arises. What I like about this structure is that a simple constructor sets up all the initial conditions we need for a simple sprite (without any animation). So it will be very easy to use the structure to handle very simple sprites without having to set all of the properties manually each time.

```
struct SPRITE
{
    float x,y;
    int frame, columns;
    int width, height;
    float scaling, rotation;
    int startframe, endframe;
    int starttime, delay;
    int direction;
    float velx, vely;
    D3DCOLOR color;

    SPRITE()
    {
        frame = 0;
        columns = 1;
        width = height = 0;
        scaling = 1.0f;
        rotation = 0.0f;
        startframe = endframe = 0;
        direction = 1;
        starttime = delay = 0;
        velx = vely = 0.0f;
        color = D3DCOLOR_XRGB(255,255,255);
    }
};
```

Adjusting for Sprite Scaling

If you change the scale of your sprite, then the Collision function will not work properly because it only takes into account the original bounding box. What we need to do is adjust the Collision function so that it takes into account the scaling factor. Technically, we should recalculate the bounding box after doing any kind of transform, because rotation (in particular) tends to change the size of the bounding box; but we'll err on the simple side in that situation and ignore rotation. My real concern is just with scaling since it definitely has an impact on the validity of collisions.

To account for the scaling factor, what we must do is multiply the sprite's width and height by the scaling value when creating the bounding box (in the form of a RECT). In order for this to work for sprites with default scaling, we must be sure to set that default scaling value to 1.0. (You might mistakenly set it to 0, since it's very common to initialize variables to 0, but we want the scale factor to be 1.0, which represents 100% of its size.) If a simple sprite is created and tested for collision, the default 1.0 will work. But if a sprite is created and scaled to some other factor (larger or smaller than 1.0), then the scaling factor in the Collision function should take that into account. Here's a new version with the changes in bold:

```
int Collision(SPRITE sprite1, SPRITE sprite2)
{
    RECT rect1;
    rect1.left = (long)sprite1.x;
    rect1.top = (long)sprite1.y;
    rect1.right = (long)sprite1.x + sprite1.width * sprite1.scaling;
    rect1.bottom = (long)sprite1.y + sprite1.height * sprite1.scaling;

    RECT rect2;
    rect2.left = (long)sprite2.x;
    rect2.top = (long)sprite2.y;
    rect2.right = (long)sprite2.x + sprite2.width * sprite2.scaling;
    rect2.bottom = (long)sprite2.y + sprite2.height * sprite2.scaling;

    RECT dest; //ignored
    return IntersectRect(&dest, &rect1, &rect2);
}
```

The Bounding Box Demo Program

We need a complete (but simple) example to demonstrate this type of collision detection. I have a program to share with you called Bounding Box Demo, and the source code is below. This program requires a minor change to the framework files in order to incorporate the Collision function into our growing game library. You may use the DirectX_Project template project located on the CD in the .\chapter08 folder as a starting point for this project (it is up to date through the previous chapter for your convenience).

Adding Code to MyDirectX.h

Open the MyDirectX.h header file and add this function prototype:

```
//bounding box collision detection
int Collision(SPRITE sprite1, SPRITE sprite2);
```

We also must add the SPRITE structure to this file so it will be visible in our main program, as well as available (as a dependency) to the Collision function. You may add the SPRITE struct somewhere near the top of the MyDirectX.h file:

```
//sprite structure
struct SPRITE
{
    float x,y;
    int frame, columns;
    int width, height;
    float scaling, rotation;
    int startframe, endframe;
    int starttime, delay;
    int direction;
    float velx, vely;
    D3DCOLOR color;

    SPRITE()
    {
        frame = 0;
        columns = 1;
        width = height = 0;
        scaling = 1.0f;
        rotation = 0.0f;
        startframe = endframe = 0;
        direction = 1;
        starttime = delay = 0;
        velx = vely = 0.0f;
        color = D3DCOLOR_XRGB(255,255,255);
    }
};
```

Adding Code to MyDirectX.cpp

Next, open the MyDirectX.cpp file and add the complete function:

```
//bounding box collision detection
int Collision(SPRITE sprite1, SPRITE sprite2)
{
    RECT rect1;
    rect1.left = (long)sprite1.x;
    rect1.top = (long)sprite1.y;
    rect1.right = (long)sprite1.x + sprite1.width * sprite1.scaling;
    rect1.bottom = (long)sprite1.y + sprite1.height * sprite1.scaling;

    RECT rect2;
    rect2.left = (long)sprite2.x;
    rect2.top = (long)sprite2.y;
    rect2.right = (long)sprite2.x + sprite2.width * sprite2.scaling;
    rect2.bottom = (long)sprite2.y + sprite2.height * sprite2.scaling;

    RECT dest; //ignored
    return IntersectRect(&dest, &rect1, &rect2);
}
```

MyGame.cpp

Now we can address the source code in the MyGame.cpp file for this Bounding Box Demo program. What I had in mind for this program was a spaceship that you can move up and down on the screen, and two asteroids moving left to right on the screen. When you move the ship into the path of an asteroid, the two sprites will collide and cause the asteroid to rebound in the opposite direction. Figure 8.1 shows the program in action.

```
#include "MyDirectX.h"
using namespace std;

const string APPTITLE = "Bounding Box Demo";
const int SCREENW = 1024;
const int SCREENH = 768;

SPRITE ship, asteroid1, asteroid2;
LPDIRECT3DTEXTURE9 imgShip = NULL;
LPDIRECT3DTEXTURE9 imgAsteroid = NULL;

bool Game_Init(HWND window)
```

Figure 8.1
The Bounding Box Demo program demonstrates basic collision detection.

```
{
    //initialize Direct3D
    Direct3D_Init(window, SCREENW, SCREENH, false);

    //initialize DirectInput
    DirectInput_Init(window);

    //load the sprite textures
    imgShip = LoadTexture("fatship.tga");
    if (!imgShip) return false;
    imgAsteroid = LoadTexture("asteroid.tga");
    if (!imgAsteroid) return false;

    //set properties for sprites
    ship.x = 450;
    ship.y = 300;
    ship.width = ship.height = 128;
```

```
        asteroid1.x = 50;
        asteroid1.y = 200;
        asteroid1.width = asteroid1.height = 60;
        asteroid1.columns = 8;
        asteroid1.startframe = 0;
        asteroid1.endframe = 63;
        asteroid1.velx = -2.0f;

        asteroid2.x = 900;
        asteroid2.y = 500;
        asteroid2.width = asteroid2.height = 60;
        asteroid2.columns = 8;
        asteroid2.startframe = 0;
        asteroid2.endframe = 63;
        asteroid2.velx = 2.0f;

        return true;
    }

void Game_Run(HWND window)
{
    if (!d3ddev) return;
    DirectInput_Update();
    d3ddev->Clear(0, NULL, D3DCLEAR_TARGET | D3DCLEAR_ZBUFFER,
        D3DCOLOR_XRGB(0,0,100), 1.0f, 0);

    //move the ship up/down with arrow keys
    if (Key_Down(DIK_UP))
    {
        ship.y -= 1.0f;
        if (ship.y < 0) ship.y = 0;
    }

    if (Key_Down(DIK_DOWN))
    {
        ship.y += 1.0f;
        if (ship.y > SCREENH - ship.height)
            ship.y = SCREENH - ship.height;
    }

    //move and animate the asteroids
    asteroid1.x += asteroid1.velx;
    if (asteroid1.x < 0 || asteroid1.x > SCREENW-asteroid1.width)
        asteroid1.velx *= -1;
```

```
    Sprite_Animate(asteroid1.frame, asteroid1.startframe, asteroid1.endframe,
        asteroid1.direction, asteroid1.starttime, asteroid1.delay);

    asteroid2.x += asteroid2.velx;
    if (asteroid2.x < 0 || asteroid2.x > SCREENW-asteroid2.width)
        asteroid2.velx *= -1;
    Sprite_Animate(asteroid2.frame, asteroid2.startframe, asteroid2.endframe,
        asteroid2.direction, asteroid2.starttime, asteroid2.delay);

    //test for collisions
    if (Collision(ship, asteroid1))
        asteroid1.velx *= -1;

    if (Collision(ship, asteroid2))
        asteroid2.velx *= -1;

    if (d3ddev->BeginScene())
    {
        spriteobj->Begin(D3DXSPRITE_ALPHABLEND);

        Sprite_Transform_Draw(imgShip, ship.x, ship.y, ship.width,
        ship.height, ship.frame, ship.columns);

        Sprite_Transform_Draw(imgAsteroid, asteroid1.x, asteroid1.y,
            asteroid1.width, asteroid1.height, asteroid1.frame,
            asteroid1.columns);

        Sprite_Transform_Draw(imgAsteroid, asteroid2.x, asteroid2.y,
            asteroid2.width, asteroid2.height, asteroid2.frame,
            asteroid2.columns);

        spriteobj->End();
        d3ddev->EndScene();
        d3ddev->Present(NULL, NULL, NULL, NULL);
    }

    if (KEY_DOWN(VK_ESCAPE)) gameover = true;
    if (controllers[0].wButtons & XINPUT_GAMEPAD_BACK)
        gameover = true;
}

void Game_End()
{
```

```
    if (imgShip) imgShip->Release();
    if (imgAsteroid) imgAsteroid->Release();

    DirectInput_Shutdown();
    Direct3D_Shutdown();
}
```

Distance-Based Collision Detection

Bounding box collision detection produces reasonably accurate collision results and is very fast. But there are some cases where this method does not do very well, such as when you are using artwork with rounded edges or very complex shapes (such as an airplane with protruding wings). In the unusual cases, it's beneficial to have an alternate way to detect collisions, and for these cases we can use the distance-based collision algorithm.

When using distance to determine whether two sprites are colliding, what we must do is calculate the center point of each sprite, calculate the radius of the sprite (from the center point to the edge), and then check the distance between the two center points. If the distance is less than the two radii combined, then you know the sprites are overlapping. Why? The radius of each sprite, when added together, should be less than the distance between the two sprites.

Calculating Distance

To calculate the distance between any two points, we need only refer to the classic mathematical distance formula. Any two points can be converted into a right triangle by treating them as the end points of the two sides. Take the delta value of the X and Y of each point, square each delta value, add them together, then take the square root, and you have the distance between the two points. See Figure 8.2.

```
delta_x = x1 - x2
delta_y = y1 - y2
distance = square root ( (delta_x * delta_x) + (delta_y * delta_y) )
```

Codifying Distance

You can code this into a function that takes two sprites as parameters and calculates the delta values and the distance from the sprites' properties. The scaling factor must also be taken into account, as it was with bounding box

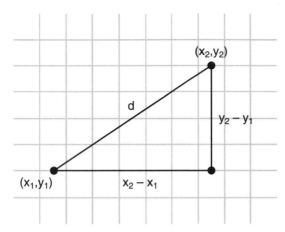

Figure 8.2
The distance between two points can be calculated by forming a right triangle that connects them.

collision. In addition, the largest dimension of a sprite (either the width or the height) will be used to calculate the radius. Let's first calculate the radius for the first sprite:

```
if (sprite1.width > sprite1.height)
    radius1 = (sprite1.width * sprite1.scaling) / 2.0;
else
    radius1 = (sprite1.height * sprite1.scaling) / 2.0;
```

When you have the radius, then you can calculate the center point of the first sprite. I will store the center value in a vector:

```
double x1 = sprite1.x + radius1;
double y1 = sprite1.y + radius1;
D3DXVECTOR2 vector1(x1, y1);
```

This new vector, called vector1, contains the center point of the first sprite—wherever it is located on the screen. By duplicating this code for the second sprite, you end up with the center points for both sprites. Once you have those values, then you can begin working on the distance calculation. That involves first calculating the delta values for X and Y:

```
double deltax = vector1.x - vector2.x;
double deltay = vector2.y - vector1.y;
```

Calculating distance is very easy when you finally have those delta values:

```
double dist = sqrt((deltax * deltax) + (deltay * deltay));
```

Let's code it up into a reusable function. I've named this function CollisionD to differentiate it from the bounding box version, which is just called Collision (because you will likely want to use that one more often—it's much, much faster after all).

```
bool CollisionD(SPRITE sprite1, SPRITE sprite2)
{
    double radius1, radius2;

    //calculate radius 1
    if (sprite1.width > sprite1.height)
        radius1 = (sprite1.width * sprite1.scaling) / 2.0;
    else
        radius1 = (sprite1.height * sprite1.scaling) / 2.0;

    //center point 1
    double x1 = sprite1.x + radius1;
    double y1 = sprite1.y + radius1;
    D3DXVECTOR2 vector1(x1, y1);

    //calculate radius 2
    if (sprite2.width > sprite2.height)
        radius2 = (sprite2.width * sprite2.scaling) / 2.0;
    else
        radius2 = (sprite2.height * sprite2.scaling) / 2.0;

    //center point 2
    double x2 = sprite2.x + radius2;
    double y2 = sprite2.y + radius2;
    D3DXVECTOR2 vector2(x2, y2);

    //calculate distance
    double deltax = vector1.x - vector2.x;
    double deltay = vector2.y - vector1.y;
    double dist = sqrt((deltax * deltax) + (deltay * deltay));

    //return distance comparison
    return (dist < radius1 + radius2);
}
```

Now would be a good time to just copy this function over to the framework, so let's do that now. Add this function to MyDirectX.cpp, and this prototype to MyDirectX.h:

```
bool CollisionD(SPRITE sprite1, SPRITE sprite2);
```

Testing Distance-Based Collision

I have a new example program that demonstrates distance-based collision detection, but it's based on the previous Bounding Box Collision Demo, and only involves changes to two lines of code, so I won't repeat the code listing here. Just note that if you load up the Distance_Demo project from the CD, it will have these two lines that differ simply by calling the new `CollisionD` function; otherwise, the programs are identical:

```
//test for collisions
if (CollisionD(ship, asteroid1))
    asteroid1.velx *= -1;

if (CollisionD(ship, asteroid2))
    asteroid2.velx *= -1;
```

What You Have Learned

In this chapter, we have gone over the two common forms of 2D sprite-based collision detection: bounding box and distance. Although the two example programs in this chapter showed how to implement collision, we have yet to see this in a real game so it may be a bit hard to visualize how the concept of collision detection (and response) is helpful in a game project at this early stage. Hang in there; we'll get to a complete game in Chapter 16.

Here are the key points:

- Bounding box-based collision detection

- Distance-based collision detection

Review Questions

Here are some review questions to see how much you have retained from this chapter.

1. What type of object do we need to fill with the bounds of each sprite to use the `IntersectRect` function?

2. What is the first parameter passed to `IntersectRect` used for?

3. What type of triangle do we use (conceptually) to calculate the distance between two points?

4. Briefly describe how the bounding box method handles sprite scaling.

5. In a fast-paced arcade game with hundreds of sprites on the screen at once, where precision is not as important, which of the two collision detection techniques should be used?

6. In a slower game (such as an RPG) where precision is important to the gameplay, and few sprites will be on the screen at a time, which collision technique should be used?

7. When calculating the distance between two sprites, where is the X,Y point on each sprite normally located?

8. After a collision between two sprites occurs, why would you want to move the sprites away from each other before the next frame?

9. What are the second and third parameters of the `IntersectRect` function?

10. Briefly describe a situation in a game where you might want to use *both* collision techniques with the same two sprites to determine if they are touching.

On Your Own

The following exercises will help to challenge your grasp of the information presented in this chapter.

Exercise 1. The Bounding Box Demo project is very simplistic in order to properly illustrate how collision detection works. But we can do something more interesting with it. For instance, let's try this: Modify the program so that the asteroids move all around the screen in random directions rather than just horizontally at a fixed row.

Exercise 2. The Distance Demo illustrates distance-based collision detection with the same project code. Let's play with the values a bit. Modify the program so that it uses a smaller radius for each of the sprites when calling the distance function. You might try one-half or one-fourth of the original radius value. What happens?

CHAPTER 9

PRINTING TEXT

In this chapter you will learn how to create a font and print text to the screen using ID3DXFont. This class makes it possible to print text using any TrueType font installed in your Windows system, although I recommend sticking with standard fonts (like Times New Roman and Verdana) so the text will look exactly as planned on every PC. (If you use an unusual font, then Windows will try to approximate it, which we do not want to happen in a game.)

Here is what you will learn in this chapter:

- How to create a new font with ID3DXFont.

- How to print text to the screen using a font.

- How to wrap text inside a region.

Creating a Font

We are going to use the ID3DXFont interface to print text to the screen using any desired TrueType font installed in the system. In the past I have favored using a bitmap-based font, in which the character set of a font is stored in a bitmap file in ASCII order. After loading the bitmap, the font borrows features used by sprites to render each character in a string. The end result is a font that looks *exactly* how you expect it to, because you are in control of the source bitmap.

Advice

ASCII stands for American Standard Code for Information Interchange and is a standard used for character set codes. For instance, the ASCII code of Space is 32, while the ASCII code of Enter is 13. ASCII codes differ from Windows virtual key codes and DirectInput key codes (which are specific to Windows).

DirectX provides a font class that abstracts the process for us so we can focus less on logistics (like the font-laden bitmap image) and more time on game code. The ID3DXFont interface is used to create a font, and the pointer version is already predefined for us:

```
LPD3DXFONT font;
```

We will use a function called D3DXCreateFontIndirect to create the font and prepare it for printing out text. But before doing that, we must first set up the properties desired for the font using the D3DXFONT_DESC structure.

The Font Descriptor

The D3DXFONT_DESC structure is comprised of these properties:

- INT Height;

- UINT Width;

- UINT Weight;

- UINT MipLevels;

- BOOL Italic;

- BYTE CharSet;

- BYTE OutputPrecision;

- BYTE Quality;

- BYTE PitchAndFamily;

- CHAR FaceName[LF_FACESIZE];

Don't let these descriptor properties intimidate you, since most are set to zero or default values. The only two properties that are *really* important are Height and FaceName. Here is an example font descriptor variable being initialized with working values for an Arial 24-point font.

```
D3DXFONT_DESC desc = {
    24,                         //height
    0,                          //width
    0,                          //weight
    0,                          //miplevels
    false,                      //italic
    DEFAULT_CHARSET,            //charset
    OUT_TT_PRECIS,              //output precision
    CLIP_DEFAULT_PRECIS,        //quality
    DEFAULT_PITCH,              //pitch and family
    "Arial"                     //font name
};
```

Creating the Font Object

After setting up the font descriptor, we can then create the font object with the D3DXCreateFontIndirect function. This function expects three parameters:

- Direct3D device

- D3DXFONT_DESC

- LPD3DXFONT

Let's see an example of how to create a font using this function:

```
D3DXCreateFontIndirect(d3ddev, &desc, &font);
```

A Reusable MakeFont Function

Let's put all of this code into a reusable function which can then be added to the game library. This function expects a font name and font point size, and it returns a pointer to an LPD3DXFONT object.

```
LPD3DXFONT MakeFont(string name, int size)
```

```
{
    LPD3DXFONT font = NULL;
    D3DXFONT_DESC desc = {
        size,                       //height
        0,                          //width
        0,                          //weight
        0,                          //miplevels
        false,                      //italic
        DEFAULT_CHARSET,            //charset
        OUT_TT_PRECIS,              //output precision
        CLIP_DEFAULT_PRECIS,        //quality
        DEFAULT_PITCH,              //pitch and family
        ""                          //font name
    };
    strcpy(desc.FaceName, name.c_str());
    D3DXCreateFontIndirect(d3ddev, &desc, &font);
    return font;
}
```

Printing Text with ID3DXFont

You have learned how to create a font object, but not how to print text to the screen with it yet. That is what we'll learn about in this section. To print text using an existing font (which you will have previously created and initialized), you can use the ID3DXFont::DrawText() function. The DrawText function expects these properties:

LPD3DXSPRITE pSprite	Sprite renderer object
LPCSTR pString	Text to be printed
INT count	Length of the text
LPRECT pRect	Rectangle that specifies position and boundary
DWORD format	Formatting options such as DT_WORDBREAK
D3DCOLOR color	Output color for the text

Printing with DrawText

Let's assume I've created a font object called "font," and want to print out something using the DrawText function. Here is an example:

```
RECT rect = { 10, 10, 0, 0 };
D3DCOLOR white = D3DCOLOR_XRGB(255,255,255);
string text = "This is a text message that will be printed.";
```

```
font->DrawText(
    spriteobj,
    text.c_str(),
    text.length(),
    &rect,
    DT_LEFT,
    white
);
```

I think we can wrap this code into a reusable function. Here's what I've come up with. The last parameter, which specifies the color, defaults to white if you want to just ignore it.

```
void Print(
    LPD3DXFONT font,
    int x,
    int y,
    string text,
    D3DCOLOR color = D3DCOLOR_XRGB(255,255,255))
{
    //figure out the text boundary
    RECT rect = { x, y, 0, 0 };
    font->DrawText(NULL,text.c_str(),text.length(),&rect,DT_CALCRECT,color);

    //print the text
    font->DrawText(spriteobj,text.c_str(),text.length(),&rect,DT_LEFT,
        color);
}
```

Wrapping Text

There's an option you can take advantage of if you want to cause the text to be formatted inside a rectangular region that defines a boundary for the text. When you set this up, the text will automatically wrap at each word (using the space character as a separator). This can be very helpful when working with your own custom GUI controls, for instance. Normally, the rectangle is defined with a width and height of zero, so no boundary is used at all. But if you specify a width and height, and use the DT_CALCRECT option, then DrawText will do automatic word wrapping! Here is an example:

```
RECT rect = { 60, 250, 350, 700 };
D3DCOLOR white = D3DCOLOR_XRGB(255,255,255);
```

```
string text = "This is a long string that will be wrapped.";
font->DrawText(
    spriteobj,
    text.c_str(),
    text.length(),
    &rect,
    DT_WORDBREAK,
    white);
```

Note that the RECT is defined with a width of 290 pixels (left = 60, right = 250), while the bottom property is set to an especially high value (and it is not as important as the width here). While DrawText is doing its thing, when it reaches the right edge (350, in this example) it will locate the nearest space character and wrap the word around to the next line. DrawText does this by printing whole words and calculating whether each word will fit before beginning to draw each character. It can be incredibly helpful!

Testing Font Output

Now we'll see an example program that demonstrates ID3DXFont::DrawText with most of the options. First, let's add the font functions to our helper files so they can be used in future projects. Open the MyDirectX.h header file and add the function prototypes:

```
//font functions
LPD3DXFONT MakeFont(
    string name,
    int size
);
void FontPrint(
    LPD3DXFONT font,
    int x,
    int y,
    string text,
    D3DCOLOR color = D3DCOLOR_XRGB(255,255,255)
);
```

Next, open the MyDirectX.cpp file and add the following functions:

```
LPD3DXFONT MakeFont(string name, int size)
{
    LPD3DXFONT font = NULL;
```

```
        D3DXFONT_DESC desc = {
            size,                   //height
            0,                      //width
            0,                      //weight
            0,                      //miplevels
            false,                  //italic
            DEFAULT_CHARSET,        //charset
            OUT_TT_PRECIS,          //output precision
            CLIP_DEFAULT_PRECIS,    //quality
            DEFAULT_PITCH,          //pitch and family
            ""                      //font name
        };
        strcpy(desc.FaceName, name.c_str());
        D3DXCreateFontIndirect(d3ddev, &desc, &font);
        return font;
}


void FontPrint(LPD3DXFONT font, int x, int y, string text, D3DCOLOR color)
{
    //figure out the text boundary
    RECT rect = { x, y, 0, 0 };
    font->DrawText( NULL, text.c_str(), text.length(), &rect, DT_CALCRECT, color);

    //print the text
    font->DrawText(spriteobj, text.c_str(), text.length(), &rect, DT_LEFT,
    color);
}
```

Now that the font support functions are in the game library files, we can test font output with an example program. The Font Demo program produces the output shown in Figure 9.1.

```
#include "MyDirectX.h"
using namespace std;

const string APPTITLE = "Font Demo";
const int SCREENW = 1024;
const int SCREENH = 768;

//declare some font objects
LPD3DXFONT fontArial24 = NULL;
LPD3DXFONT fontGaramond36 = NULL;
LPD3DXFONT fontTimesNewRoman40 = NULL;
```

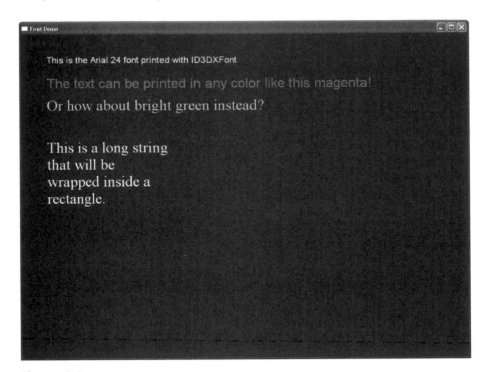

Figure 9.1
The Font Demo program demonstrates how to print text using ID3DXFont.

```
bool Game_Init(HWND window)
{
    Direct3D_Init(window, SCREENW, SCREENH, false);
    DirectInput_Init(window);

    //create some fonts
    fontArial24 = MakeFont("Arial",24);
    fontGaramond36 = MakeFont("Garamond",36);
    fontTimesNewRoman40 = MakeFont("Times New Roman", 40);

    return true;
}

void Game_Run(HWND window)
{
    //make sure the Direct3D device is valid
    if (!d3ddev) return;

    //update input devices
    DirectInput_Update();

    d3ddev->Clear(0, NULL, D3DCLEAR_TARGET | D3DCLEAR_ZBUFFER,
        D3DCOLOR_XRGB(0,0,100), 1.0f, 0);
```

```
        //start rendering
        if (d3ddev->BeginScene())
        {
            spriteobj->Begin(D3DXSPRITE_ALPHABLEND);

            //demonstrate font output
            FontPrint(fontArial24, 60, 50,
                "This is the Arial 24 font printed with ID3DXFont");

            FontPrint(fontGaramond36, 60, 100,
                "The text can be printed in any color like this magenta!",
                D3DCOLOR_XRGB(255,0,255));

            FontPrint(fontTimesNewRoman40, 60, 150,
                "Or how about bright green instead?",
                D3DCOLOR_XRGB(0,255,0));

            //demonstrate text wrapping inside a rectangular region
            RECT rect = { 60, 250, 350, 700 };
            D3DCOLOR white = D3DCOLOR_XRGB(255,255,255);
            string text = "This is a long string that will be ";
            text += "wrapped inside a rectangle.";
            fontTimesNewRoman40->DrawText( spriteobj, text.c_str(),
                text.length(), &rect, DT_WORDBREAK, white);

            spriteobj->End();
            d3ddev->EndScene();
            d3ddev->Present(NULL, NULL, NULL, NULL);
        }

    if (KEY_DOWN(VK_ESCAPE)) gameover = true;
    if (controllers[0].wButtons & XINPUT_GAMEPAD_BACK)
        gameover = true;
}

void Game_End()
{
    if (fontArial24) fontArial24->Release();
    if (fontGaramond36) fontGaramond36->Release();
    if (fontTimesNewRoman40) fontTimesNewRoman40->Release();

    DirectInput_Shutdown();
    Direct3D_Shutdown();
}
```

What You Have Learned

In this chapter, you have learned to use `ID3DXFont` to print text out to the Direct3D-based screen with support for TrueType fonts. Here are the key points:

- You learned how to create a new font.

- You learned how to print text using a font.

- You learned how to wrap text inside a rectangle.

Review Questions

Here are some review questions to see how much you have retained from this chapter.

1. What is the name of the font object used to print text on the screen?

2. What is the name of the long pointer version of the font object?

3. What is the name of the function used to print text on the screen?

4. Which function is used to create a new font object based on certain font properties?

5. What is the name of the constant used to specify that text will be wrapped inside a supplied rectangular region on the screen?

6. If the sprite object is not supplied to the font renderer, will it create its own sprite object for 2D output when rendering the font to the screen?

7. Which `std::string` function converts the string data into a C-style character array for use by functions such as `strcpy`?

8. Which `std::string` function returns the length of the string (i.e., the number of characters in the string)?

9. What Direct3D data type would you use to define a color for text output?

10. Which function returns a Direct3D color with an alpha channel component?

On Your Own

The following exercises will help to challenge your grasp of the information presented in this chapter.

Exercise 1. Modify the Font Test project so that it prints out your own name rather than the sample text provided in the demo.

Exercise 2. Modify the Font Test project so that it moves a text message around on the screen like a moving sprite.

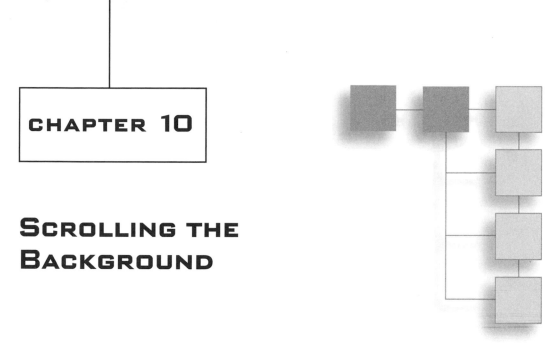

CHAPTER 10

SCROLLING THE BACKGROUND

Most action and arcade games use the technique of tile-based scrolling to achieve the moving background you see in such games. Although this technique is now decades old, it is still employed for rendering backgrounds, and this style of 2D game is still used frequently today. Back in the old days, when computer memory was very limited, tile-based scrolling was used because it is very efficient. We take for granted multiple gigabytes of memory today, but that much memory was unbelievable in the earlier days of video games, even in a hard drive, let alone main memory (RAM). The concept of a *virtual screen buffer*, which you will learn about in this chapter, was used with very limited video cards at the time (with 256 to 1024 KB of video memory). Back then, you would be very lucky to have two 320 × 240 screens (or buffers), let alone enough memory for a large scrolling world. This chapter focuses on two different ways to create a scrolling background: bitmap-based and tile-based.

Here is a breakdown of the major topics in this chapter:

- Introduction to scrolling.

- Creating tile-based backgrounds.

- Using a single large scroll buffer.

- Using dynamically drawn tiles.

Scrolling

What is scrolling? In today's gaming world, where 3D is the focus of everyone's attention, it's not surprising to find gamers and programmers who have never heard of scrolling. What a shame! The heritage of modern games is a long and fascinating one that is still relevant today, even if it is not understood or appreciated. The console industry puts great effort and value into scrolling, particularly on handheld systems, such as the Game Boy Advance. Given the extraordinary sales market for the GBA, would you be surprised to learn that more 2D games may be sold in a given day than 3D games. Figure 10.1 illustrates the concept of scrolling.

GAME WORLD / MEMORY BITMAP

1600 x 1200

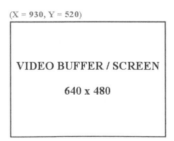

(X = 930, Y = 520)

VIDEO BUFFER / SCREEN

640 x 480

Figure 10.1
The scroll window shows a small part of a larger game world.

Advice

Scrolling is the process of displaying a small portion of a large virtual game world in a window on the screen, and moving the view of that window to reflect the changing position within the game world.

You could display one huge bitmap image in the virtual game world, representing the current level of the game, and then copy (blit) a portion of that virtual world onto the screen. This is the simplest form of scrolling. Another method uses tiles to create the game world, which I'll cover shortly. First, you'll write a short program to demonstrate how to use bitmap scrolling.

You have seen what a simple scroller looks like, even though it relied on keyboard input to scroll. A high-speed scrolling arcade game would automatically scroll horizontally or vertically, displaying a ground-, air-, or space-based terrain below the player (usually represented by an airplane or a spaceship). The point of these games is to keep the action moving so fast that the player doesn't have a chance to rest from one wave of enemies to the next. Two upcoming chapters have been dedicated to these very subjects! For the time being, I want to keep things simple to cover the basics of scrolling before you delve into these advanced chapters.

Backgrounds and Scenery

A background is comprised of imagery or terrain in one form or another, upon which the sprites are drawn. The background might be nothing more than a pretty picture behind the action in a game, or it might take an active part, as in a scroller. When you are talking about scrollers, they need not be relegated only to the high-speed arcade games. Role-playing games are usually scrollers too, as are most sports games.

You should design the background around the goals of your game, not the other way around. You should not come up with some cool background and then try to build the game around it. (However, I admit that this is often how games are started.) You never want to rely on a single cool technology as the basis for an entire game, or the game will be forever remembered as a trendy game that tried to cash in on the latest fad. Instead of following and imitating, set your own precedents and make your own standards!

What am I talking about, you might ask? You might have the impression that anything and everything that could possibly have been done with a scrolling game has already been done ten times over. Not true. Not true! Remember when

Doom first came out? Everyone had been imitating *Wolfenstein 3D* when Carmack and Romero bumped up the notch a few hundred points and raised everyone's expectations so high that shock waves reverberated through the game industry—console and PC alike.

Do you really think it has all been done before and there is no more room for innovation, that the game industry is saturated and it's impossible to make a successful "indie" game? That didn't stop Bungie from going for broke on their first game project. *Halo* has made its mark in gaming history by upping everyone's expectations for superior physics and intelligent opponents. Now, a few years hence, what kinds of games are coming out? What is the biggest industry buzzword? Physics. Design a game today without it, and suddenly your game is so 1990s in the gaming press. It's all about physics and AI now, and that started with *Halo*. Rather, it was perfected with *Halo*—I can't personally recall a game with that level of interaction before *Halo* came along. There is absolutely no reason why you can't invent the next innovation or revolution in gaming, even in a 2D game.

Creating Backgrounds from Tiles

The real power of a scrolling background comes from a technique called tiling. Tiling is a process in which there really is no background, just an array of tiles that make up the background as it is displayed. In other words, it is a virtual virtual background and it takes up very little memory compared to a full bit-mapped background. Take a look at Figure 10.2 for an example.

Figure 10.2
A bitmap image constructed of tiles.

Can you count the number of tiles used to construct the background in Figure 10.2? Eighteen tiles make up this image, actually. Imagine that—an entire game screen built using a handful of tiles, and the result is pretty good! Obviously, a real game would have more than just grass, roads, rivers, and bridges; a real game would have sprites moving on top of the background. How about an example? I thought you'd like that idea.

Tile-Based Scrolling

The Tile_Static_Scroll program, which you will write soon, uses tiles to fill the large background bitmap when the program starts. It loads up the tiles from a bitmap (containing the tiles arranged in rows and columns), and then uses the map data to fill in the virtual scroll surface represented by a large bitmap in memory. Take a look at Figure 10.3.

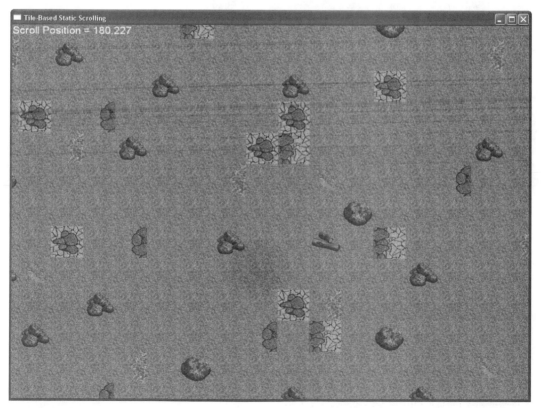

Figure 10.3
The Tile_Static_Scroll program demonstrates how to perform tile-based scrolling.

This program creates the tiles that you see in this figure by drawing the tiles onto a large bitmap image created in memory (which is actually a Direct3D surface— and we're using a surface rather than a texture because no transparency is needed). The actual bitmap containing the tiles is shown in Figure 10.4. These tiles were created by Ari Feldman (http://www.flyingyogi.com) as part of his free SpriteLib.

I have prepared a legend of the tiles and the value for each in Figure 10.5. You can use the legend while building your own maps.

Figure 10.4
The source file containing the tiles used in the Tile_Static_Scroll program.

Figure 10.5
A legend of the tile map used in the Tile_Static_Scroll program.

Tile-Based Static Scrolling Project

Now, let's write a test program to demonstrate, because theory only gets one so far when trying to build an actual game. I don't know about you, but I learn better by doing rather than by just reading. I'm assuming that you're going to follow the same steps from the previous chapter for creating a new project, and adding the necessary library files.

```cpp
/*
    Beginning Game Programming, Third Edition
    MyGame.cpp
*/

#include "MyDirectX.h"
#include <sstream>
using namespace std;

const string APPTITLE = "Tile-Based Static Scrolling";
const int SCREENW = 1024;
const int SCREENH = 768;

LPD3DXFONT font;

//settings for the scroller
const int TILEWIDTH = 64;
const int TILEHEIGHT = 64;
const int MAPWIDTH = 25;
const int MAPHEIGHT = 18;

//scrolling window size
const int WINDOWWIDTH = (SCREENW / TILEWIDTH) * TILEWIDTH;
const int WINDOWHEIGHT = (SCREENH / TILEHEIGHT) * TILEHEIGHT;

//entire game world dimensions
const int GAMEWORLDWIDTH = TILEWIDTH * MAPWIDTH;
const int GAMEWORLDHEIGHT = TILEHEIGHT * MAPHEIGHT;

int ScrollX, ScrollY;
int SpeedX, SpeedY;
long start;
LPDIRECT3DSURFACE9 gameworld = NULL;
```

```
int MAPDATA[MAPWIDTH*MAPHEIGHT] = {
80,81,81,81,81,81,81,81,81,81,81,81,81,81,81,81,81,81,81,81,
81,81,81,82,90,3,3,3,3,3,3,3,3,3,3,3,3,3,3,3,92,3,3,3,3,3,92,3,
92,90,3,13,83,96,3,3,23,3,92,3,13,92,3,3,3,3,3,3,11,3,13,3,3,92,
90,3,3,3,3,3,3,3,10,3,3,3,3,3,23,3,3,3,3,3,3,3,3,13,3,92,90,3,96,
3,13,3,3,3,3,3,3,3,3,3,3,3,3,96,3,23,3,96,3,3,92,90,3,3,3,3,3,3,
13,3,3,3,13,3,3,11,3,3,3,3,3,3,13,3,92,90,3,83,11,3,92,3,3,3,
3,3,11,3,3,3,3,3,3,3,83,3,3,3,92,92,90,3,3,3,96,3,13,3,3,3,11,
10,3,3,3,3,3,13,3,3,13,3,3,3,92,90,3,23,3,3,3,3,3,3,96,3,3,83,
3,3,3,92,3,3,3,3,3,13,3,92,90,3,3,3,3,3,3,3,3,3,3,3,3,3,23,3,3,3,
3,3,3,3,3,3,3,92,90,3,3,3,11,3,92,3,3,13,3,3,131,3,10,3,3,3,96,
3,92,3,96,3,92,90,3,13,83,3,3,3,3,3,3,3,3,3,3,3,13,3,3,3,3,3,3,
3,3,92,90,3,3,3,3,13,3,3,3,3,3,3,11,96,3,3,3,3,3,3,13,3,13,3,11,
92,90,92,3,13,3,3,3,3,3,3,92,3,10,3,23,3,3,3,3,3,3,3,3,3,92,90,
3,3,3,3,3,96,3,23,3,3,3,3,3,3,3,3,83,3,3,13,3,96,3,92,90,3,3,3,
3,92,3,3,3,3,3,13,3,3,3,13,3,3,3,11,3,3,3,3,92,90,3,13,3,3,3,3,
3,3,3,96,3,3,3,3,3,3,3,3,3,92,3,3,92,100,101,101,101,101,101,
101,101,101,101,101,101,101,101,101,101,101,101,101,101,101,101,
101,101,102
};

void DrawTile(
    LPDIRECT3DSURFACE9 source,    // source surface image
    int tilenum,                  // tile #
    int width,                    // tile width
    int height,                   // tile height
    int columns,                  // columns of tiles
    LPDIRECT3DSURFACE9 dest,      // destination surface
    int destx,                    // destination x
    int desty)                    // destination y
{
    //create a RECT to describe the source image
    RECT r1;
    r1.left = (tilenum % columns) * width;
    r1.top = (tilenum / columns) * height;
    r1.right = r1.left + width;
    r1.bottom = r1.top + height;

    //set destination rect
    RECT r2 = {destx,desty,destx+width,desty+height};

    //draw the tile
    d3ddev->StretchRect(source, &r1, dest, &r2, D3DTEXF_NONE);
}
```

```
void BuildGameWorld()
{
    HRESULT result;
    int x, y;
    LPDIRECT3DSURFACE9 tiles;

    //load the bitmap image containing all the tiles
    tiles = LoadSurface("groundtiles.bmp");

    //create the scrolling game world bitmap
    result = d3ddev->CreateOffscreenPlainSurface(
        GAMEWORLDWIDTH,              //width of the surface
        GAMEWORLDHEIGHT,             //height of the surface
        D3DFMT_X8R8G8B8,
        D3DPOOL_DEFAULT,
        &gameworld,                  //pointer to the surface
        NULL);

    if (result != D3D_OK)
    {
        MessageBox(NULL,"Error creating working surface!","Error",0);
        return;
    }

    //fill the gameworld bitmap with tiles
    for (y=0; y < MAPHEIGHT; y++)
        for (x=0; x < MAPWIDTH; x++)
            DrawTile(tiles, MAPDATA[y * MAPWIDTH + x], 64, 64, 16,
            gameworld, x * 64, y * 64);

    //now the tiles bitmap is no longer needed
    tiles->Release();
}

bool Game_Init(HWND window)
{
    Direct3D_Init(window, SCREENW, SCREENH, false);
    DirectInput_Init(window);

    //create pointer to the back buffer
    d3ddev->GetBackBuffer(0, 0, D3DBACKBUFFER_TYPE_MONO, &backbuffer);
```

```cpp
    //create a font
    font = MakeFont("Arial", 24);

    BuildGameWorld();

    start = GetTickCount();

    return true;
}

void Game_End()
{
    if (gameworld) gameworld->Release();
    DirectInput_Shutdown();
    Direct3D_Shutdown();
}

void ScrollScreen()
{
    //update horizontal scrolling position and speed
    ScrollX += SpeedX;
    if (ScrollX < 0)
      {
        ScrollX = 0;
        SpeedX = 0;
      }
    else if (ScrollX > GAMEWORLDWIDTH - SCREENW)
    {
        ScrollX = GAMEWORLDWIDTH - SCREENW;
        SpeedX = 0;
    }

    //update vertical scrolling position and speed
    ScrollY += SpeedY;
    if (ScrollY < 0)
    {
        ScrollY = 0;
        SpeedY = 0;
    }
    else if (ScrollY > GAMEWORLDHEIGHT - SCREENH)
    {
        ScrollY = GAMEWORLDHEIGHT - SCREENH;
        SpeedY = 0;
    }
```

```
    //set dimensions of the source image
    RECT r1 = {ScrollX, ScrollY, ScrollX+SCREENW-1, ScrollY+SCREENH-1};

    //set the destination rect
    RECT r2 = {0, 0, SCREENW-1, SCREENH-1};

    //draw the current game world view
    d3ddev->StretchRect(gameworld, &r1, backbuffer, &r2,
        D3DTEXF_NONE);

}

void Game_Run(HWND window)
{
    if (!d3ddev) return;
    DirectInput_Update();
    d3ddev->Clear(0, NULL, D3DCLEAR_TARGET | D3DCLEAR_ZBUFFER,
        D3DCOLOR_XRGB(0,0,100), 1.0f, 0);

    //scroll based on key or controller input
    if (Key_Down(DIK_DOWN) || controllers[0].sThumbLY < -2000)
        ScrollY += 1;

    if (Key_Down(DIK_UP) || controllers[0].sThumbLY > 2000)
        ScrollY -= 1;

    if (Key_Down(DIK_LEFT) || controllers[0].sThumbLX < -2000)
        ScrollX -= 1;

    if (Key_Down(DIK_RIGHT) || controllers[0].sThumbLX > 2000)
        ScrollX += 1;

    //keep the game running at a steady frame rate
    if (GetTickCount() - start >= 30)
    {
        //reset timing
        start = GetTickCount();

        //start rendering
        if (d3ddev->BeginScene())
        {
            //update the scrolling view
            ScrollScreen();
```

```
            spriteobj->Begin(D3DXSPRITE_ALPHABLEND);

            std::ostringstream oss;
            oss << "Scroll Position = " << ScrollX << "," << ScrollY;
            FontPrint(font, 0, 0, oss.str());

            spriteobj->End();

            //stop rendering
            d3ddev->EndScene();
            d3ddev->Present(NULL, NULL, NULL, NULL);
        }
    }

    //to exit
    if (KEY_DOWN(VK_ESCAPE) ||
        controllers[0].wButtons & XINPUT_GAMEPAD_BACK)
        gameover = true;

}
```

Dynamically Rendered Tiles

Displaying tiles just to make a proof-of-concept is one thing, but it is not very useful. True, you have some code to create a virtual background, load tiles onto it, and then scroll the game world. In the past, I have generated a realistic-looking game map with source code, using an algorithm that matched terrain curves and straights (such as the road, bridge, and river) so that I created an awesome map from scratch, all by myself. Building an algorithmic landscape is one thing, but constructing it at run time is not a great solution—even if your map-generating routine is very good.

For instance, many games, such as *Warcraft III*, *Age of Mythology*, and *Civilization IV* can generate the game world on the fly. Obviously, the programmers spent a lot of time perfecting the world-generating routines. If your game would benefit by featuring a randomly generated game world, then your work is cut out for you, but the results will be worth it. This is simply one of those design considerations that you must make, given that you have time to develop it.

The Tile Map

Assuming you don't have the means to generate a random map (or simply do not want to go that route), you can simply create one within an array, as we did in the

previous project. But where did this map data actually come from? And, furthermore, where do you start? First of all, you should realize that the tiles are
numbered and should be referenced this way in the map array. Each number in
the tile map represents a tile image in a bitmap file. Here is what the array looks
like, as defined in the Tile_Dynamic_Scroll program (which we'll cover here in a
minute).

```
int MAPDATA[MAPWIDTH*MAPHEIGHT] = {
1,2,3,4,5,6,7,8,9,10,11,12,13,14,15,16,
17,18,19,20,21,22,23,24,25,26,27,28,29,30,31,32,
33,34,35,36,37,38,39,40,41,42,43,44,45,46,47,48,
49,50,51,52,53,54,55,56,57,58,59,60,61,62,63,64,
65,66,67,68,69,70,71,72,73,74,75,76,77,78,79,80,
81,82,83,84,85,86,87,88,89,90,91,92,93,94,95,96,
97,98,99,100,101,102,103,104,105,106,107,108,109,110,111,112,
113,114,115,116,117,118,119,120,121,122,123,124,125,126,127,128,
129,130,131,132,133,134,135,136,137,138,139,140,141,142,143,144,
145,146,147,148,149,150,151,152,153,154,155,156,157,158,159,160,
161,162,163,164,165,166,167,168,169,170,171,172,173,174,175,176,
177,178,179,180,181,182,183,184,185,186,187,188,189,190,191,192,
1,2,3,4,5,6,7,8,9,10,11,12,13,14,15,16,
17,18,19,20,21,22,23,24,25,26,27,28,29,30,31,32,
33,34,35,36,37,38,39,40,41,42,43,44,45,46,47,48,
49,50,51,52,53,54,55,56,57,58,59,60,61,62,63,64,
65,66,67,68,69,70,71,72,73,74,75,76,77,78,79,80,
81,82,83,84,85,86,87,88,89,90,91,92,93,94,95,96,
97,98,99,100,101,102,103,104,105,106,107,108,109,110,111,112,
113,114,115,116,117,118,119,120,121,122,123,124,125,126,127,128,
129,130,131,132,133,134,135,136,137,138,139,140,141,142,143,144,
145,146,147,148,149,150,151,152,153,154,155,156,157,158,159,160,
161,162,163,164,165,166,167,168,169,170,171,172,173,174,175,176,
177,178,179,180,181,182,183,184,185,186,187,188,189,190,191,192
};
```

The trick here is that this is really only a single-dimensional array, but the listing
makes it obvious how the map will look because there are 16 numbers in each
row—the same number of tiles in each row of the bitmap file, which is shown in
Figure 10.6. I did this intentionally so you can use this as a template for creating
your own maps. And you can create more than one map if you want. Simply
change the name of each map and reference the map you want to draw so that
your new map will show up. You are not limited in adding more tiles to each row.
One interesting thing you can try is making MAPDATA a two-dimensional array

Figure 10.6
Starfield image used to create a tile map for the Tile_Dynamic_Scroll program (courtesy of Space Telescope Science Institute, www.scsti.edu).

containing many maps, and then changing the map at run time! You could use this simple scrolling code as the basis for any of a hundred different games if you have the creative gumption to do so.

Creating a Tile Map Using Mappy

I'm going to go through the steps with you for creating a very simple tile map using the awesome (and free) tile-editing program, Mappy. This program is available at http://www.tilemap.co.uk, and is provided on the CD-ROM in \software\Mappy. It is my favorite level editing program for tile-based games, and is used by many professional game developers as well (especially those working on handheld and strategy games). I wish we had time for a full tutorial on using Mappy, because it really is jam packed with an amazing assortment of features (tucked away in its various submenus). We'll have to rely on simplistic coverage of Mappy here, just enough to read in a large photograph and convert it to a tile map.

Note

If you enjoy the subject of tile-based game level editing and development, I recommend *Game Programming All in One, Third Edition*, which contains several chapters on scrolling backgrounds, including a comprehensive tutorial chapter on using Mappy.

Let's start by firing up Mappy. When it starts running, open the File menu and select New Map. This will bring up the New Map dialog box shown in Figure 10.7. As shown in this figure, type in **64 × 64** for the tile size and **16 × 24** for the map size (which is a count of the number of tiles in the tile map). The new map will be created, but will be void of any tiles as of yet, as you can see in Figure 10.8.

Figure 10.7
Creating a new map using Mappy.

Figure 10.8
The new map that has been created by Mappy, awaiting your custom tiles.

Importing an Existing Bitmap File

Next, we're going to import the space photograph taken by Hubble into Mappy and convert it to a tile map. As shown in Figure 10.9, open the MapTools menu, and select Useful Functions, followed by the option "Create map from big picture." Browse for the space1.bmp file, located in \sources\chapter10\Tile Dynamic Scrolling Demo\map on the CD-ROM. When you select this file, Mappy will import it into the palette of tiles, as shown in Figure 10.10.

As you can see from this figure, there are a *lot* of tiles that made up the image! If you are curious about the number of tiles in this palette, let's take a look! Open up the MapTools menu and select Map Properties. This brings up the Map Properties dialog box, shown in Figure 10.11. Take a look at the text values on the left side of the dialog: Map Array, Block Str, Graphics, and so on. The Map Array text tells you the size of the map in tiles (16 × 24, just as we specified). Now take a look at the Graphics information. Here we see that there are 193 tiles in this tile map, and they are all 64 × 64 pixels in size, and have a color depth of 24 bits.

Figure 10.9
Preparing to import a large bitmap file as the source for our tiles.

Figure 10.10
The palette of tiles has been imported from the large space photograph.

Figure 10.11
The Map Properties dialog box shows the properties of the tile map.

When you import a large bitmap into Mappy, it grabs tiles starting at the upper-left corner of the bitmap, and goes through the image in a grid, from left to right and from top to bottom, until the entire image has been encoded into tiles. It then constructs the tile map using those tile numbers and inserts the tile map into the editor, so that it resembles the original bitmap image. Note that you must create the tile map in the first place so that it is at least as large as the bitmap image (in this case, 1024 × 768) or larger.

Exporting the Tile Map

First, let's just save the tile map in the native Mappy file format, so it can be edited later. Open the File menu and select Save. I have named this tile map "spacemap". The default extension for a Mappy file is .fmp.

Now, you can go ahead and edit the tile map if you want, but I'm going to just go ahead and export the tile map now and show you how to do that. First, open up the File menu and select the Export option. This brings up the Export dialog, shown in Figure 10.12. Select the options on this dialog as follows:

- Map array as comma values only (?.CSV)

- Graphics Blocks as picture (?.BMP)

- 16 Blocks a row

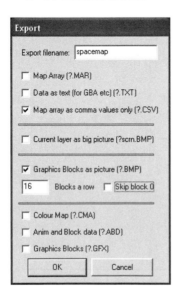

Figure 10.12
The Export dialog box is used to export a tile map to a text file.

These options will cause Mappy to export a new bitmap file comprised of the tiles in the order that they appear in the palette—which means this bitmap image will then be used to draw the tiles in your game. Note that Mappy automatically inserts a blank tile first in the palette. You want to keep that blank tile in place, because the tile map values begin with that first blank tile (index number zero). I have named the export file spacemap.

Click the Okay button and Mappy will save two new files for your use:

- spacemap.csv

- spacemap.bmp

The .csv file is a comma-separated values file, which is actually just stored in a text format (which can be opened in Notepad or any text editor). If you have Microsoft Excel installed, it will try to open the .csv file if you double-click it, because Excel uses that format for text-based spreadsheets as well. You can rename it to spacemap.txt to make it easier to open the file if you wish. Once open, copy the contents out of this file and paste it into your source code over any pre-existing tile map (defined by the array called MAPDATA in the examples in this chapter).

The Tile_Dynamic_Scroll Project

Now let's create a new project. You may just re-use one of the projects from the previous chapter if you want, since it will already be configured with the proper library files and so forth. Or, if you already created the Tile_Static_Scroll program, feel free to reuse that project.

If you are creating a new project file, call it Tile_Dynamic_Scroll, since that is the name of this program. This program is similar to the static demo, but it draws the tiles directly to the screen without the need for a large bitmap in memory. This program will also use a smaller virtual background to cut down on the size of the map array. Why? Not to save memory, but to make the program more manageable. Because the virtual background was 1600×1200 in the previous program, it would require 50 columns of tiles across and 37 rows of tiles down to fill it! That is no problem at all for a map editor program, but it's too much data to type in manually.

To make it more manageable, the new virtual background will be 1024 pixels across, which also happens to be the width of the screen in this program. That was intentional, because the dynamic scroll program will simulate a vertically scrolling arcade shooter game! The point is to demonstrate how it will work, not to build a game engine, so don't worry about precision at this point. If you want to type in the values to create a bigger map, by all means, go for it! That would be a great learning experience, as a matter of fact. For your purposes here (and with my primary goal of being able to print an entire row of numbers in a single source code line in the book), I'll stick to 16 tiles across and 24 tiles down.

In the example tile map, I have doubled its size by copying the entire tile map of values and pasting them at the end, which effectively doubles the map size; otherwise, you would not be able to scroll it. We're just going to scroll the screen of tiles over and over again in such a game, but in this example, the scrolling will be controlled by the mouse. You can work with a map that is deeper than it is wide, so that will allow you to test scrolling up and down fairly well. Figure 10.13 shows the output from the dynamic scroll demo program.

Figure 10.13
The dynamic scrolling demo scrolls a map that was defined in the map array.

Tile_Dynamic_Scroll Source Code

Now let's type in the source code for the dynamic scrolling demo project. This code goes in the MyGame.cpp file.

```cpp
/*
    Beginning Game Programming, Third Edition
  MyGame.cpp
*/

#include "MyDirectX.h"
#include <sstream>
using namespace std;

const string APPTITLE = "Tile-Based Dynamic Scrolling";
const int SCREENW = 1024;
const int SCREENH = 768;

LPD3DXFONT font;

//settings for the scroller
const int TILEWIDTH = 64;
const int TILEHEIGHT = 64;
const int MAPWIDTH = 16;
const int MAPHEIGHT = 24;

//scrolling window size
const int WINDOWWIDTH = (SCREENW / TILEWIDTH) * TILEWIDTH;
const int WINDOWHEIGHT = (SCREENH / TILEHEIGHT) * TILEHEIGHT;

int ScrollX, ScrollY;
int SpeedX, SpeedY;
long start;
LPDIRECT3DSURFACE9 scrollbuffer=NULL;
LPDIRECT3DSURFACE9 tiles=NULL;

int MAPDATA[MAPWIDTH*MAPHEIGHT] = {
1,2,3,4,5,6,7,8,9,10,11,12,13,14,15,16,17,18,19,20,21,22,23,24,25,
26,27,28,29,30,31,32,33,34,35,36,37,38,39,40,41,42,43,44,45,46,47,
48,49,50,51,52,53,54,55,56,57,58,59,60,61,62,63,64,65,66,67,68,69,
70,71,72,73,74,75,76,77,78,79,80,81,82,83,84,85,86,87,88,89,90,91,
92,93,94,95,96,97,98,99,100,101,102,103,104,105,106,107,108,109,
110,111,112,113,114,115,116,117,118,119,120,121,122,123,124,125,
```

```
126,127,128,129,130,131,132,133,134,135,136,137,138,139,140,141,
142,143,144,145,146,147,148,149,150,151,152,153,154,155,156,157,
158,159,160,161,162,163,164,165,166,167,168,169,170,171,172,173,
174,175,176,177,178,179,180,181,182,183,184,185,186,187,188,189,
190,191,192,1,2,3,4,5,6,7,8,9,10,11,12,13,14,15,16,17,18,19,20,
21,22,23,24,25,26,27,28,29,30,31,32,33,34,35,36,37,38,39,40,41,
42,43,44,45,46,47,48,49,50,51,52,53,54,55,56,57,58,59,60,61,62,
63,64,65,66,67,68,69,70,71,72,73,74,75,76,77,78,79,80,81,82,83,
84,85,86,87,88,89,90,91,92,93,94,95,96,97,98,99,100,101,102,103,
104,105,106,107,108,109,110,111,112,113,114,115,116,117,118,119,
120,121,122,123,124,125,126,127,128,129,130,131,132,133,134,135,
136,137,138,139,140,141,142,143,144,145,146,147,148,149,150,151,
152,153,154,155,156,157,158,159,160,161,162,163,164,165,166,167,
168,169,170,171,172,173,174,175,176,177,178,179,180,181,182,183,
184,185,186,187,188,189,190,191,192
};


bool Game_Init(HWND window)
{
    Direct3D_Init(window, SCREENW, SCREENH, false);
    DirectInput_Init(window);

    //create pointer to the back buffer
    d3ddev->GetBackBuffer(0, 0, D3DBACKBUFFER_TYPE_MONO, &backbuffer);

    //create a font
    font = MakeFont("Arial", 24);

    //load the tile images
    tiles = LoadSurface("spacemap.bmp");
    if (!tiles) return false;

    //create the scroll buffer surface in memory, slightly bigger
    //than the screen
    const int SCROLLBUFFERWIDTH = SCREENW + TILEWIDTH * 2;
    const int SCROLLBUFFERHEIGHT = SCREENH + TILEHEIGHT * 2;

    HRESULT result = d3ddev->CreateOffscreenPlainSurface(
        SCROLLBUFFERWIDTH, SCROLLBUFFERHEIGHT,
        D3DFMT_X8R8G8B8, D3DPOOL_DEFAULT,
        &scrollbuffer,
        NULL);
```

```
    if (result != S_OK) return false;

    start = GetTickCount();

    return true;
}

void Game_End()
{
    if (scrollbuffer) scrollbuffer->Release();
    if (tiles) tiles->Release();
    DirectInput_Shutdown();
    Direct3D_Shutdown();
}

//This function updates the scrolling position and speed
void UpdateScrollPosition()
{
    const int GAMEWORLDWIDTH = TILEWIDTH * MAPWIDTH;
    const int GAMEWORLDHEIGHT = TILEHEIGHT * MAPHEIGHT;

    //update horizontal scrolling position and speed
    ScrollX += SpeedX;

    if (ScrollX < 0)
    {
        ScrollX = 0;
        SpeedX = 0;
    }
    else if (ScrollX > GAMEWORLDWIDTH - WINDOWWIDTH)
    {
        ScrollX = GAMEWORLDWIDTH - WINDOWWIDTH;
        SpeedX = 0;
    }

    //update vertical scrolling position and speed
    ScrollY += SpeedY;
    if (ScrollY < 0)
    {
        ScrollY = 0;
        SpeedY = 0;
    }
    else if (ScrollY > GAMEWORLDHEIGHT - WINDOWHEIGHT)
```

```
        {
            ScrollY = GAMEWORLDHEIGHT - WINDOWHEIGHT;
            SpeedY = 0;
        }
    }


    //This function does the real work of drawing a single tile from the
    //source image onto the tile scroll buffer
    void DrawTile(
        LPDIRECT3DSURFACE9 source,  // source surface image
        int tilenum,               // tile #
        int width,                 // tile width
        int height,                // tile height
        int columns,               // columns of tiles
        LPDIRECT3DSURFACE9 dest,    // destination surface
        int destx,                 // destination x
        int desty)                 // destination y
    {

        //create a RECT to describe the source image
        RECT r1;
        r1.left = (tilenum % columns) * width;
        r1.top = (tilenum / columns) * height;
        r1.right = r1.left + width;
        r1.bottom = r1.top + height;

        //set destination rect
        RECT r2 = {destx,desty,destx+width,desty+height};

        //draw the tile
        d3ddev->StretchRect(source, &r1, dest, &r2, D3DTEXF_NONE);
    }


    //This function fills the tilebuffer with tiles representing
    //the current scroll display based on scrollx/scrolly.
    void DrawTiles()
    {
        int tilex, tiley;
        int columns, rows;
        int x, y;
        int tilenum;

        //calculate starting tile position
```

```
    tilex = ScrollX / TILEWIDTH;
    tiley = ScrollY / TILEHEIGHT;

    //calculate the number of columns and rows
    columns = WINDOWWIDTH / TILEWIDTH;
    rows = WINDOWHEIGHT / TILEHEIGHT;

    //draw tiles onto the scroll buffer surface
    for (y=0; y<=rows; y++)
    {
        for (x=0; x<=columns; x++)
        {
            //retrieve the tile number from this position
            tilenum = MAPDATA[((tiley + y) * MAPWIDTH + (tilex + x))];

            //draw the tile onto the scroll buffer
            DrawTile(tiles,tilenum,TILEWIDTH,TILEHEIGHT,16,scrollbuffer,
                x*TILEWIDTH,y*TILEHEIGHT);
        }
    }
}

//This function draws the portion of the scroll buffer onto the back
//buffer according to the current "partial tile" scroll position.
void DrawScrollWindow(bool scaled = false)
{
    //calculate the partial sub-tile lines to draw using modulus
    int partialx = ScrollX % TILEWIDTH;
    int partialy = ScrollY % TILEHEIGHT;

    //set dimensions of the source image as a rectangle
    RECT r1 = {partialx,partialy,partialx+WINDOWWIDTH-1,
        partialy+WINDOWHEIGHT-1};

    //set the destination rectangle
    RECT r2;
    if (scaled) {
        //use this line for scaled display
        RECT r = {0, 0, WINDOWWIDTH-1, WINDOWHEIGHT-1};
        r2 = r;
    }
    else {
        //use this line for non-scaled display
```

```
        RECT r = {0, 0, SCREENW-1, SCREENH-1};
        r2 = r;
    }

    //draw the "partial tile" scroll window onto the back buffer
    d3ddev->StretchRect(scrollbuffer, &r1, backbuffer, &r2,
        D3DTEXF_NONE);
}


void Game_Run(HWND window)
{
    if (!d3ddev) return;
    DirectInput_Update();
    d3ddev->Clear(0, NULL, D3DCLEAR_TARGET | D3DCLEAR_ZBUFFER,
        D3DCOLOR_XRGB(0,0,100), 1.0f, 0);

    //scroll based on key or controller input
    if (Key_Down(DIK_DOWN) || controllers[0].sThumbLY < -2000)
        ScrollY += 1;

    if (Key_Down(DIK_UP) || controllers[0].sThumbLY > 2000)
        ScrollY -= 1;

    //keep the game running at a steady frame rate
    if (GetTickCount() - start >= 30)
    {
        //reset timing
        start = GetTickCount();

        //update the scrolling view
        UpdateScrollPosition();

        //start rendering
        if (d3ddev->BeginScene())
        {
            //draw tiles onto the scroll buffer
            DrawTiles();

            //draw the scroll window onto the back buffer
            DrawScrollWindow();
```

```
            spriteobj->Begin(D3DXSPRITE_ALPHABLEND);

            std::ostringstream oss;
            oss << "Scroll Position = " << ScrollX << "," << ScrollY;
            FontPrint(font, 0, 0, oss.str());

            spriteobj->End();

            //stop rendering
            d3ddev->EndScene();
            d3ddev->Present(NULL, NULL, NULL, NULL);
        }
    }

    //to exit
    if (KEY_DOWN(VK_ESCAPE) ||
        controllers[0].wButtons & XINPUT_GAMEPAD_BACK)
        gameover = true;
}
```

This program was quite a bit to chew on all at once, and we didn't explain every detail very carefully—because we have to move on to 3D and can't spare any more time on 2D graphics at this point! But all of this code is reusable and you can build a scrolling arcade game with it very easily. Just get your scroller moving on its own (without requiring user input), and then add some sprites over the top, and presto—you have a scrolling arcade game!

Bitmap-Based Scrolling

There is another way to perform background scrolling using a Direct3D surface object—with full bitmap scrolling. It requires some very complex programming to produce the algorithm that will wrap a single bitmap onto a scroll window without using tiles (like we used in the previous two example programs). Not only does the code become complex, but the rendering of a bitmap-based scroller using wrapping of the image is rather slow as well.

Theory of Bitmap-Based Scrolling

To perform bitmap-based scrolling as efficiently as possible, I recommend keeping the source image the same size as the screen. This might make the scroller

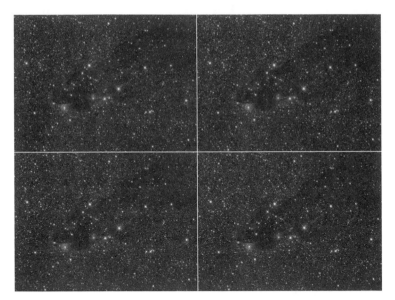

Figure 10.14
The scroll buffer is a surface that is four times the size of the source bitmap.

less versatile than one that supports any resolution, but you can always go that route if you really need the versatility (at the expense of a bit of performance—since you will need to scale the resulting scroll buffer to the screen).

So, what we'll do is make sure our source bitmap is the same size as the screen, just for starters. Then, what we must do is create a larger scroll buffer that is four times (4 ×) as large as the source image (i.e., the screen size). We can do this by creating a large Direct3D surface in memory and then pasting the source image onto the four corners of the scroll buffer. This takes up a lot of memory, but it allows us to scroll in *any direction*! Figure 10.14 shows what the scroll buffer looks like after the source image has been pasted onto it four times (the white lines separating the four images is only illustrative; the actual scroll buffer has no such divisions).

The key to performing this kind of scrolling involves these steps:

1. Load the source bitmap used for the scroller.

2. Create the scroll buffer at four times the size of the source bitmap.

3. Copy the source bitmap onto the four corners of the scroll buffer.

4. Render the portion of the scroll buffer that corresponds to the scroll position.

Bitmap Scrolling Demo

The Bitmap_Scrolling demo, shown in Figure 10.15, demonstrates bitmap-based scrolling. This program is interesting in that, unlike the previous two projects, you can scroll in any direction—not just horizontally and vertically, but also at any diagonal angle as well.

```
/*
    Beginning Game Programming, Third Edition
    MyGame.cpp
*/

#include "MyDirectX.h"
#include <sstream>
using namespace std;
```

Figure 10.15
The Bitmap_Scrolling demo (space image courtesy of Space Telescope Science Institute, www.scsti.edu).

```cpp
const string APPTITLE = "Bitmap Scrolling Demo";
const int SCREENW = 1024;
const int SCREENH = 768;

const int BUFFERW = SCREENW * 2;
const int BUFFERH = SCREENH * 2;

LPDIRECT3DSURFACE9 background = NULL;

LPD3DXFONT font;

double scrollx=0, scrolly=0;


bool Game_Init(HWND window)
{
    Direct3D_Init(window, SCREENW, SCREENH, false);
    DirectInput_Init(window);

    //create a font
    font = MakeFont("Arial", 24);

    //load background
    LPDIRECT3DSURFACE9 image = NULL;
    image = LoadSurface("space2.bmp");
    if (!image) return false;

    //create background
    HRESULT result =
    d3ddev->CreateOffscreenPlainSurface(
        BUFFERW,
        BUFFERH,
        D3DFMT_X8R8G8B8,
        D3DPOOL_DEFAULT,
        &background,
        NULL);
    if (result != D3D_OK) return false;

    //copy image to upper left corner of background
    RECT source_rect = {0, 0, 1024, 768 };
    RECT dest_ul = { 0, 0, 1024, 768 };
    d3ddev->StretchRect(image, &source_rect, background, &dest_ul, D3DTEXF_NONE);
```

```cpp
    //copy image to upper right corner of background
    RECT dest_ur = { 1024, 0, 1024*2, 768 };
    d3ddev->StretchRect(image, &source_rect, background, &dest_ur, D3DTEXF_NONE);

    //copy image to lower left corner of background
    RECT dest_ll = { 0, 768, 1024, 768*2 };
    d3ddev->StretchRect(image, &source_rect, background, &dest_ll, D3DTEXF_NONE);

    //copy image to lower right corner of background
    RECT dest_lr = { 1024, 768, 1024*2, 768*2 };
    d3ddev->StretchRect(image, &source_rect, background, &dest_lr, D3DTEXF_NONE);

    //get pointer to the back buffer
    d3ddev->GetBackBuffer(0, 0, D3DBACKBUFFER_TYPE_MONO, &backbuffer);

    //remove scratch image
    image->Release();

    return true;
}


void Game_Run(HWND window)
{
    if (!d3ddev) return;
    DirectInput_Update();
    d3ddev->Clear(0, NULL, D3DCLEAR_TARGET | D3DCLEAR_ZBUFFER,
        D3DCOLOR_XRGB(0,0,100), 1.0f, 0);

    if (Key_Down(DIK_UP) || controllers[0].sThumbLY > 2000)
        scrolly -= 1;

    if (Key_Down(DIK_DOWN) || controllers[0].sThumbLY < -2000)
        scrolly += 1;

    if (Key_Down(DIK_LEFT) || controllers[0].sThumbLX < -2000)
        scrollx -= 1;

    if (Key_Down(DIK_RIGHT) || controllers[0].sThumbLX > 2000)
        scrollx += 1;
```

```
        //keep scrolling within boundary
        if (scrolly < 0)
            scrolly = BUFFERH - SCREENH;
        if (scrolly > BUFFERH - SCREENH)
            scrolly = 0;
        if (scrollx < 0)
            scrollx = BUFFERW - SCREENW;
        if (scrollx > BUFFERW - SCREENW)
            scrollx = 0;

        if (d3ddev->BeginScene())
        {
            RECT source_rect = {scrollx, scrolly, scrollx+1024, scrolly+768 };
            RECT dest_rect = { 0, 0, 1024, 768};

            d3ddev->StretchRect(background, &source_rect, backbuffer,
                &dest_rect, D3DTEXF_NONE);

            spriteobj->Begin(D3DXSPRITE_ALPHABLEND);

            std::ostringstream oss;
            oss << "Scroll Position = " << scrollx << "," << scrolly;
            FontPrint(font, 0, 0, oss.str());

            spriteobj->End();
            d3ddev->EndScene();
            d3ddev->Present(NULL, NULL, NULL, NULL);
        }

        if (KEY_DOWN(VK_ESCAPE)) gameover = true;
        if (controllers[0].wButtons & XINPUT_GAMEPAD_BACK)
            gameover = true;
    }

void Game_End()
{
    background->Release();
    font->Release();
    DirectInput_Shutdown();
    Direct3D_Shutdown();
}
```

What You Have Learned

In this chapter we learned about scrolling backgrounds. You learned how they are created and how to use them in a game. Working with tiles to create a scrolling game world is by no means an easy subject! Here are the key points:

- You learned how to create a virtual scroll buffer.

- You learned how to use Mappy to create a tile map.

- You learned how to dynamically draw tiles onto the screen.

Review Questions

The following review questions will challenge your comprehension of the subject material covered in this chapter.

1. What was the resolution of the virtual scroll buffer used in the static scrolling program?

2. Likewise, what was the resolution of the buffer used in the dynamic scrolling program?

3. What is the difference between the tile drawing code in the two example programs?

4. How would you create a tile map using Mappy with a *gigantic* level with thousands of tiles?

5. What is the effective limit on map size for a game that draws tiles dynamically?

6. What is the file extension for a native Mappy level file?

7. What type of export do we want to perform to convert a Mappy level file into a form usable in a DirectX program?

8. How many times do we need to blit the source background image onto the scroll buffer for a bitmap scroller?

9. What term is used by Mappy to refer to individual tiles in a level?

10. If you wanted to create a game similar to the old Mario platformer games, would you use a bitmap scroller or a tile scroller?

On Your Own

The following exercises will challenge your retention of the information presented in this chapter.

Exercise 1. The dynamic scrolling program sure has a lot of potential and we have only scratched the surface here! See if you can get the program to automatically scroll the tile map without user input.

Exercise 2. The dynamic scrolling program almost looks like a rudimentary game with automatic scrolling, so let's take it one step further. Load up a sprite representing a space ship and draw it on the screen over the top of the scroller. Then, allow the player to move the sprite left and right using the arrow keys.

CHAPTER 11

PLAYING AUDIO

Audio is essential to a game! Sound effects and music contribute dramatically to the player's immersion in the fictional game experience (which is called the suspension of disbelief), and creating an emotional reaction in the player. Players will respond differently to the same game when audio is removed from the game. But when the same game game features dynamic, powerful sound effects and appropriate background music, it changes the entire experience. This chapter will show you how to use DirectSound to audibly enhance a game. A talented game designer will use audio to affect the mood of the player. While exploring

DirectSound in this chapter, we'll use the opportunity to work with sprite collision some more. Here is what you will learn:

- How to initialize DirectSound.

- How to load audio from a wave file.

- How to play an audio effect with mixing.

- How to loop an audio effect with mixing.

Using DirectSound

DirectSound is the DirectX component that handles all sound output for your game, and features a multi-channel sound mixer. Basically, you just tell DirectSound to play a sound and it takes care of all the details (including combining that sound with any currently playing sounds). The code required to create, initialize, load, and play a wave file using DirectSound is a bit more involved than the bitmap and sprite code you learned about in the last several chapters. For this reason, and to avoid re-inventing the wheel, I will show you how to use Microsoft's own wrapper for DirectSound.

Using a wrapper is generally against my own instincts as a programmer, as I prefer to know everything about the code I'm using, and often prefer to write my own rather than use someone else's code. However, there comes a time when, in the interest of time, you have to give in and use what's already available. After all, DirectX itself is a game library written by someone else, and it makes no sense to adhere to a strict philosophy in game programming when all it does is slow you down. It's okay if you are writing mostly C, as I am doing in this book, because once in a while you may be required to delve a little into C++ in order to re-use code. In this case, we'll use the DirectSound Utility classes—but I have chosen not go into detail on how they work. You might think of it as going over an SDK, such as DirectX itself—there is a lot of code that you don't understand, but as long as it works, you can work on your game without worrying about it.

The DirectX SDK includes a Utility library called DXUTsound. We won't be using this because it has too many support files with it. Instead, we'll use an older version that I hung onto from a previous version of DirectX 9.0c. The old "DXUT" version of DirectSound is found in a pair of files called dsutil.cpp and dsutil.h.

Microsoft has been very unpredictable with it's DirectX Utility library (DXUT). The consistency problem is especially acute with regard to the DirectSound helper functions and classes: CSoundManager, CSound, and CWaveFile, which we need in order to load and play wave files with DirectSound.

In older versions of DirectX, these helper classes were located in the files dsutil.h and dsutil.cpp. In a later version of DirectX, they were combined in DXUT-sound.h and DXUTsound.cpp. The latest version of DirectX (at the time of this writing) hides these classes in yet another set of filenames: SDKsound.h, SDKsound.cpp, and SDKwavefile.h. The inconsistencies continue! Inside the SDKsound.h file it is referred to in the header comment as DXUTsound.h!

Since this is such a recurring problem, I have created a new pair of audio files for our own use, which shall be called DirectSound.h and DirectSound.cpp. These files contain the source code from the old dsutil files (since the code has not changed even in the latest DirectX SDK). We will simply add these files to our reusable "DirectX_Project" template.

There are three classes defined in the SDKsound (formerly DXUTSound) that we're interested in here:

CSoundManager	The primary DirectSound device.
CSound	Used to create DirectSound buffers.
CWaveFile	Helps load a wave file into a CSound buffer.

Initializing DirectSound

The first thing to do in order to use DirectSound is create an instance of the CSoundManager class (which creates an "object" of the "class").

```
CSoundManager *dsound = new CSoundManager();
```

The next step requires you to call the Initialize function to initialize the DirectSound manager:

```
dsound->Initialize(window_handle, DSSCL_PRIORITY);
```

The first parameter is the window handle for your program, while the second parameter specifies the DirectSound cooperative level, of which there are three choices:

DSSCL_NORMAL. Shares sound device with other programs.

DSSCL_PRIORITY. Gains higher priority over sound device (recommended for games).

DSSCL_WRITEPRIMARY. Provides access to modify the primary sound buffer.

The most common cooperative level is DSSCL_PRIORITY, which gives your game a higher priority on the sound device than other programs that may be running.

After initializing DirectSound, we must set the audio buffer format. This is usually not something you will need to mess with but we do have the option of changing the sound mixer's internal format (used to adjust the audio playback quality) if we want to. In the following line of code, I've configured the audio buffer to *stereo, 22 kHz, 16-bit*. If you are making a game that requires CD-quality audio, then you may bump the settings up a notch or two if you wish. (For instance, CD quality audio is approximately 44 kHz, but most wave files are encoded at a lower rate.)

```
dsound->SetPrimaryBufferFormat(2, 22050, 16);
```

Creating a Sound Buffer

After you have initialized the DirectSound manager (via CSoundManager), you will then usually load all of the sound effects for your game. You access sound effects using CSound pointer variables that are declared like this:

```
CSound *wave;
```

The CSound object that you create is a wrapper for a secondary sound buffer called LPDIRECTSOUNDBUFFER8 that, thanks to the utility classes, you do not need to program yourself.

Loading a Wave File

The sound mixer created and managed by DirectSound might be thought of as the primary buffer for sound. Like Direct3D, the primary buffer is where output occurs. But in the case of DirectSound, the secondary buffers are sound data rather than bitmap data, and you play a sound by calling Play (which I'll go over shortly).

Loading a wave file into a DirectSound secondary buffer involves a single function call rather than a multi-page code listing to initialize the sound buffer, open the wave file, read it into memory, and configure all of the parameters. The CSoundManager object that you create has the function you need to load a wave file. It is called Create:

```
HRESULT Create(
    CSound** ppSound,
```

```
    LPTSTR strWaveFileName,
    DWORD dwCreationFlags = 0,
    GUID guid3DAlgorithm = GUID_NULL,
    DWORD dwNumBuffers = 1
);
```

The first parameter specifies the CSound object that you want to use for the newly loaded wave sound. The second parameter is the filename. The remaining parameters can be left at their defaults, meaning you really only need to call this function with two parameters. Here is an example:

```
dsound->Create(&wave, "snicker.wav");
```

Playing a Sound

You are free to play sounds as often as you want without worrying about the sound mixing, ending the sound playback, or any other details, because DirectSound itself handles all of those details for you. Within the CSound class itself is a function called Play that will play the sound for you. Here is what that function looks like:

```
HRESULT Play(
    DWORD dwPriority = 0,
    DWORD dwFlags = 0,
    LONG lVolume = 0,
    LONG lFrequency = -1,
    LONG lPan = 0
);
```

The first parameter is the priority, which is an advanced option and should always be set to zero. The second parameter specifies whether you want the sound to loop, meaning that it will restart at the beginning and continue playing every time it reaches the end of the wave data. If you want to play the sound with looping, use DSBPLAY_LOOPING for this parameter. The last three parameters specify the volume, frequency, and panning (left to right) of the sound, which are also usually left at their defaults, but you may experiment with them if you wish.

Here is an example of how you would usually call this function, first with normal playback. You can either fill in the parameters or leave them out entirely if you want to use the defaults.

```
wave->Play();
```

And here is how you would use looping:

```
wave->Play(0, DSBPLAY_LOOPING);
```

To stop playback of a sound while it is playing, use the Stop function. This function is particularly useful with looping sounds, which will go on forever unless you specifically stop or reset the sound by playing it again without the looping parameter.

```
HRESULT Stop();
```

An example usage of this function couldn't be much simpler:

```
wave->Stop();
```

Advice

Although DirectSound is adequate for our purposes here, there are better audio engines available for game projects. I recommend FMOD by Firelight Technologies. It is free for non-commercial use at www.fmod.org. I personally use this audio library for most of my own projects and more advanced books.

Testing DirectSound

Let's write a simple demo to test the DirectSound code you have learned how to write in this chapter. Since DirectSound is a new component, there's no support for it yet in our MyDirectX.h and MyDiretX.cpp files yet, which we'll need to rectify. After a new project has been configured and we have added the Direct-Sound code, I'll go over the code for a sample program that bounces a bunch of pinball-style balls against four bumpers (and each other) with a sound played each time as an audio demo. The Play_Sound program is shown in Figure 11.1.

The Play_Sound program does not use realistic physics for the ball movement or rebounding off the bumpers (or each other), just an approximation of rebound physics based on each object's position. The resulting rebounds of the balls are not very impressive, but this is not supposed to be a physics demo after all.

It's surprising that, of all the lines in this Play_Sound program, only a very few actually involve any audio playback! That's not a bad thing, though; on the contrary, that's the goal, to keep the audio interface as simple and painless as possible, which we have accomplished here. In the process, this Play_Sound program ended up being quite interesting! Do I see the start of a pinball game in the works here?

Figure 11.1
The Play_Sound program demonstrates how to use DirectSound.

Creating the Project

The Play_Sound project is already finished on the CD-ROM if you want to just open it up and examine it. Optionally, you may open the "DirectX_Project" template, also in this chapter's folder, and configure it and add the source code for the Play_Sound program.

If you want to create the new project from scratch, follow these basic instructions:

1. Run Visual C++.

2. Open the File menu and select New to bring up the New dialog.

3. Make sure the Projects tab is selected. Choose Win32 Application for the project type, and type **Play_Sound** for the project name.

4. Click OK to close the dialog and create the new project. As usual, don't let Visual C++ add any files for you.

From this point forward we will need to include two new files in the DirectX_Project template, and you will need them for the Play_Sound program coming up shortly. These two files contain the Microsoft code for working with DirectSound via several support classes: CSoundManager, CSound, and CWaveFile. These files have been included on the CD-ROM and are too lengthy to print here (even if I had permission to reprint them—they have a Microsoft copyright after all). The two files are as follows:

- DirectSound.h

- DirectSound.cpp

These files do not exist in the DirectX SDK; they have been adapted from the DXUT files discussed earlier and will compile on their own without the DXUT dependency. Just be sure to add these files to your project. Next, we'll need to add new audio functions to MyDirectX.h and MyDirectX.cpp that use the audio classes in a convenient way.

After you have copied these files to your new project folder, you can add them to your project in Visual C++ by opening the Project menu and selecting Add Existing Item. This will bring up the Add Existing Item dialog. Select Direct-Sound.h and DirectSound.cpp to add them to your project. After these files have been added, your project should contain these files:

- DirectSound.cpp

- DirectSound.h

- MyDirectX.cpp

- MyDirectX.h

- MyGame.cpp

- MyWindows.cpp

You can verify that your project is configured correctly by referring to Figure 11.2, which shows the Solution Explorer loaded with all of the necessary files.

Modifying the "MyDirectX" Files

Okay, this has been quite a long process, but if you have followed along and performed each step along the way, then you should now have a project that is

Figure 11.2
The framework files have been added to the project.

ready to compile. Unfortunately, the game.h and game.cpp files contain source code from a previous project that has nothing to do with DirectSound! So, conveniently, these files are already in your project—you just need to open them up and replace the code.

MyDirectX.h Additions

You can simply add the following new code to MyDirectX.h to provide support for DirectSound to the framework we've been building (and maintained in the "DirectX_Project" template in each chapter).

```
//DirectSound code added in chapter 11
#include "DirectSound.h"

#pragma comment(lib,"dsound.lib")
#pragma comment(lib,"dxerr9.lib")

//primary DirectSound object
extern CSoundManager *dsound;

//function prototypes
bool DirectSound_Init(HWND hwnd);
void DirectSound_Shutdown();
```

```
CSound *LoadSound(string filename);
void PlaySound(CSound *sound);
void LoopSound(CSound *sound);
void StopSound(CSound *sound);
```

MyDirectX.cpp Additions

Add the following code to MyDirectX.cpp:

```
// New DirectSound code

#include "DirectSound.h"

//primary DirectSound object
CSoundManager *dsound = NULL;

bool DirectSound_Init(HWND hwnd)
{
    //create DirectSound manager object
    dsound = new CSoundManager();

    //initialize DirectSound
    HRESULT result;
    result = dsound->Initialize(hwnd, DSSCL_PRIORITY);
    if (result != DS_OK) return false;

    //set the primary buffer format
    result = dsound->SetPrimaryBufferFormat(2, 22050, 16);
    if (result != DS_OK) return false;

    //return success
    return true;
}

void DirectSound_Shutdown()
{
    if (dsound) delete dsound;
}

CSound *LoadSound(string filename)
{
    HRESULT result;
```

```
    //create local reference to wave data
    CSound *wave = NULL;

    //attempt to load the wave file
    char s[255];
    sprintf(s, "%s", filename.c_str());
    result = dsound->Create(&wave, s);
    if (result != DS_OK) wave = NULL;

    //return the wave
    return wave;
}

void PlaySound(CSound *sound)
{
    sound->Play();
}

void LoopSound(CSound *sound)
{
    sound->Play(0, DSBPLAY_LOOPING);
}

void StopSound(CSound *sound)
{
    sound->Stop();
}
```

Modifying MyGame.cpp

Now that the DirectSound helper files have been added to the project, and the DirectSound helper *functions* have been added to our "MyDirectX" files, we can very easily load and play an audio file with a minimum of fuss. Here's the complete source code for the Play_Sound example program. I have highlighted the key audio code in bold for your reference.

```
#include "MyDirectX.h"
using namespace std;

const string APPTITLE = "Play Sound Program";
const int SCREENW = 1024;
const int SCREENH = 768;
```

```cpp
LPDIRECT3DTEXTURE9 ball_image = NULL;
LPDIRECT3DTEXTURE9 bumper_image = NULL;
LPDIRECT3DTEXTURE9 background = NULL;

//balls
const int NUMBALLS = 10;
SPRITE balls[NUMBALLS];

//bumpers
SPRITE bumpers[4];

//timing variable
DWORD screentimer = timeGetTime();
DWORD coretimer = timeGetTime();
DWORD bumpertimer = timeGetTime();

//the wave sounds
CSound *sound_bounce = NULL;
CSound *sound_electric = NULL;


bool Game_Init(HWND window)
{
    srand(time(NULL));

    //initialize Direct3D
    if (!Direct3D_Init(window, SCREENW, SCREENH, false))
    {
        MessageBox(window,"Error initializing Direct3D",APPTITLE.c_str(),0);
        return false;
    }

    //initialize DirectInput
    if (!DirectInput_Init(window))
    {
        MessageBox(window,"Error initializing DirectInput",
        APPTITLE.c_str(),0);
        return false;
    }

    //initialize DirectSound
    if (!DirectSound_Init(window))
```

```
{
    MessageBox(window,"Error initializing DirectSound",
    APPTITLE.c_str(),0);
    return false;
}


//load the background image
background = LoadTexture("craters.tga");
if (!background)
{
    MessageBox(window,"Error loading craters.tga",APPTITLE.c_str(),0);
    return false;
}

//load the ball image
ball_image = LoadTexture("lightningball.tga");
if (!ball_image)
{
    MessageBox(window,"Error loading lightningball.tga",
    APPTITLE.c_str(),0);
    return false;
}

//load the bumper image
bumper_image = LoadTexture("bumper.tga");
if (!ball_image)
{
    MessageBox(window,"Error loading bumper.tga",APPTITLE.c_str(),0);
    return false;
}

//set the balls' properties
for (int n=0; n<NUMBALLS; n++)
{
    balls[n].x = (float)(rand() % (SCREENW-200));
    balls[n].y = (float)(rand() % (SCREENH-200));
    balls[n].width = 64;
    balls[n].height = 64;
    balls[n].velx = (float)(rand() % 6 - 3);
    balls[n].vely = (float)(rand() % 6 - 3);
}
```

```
//set the bumpers' properties
for (int n=0; n<4; n++)
{
    bumpers[n].width = 128;
    bumpers[n].height = 128;
    bumpers[n].columns = 2;
    bumpers[n].frame = 0;
}
bumpers[0].x = 150;
bumpers[0].y = 150;
bumpers[1].x = SCREENW-150-128;
bumpers[1].y = 150;
bumpers[2].x = 150;
bumpers[2].y = SCREENH-150-128;
bumpers[3].x = SCREENW-150-128;
bumpers[3].y = SCREENH-150-128;

//load bounce wave file
sound_bounce = LoadSound("step.wav");
if (!sound_bounce)
{
    MessageBox(window,"Error loading step.wav",APPTITLE.c_str(),0);
    return false;
}

return true;
}

void rebound(SPRITE &sprite1, SPRITE &sprite2)
{
    float centerx1 = sprite1.x + sprite1.width/2;
    float centery1 = sprite1.y + sprite1.height/2;

    float centerx2 = sprite2.x + sprite2.width/2;
    float centery2 = sprite2.y + sprite2.height/2;

    if (centerx1 < centerx2)
    {
        sprite1.velx = fabs(sprite1.velx) * -1;
    }
    else if (centerx1 > centerx2)
    {
```

```
            sprite1.velx = fabs(sprite1.velx);
    }

    if (centery1 < centery2)
    {
            sprite1.vely = fabs(sprite1.vely) * -1;
    }
    else {
            sprite1.vely = fabs(sprite1.vely);
    }

    sprite1.x += sprite1.velx;
    sprite1.y += sprite1.vely;

}

void Game_Run(HWND window)
{
    int n;

    if (!d3ddev) return;
    DirectInput_Update();
    d3ddev->Clear(0, NULL, D3DCLEAR_TARGET | D3DCLEAR_ZBUFFER,
        D3DCOLOR_XRGB(0,0,100), 1,0f, 0);


    /*
     * slow ball movement
     */
    if (timeGetTime() > coretimer + 10)
    {
        //reset timing
        coretimer = GetTickCount();

        int width = balls[0].width;
        int height = balls[0].height;

        //move the ball sprites
        for (n=0; n<NUMBALLS; n++)
        {
            balls[n].x += balls[n].velx;
            balls[n].y += balls[n].vely;
```

```
            //warp the ball at screen edges
            if (balls[n].x > SCREENW)
            {
                balls[n].x = -width;
            }
            else if (balls[n].x < -width)
            {
                balls[n].x = SCREENW+width;
            }

            if (balls[n].y > SCREENH+height)
            {
                balls[n].y = -height;
            }
            else if (balls[n].y < -height)
            {
                balls[n].y = SCREENH+height;
            }
        }
    }


    //reset bumper frames
    if (timeGetTime() > bumpertimer + 250)
    {
        bumpertimer = timeGetTime();
        for (int bumper=0; bumper<4; bumper++)
        {
            bumpers[bumper].frame = 0;
        }
    }

    /*
     * check for ball collisions with bumpers
     */
    for (int ball=0; ball<NUMBALLS; ball++)
    {
        for (int bumper=0; bumper<4; bumper++)
        {
            if (CollisionD(balls[ball], bumpers[bumper]))
            {
                rebound(balls[ball], bumpers[bumper]);
                bumpers[bumper].frame = 1;
```

```
                PlaySound(sound_bounce);
            }
        }
}


/*
 * check for sprite collisions with each other
 * (as fast as possible-with no time limiter)
 */
for (int one=0; one<NUMBALLS; one++)
{
    for (int two=0; two<NUMBALLS; two++)
    {
        if (one != two)
        {
            if (CollisionD(balls[one], balls[two]))
            {
                while (CollisionD(balls[one], balls[two]))
                {
                    //rebound ball one
                    rebound(balls[one], balls[two]);

                    //rebound ball two
                    rebound(balls[two], balls[one]);

                }

            }
        }
    }
}



/*
 * slow rendering to approximately 60 fps
 */
if (timeGetTime() > screentimer + 14)
{
    screentimer = GetTickCount();

    //start rendering
    if (d3ddev->BeginScene())
    {
```

```
        //start sprite handler
        spriteobj->Begin(D3DXSPRITE_ALPHABLEND);

        //draw background
        Sprite_Transform_Draw(background, 0, 0, SCREENW, SCREENH);

        //draw the balls
        for (n=0; n<NUMBALLS; n++)
        {
            Sprite_Transform_Draw(ball_image,
                balls[n].x, balls[n].y,
                balls[n].width, balls[n].height);
        }

        //draw the bumpers
        for (n=0; n<4; n++)
        {
            Sprite_Transform_Draw(bumper_image,
                bumpers[n].x,
                bumpers[n].y,
                bumpers[n].width,
                bumpers[n].height,
                bumpers[n].frame,
                bumpers[n].columns);
        }

        //stop drawing
        spriteobj->End();


        //stop rendering
        d3ddev->EndScene();
        d3ddev->Present(NULL, NULL, NULL, NULL);
        }
    }

    //exit with escape key or controller Back button
    if (KEY_DOWN(VK_ESCAPE)) gameover = true;
    if (controllers[0].wButtons & XINPUT_GAMEPAD_BACK) gameover = true;
}

void Game_End()
{
```

```
    if (ball_image) ball_image->Release();
    if (bumper_image) bumper_image->Release();
    if (background) background->Release();
    if (sound_bounce) delete sound_bounce;

    DirectSound_Shutdown();
    DirectInput_Shutdown();
    Direct3D_Shutdown();
}
```

What You Have Learned

This chapter explained how to use some relatively painless DirectSound support routines included in the DirectX SDK to make DirectSound programming easier. Here are the key points:

- You learned how to initialize the DirectSound object.

- You learned how to load a wave file into a sound buffer.

- You learned how to play and stop a sound, with or without looping.

- You learned a little bit about sound mixing.

- You got some practice working on a project with many files.

- You learned about the value of code re-use.

Review Questions

These questions will help to challenge your understanding of the chapter:

1. What is the name of the primary DirectSound class used in this chapter?

2. What is a secondary sound buffer?

3. What is the secondary sound buffer called in DirectSound.h?

4. What is the option called that causes a sound to play with looping?

5. For reference, what is the name of the function that draws a texture (as a sprite)?

6. Which DXUT helper class handles wave file loading?

7. Which DXUT helper class do you need to use in order to create a secondary sound buffer?

8. Briefly explain how DirectSound handles sound mixing from a user's point of view.

9. Since DirectMusic is now defunct, what would be a good alternative for music playback in a game?

10. Which function must be called to initialize DirectSound?

On Your Own

The following exercises will help you to think outside the box and push your limits, which will increase your capacity for retention.

Exercise 1. The Play_Sound program played a sound effect every time a ball sprite hit one of the bumpers. Modify the program so that it draws a different number of balls of your choosing and give each ball more of a random velocity.

Exercise 2. The Play_Sound program plays just a single sound when a ball sprite hits a bumper. Modify the program by adding three more wave files, with associated code to load them, so that when a ball hits a bumper, a random sound will be played.

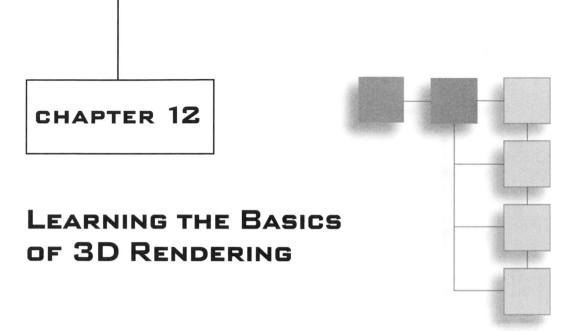

CHAPTER 12

LEARNING THE BASICS OF 3D RENDERING

This chapter covers the basics of 3D graphics. You will learn the basic concepts so that you are at least aware of the key points in 3D programming. However, this chapter will not go into great detail on 3D mathematics or graphics theory, which are far too advanced for this book. What you will learn instead is the practical implementation of 3D in order to write simple 3D games. You will get just exactly what you need to render simple 3D objects without getting bogged down in theory. If you have questions about how matrix math works and about how 3D rendering is done at a much lower level, you might want to use this chapter as a starting point and then go on and read a more advanced book (see Appendix B for recommendations). The goal of this chapter is to simply introduce you to the concepts at this point. Here is what you will learn:

- How to create and use vertices.

- How to manipulate polygons.

- How to create a textured polygon.

- How to create a cube and rotate it.

Introduction to 3D Programming

It's a foregone conclusion today that everyone has a 3D accelerated video card. Even the low-end budget video cards are equipped with a 3D graphics processing unit (GPU) that would be impressive were it not for all the competition in this market pushing out more and more polygons and new features every year. Figure 12.1 shows a typical 3D accelerated video card.

Advice

When I discuss "3D programming" in this chapter, please note that I'm specifically talking about Direct3D. Some of the 3D concepts discussed herein are specifically related to Direct3D and not necessarily any other graphics API (nor to 3D graphics theory in general).

Figure 12.1
Modern 3D video cards are capable of producing real-time photo-realistic graphics. (Image courtesy of Micro Star International.)

The Key Components of 3D Programming

There are three key components to rendering a scene in Direct3D:

1. **World transformation.** This moves 3D objects around in the "world," which is a term that describes the entire scene. In other words, the world transformation causes things in the scene to move, rotate, and scale (one object at a time).

2. **View transformation.** This is the camera, so to speak, that defines what you see on the screen. The camera can be positioned anywhere in the "world," so if you want to move the camera, you do so with the view transform.

3. **Projection transformation.** This is the final step, in which you take the view transform (what objects are visible to the camera) and draw them on the screen, resulting in a flat 2D image of pixels. The projection determines how the rendered scene will look on the screen (with whatever aspect ratio you have defined primarily affecting the output).

Direct3D provides all the functions and transformations that you need to create, render, and view a scene without using any 3D mathematics—which is good for you, the programmer, because 3D matrix math is not easy. (Even if we wanted to write our own matrix math calculations from scratch, they probably would not be as fast as Microsoft's implementation.)

A "transformation" occurs when you add, subtract, multiply, or divide one matrix with another matrix, causing a change to occur within the resulting matrix; these changes cause 3D objects to move, rotate, and scale 3D objects. A matrix is a grid or two-dimensional array that is 4×4 (or 16 cells) in size. Direct3D defines all of the standard matrices that you need to do just about everything required for a 3D game.

The 3D Scene

Before you can do anything with the scene, you must first create the 3D objects that will make up the scene. In this chapter, I will show you how to create simple 3D objects from scratch, and will also go over some of the freebie models that Direct3D provides, mainly for testing. There are standard objects, such as a cylinder, pyramid, torus, and even a teapot, that you can use to create a scene.

Of course, you can't create an entire 3D game just with source code because there are too many objects in a typical game. Eventually, you'll need to create your 3D models in a modeling program like 3ds max or the free Anim8or program (included on the CD-ROM). The next two chapters will explain how to load 3D models from a file into a scene. But in this chapter, I'll stick with programmable 3D objects.

Advice

Between this chapter and the next one, we will only cover the basics of 3D rendering with Direct3D—enough to render a textured mesh with ambient lighting, loaded from a .X file. We will not be learning about lighting or shaders or mesh animation in this beginning title. If you would like to continue to learn more about 3D graphics programming with Direct3D, please refer to Appendix B, "Resources for Further Study" for recommended books (which I personally own and can heartily recommend!).

Introducing Vertices

The advanced 3D graphics chip that powers your video card sees only vertices. A *vertex* (singular) is a point in 3D space specified with the values of X, Y, and Z. The video card itself really only "sees" the vertices that make up the three angles of each triangle. It is the job of the video card to fill in the empty space that makes up the triangle between the three vertices. See Figure 12.2. Unlike this example, though, all of the triangles in a 3D scene will be *right triangles*, which can be rendered more efficiently.

Creating and manipulating the 3D objects in a scene is a job for you, the programmer, so it helps to understand some of the basics of the 3D environment. The entire scene might be thought of as a mathematical grid with three axes. You

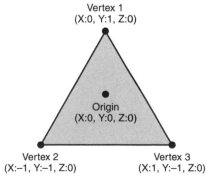

Figure 12.2
A 3D scene is made up entirely of triangles.

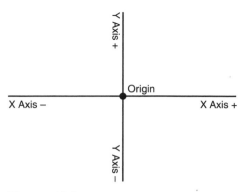

Figure 12.3
The Cartesian coordinate system.

might be familiar with the Cartesian coordinate system if you have ever studied geometry or trigonometry: The coordinate system is the basis for all geometric and trigonometric math, as there are formulas and functions for manipulating points on the Cartesian grid.

The Cartesian Coordinate System

The "grid" is really made up of two infinite lines that intersect at the origin. These lines are perpendicular. The horizontal line is called the *X axis* and the vertical line is called the *Y axis*. The origin is at position (0,0). The X axis goes up in value toward the right, and it goes down in value to the left. Likewise, the Y axis goes up in the up direction, and goes down in the down direction. See Figure 12.3.

If you have a point at a specified position that is represented on a Cartesian coordinate system, such as at (100,−50), then you can manipulate that point using mathematical calculations. There are three primary things you can do with a point:

1. **Translation**. This is the process of moving a point to a new location. See Figure 12.4.

2. **Rotation**. This causes a point to move in a circle around the origin at a radius that is based on its current position. See Figure 12.5.

3. **Scaling**. You can adjust the point relative to the origin by modifying the entire range of the two axes. See Figure 12.6.

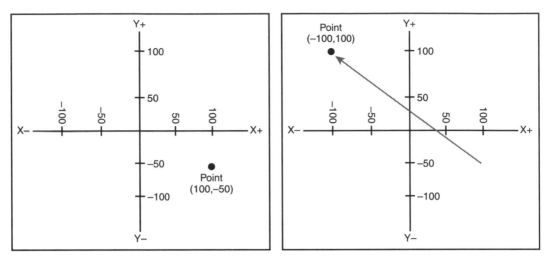

Figure 12.4
A point (100,−50) is translated by a value of (−200,150) resulting in a new position at (−100,100).

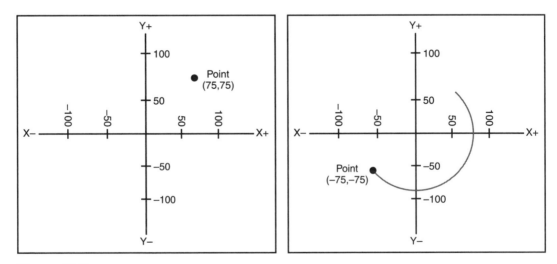

Figure 12.5
A point (75,75) is rotated by 180 degrees, resulting in a new position at (−75,−75).

The Origin of Vertices

The one thing you want to remember when working with 3D graphics is that everything works around the origin. So, when you want to rotate a 3D object on the screen, you have to remember that all rotation is based on the origin point. If you translate the object to a new location that is no longer centered at the origin, then rotating the object will cause it to move around the origin in a circle!

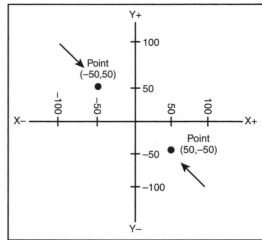

Figure 12.6
A point (100,100) is scaled by −50 percent, resulting in a new position at (−50,50)

So, what's the solution to this problem? This is the biggest sticking point most people run into with 3D programming because it's very hard to get a handle on it unless you have, say, a more senior programmer to explain it to you. In this case, you have an opportunity to learn an important lesson in 3D graphics programming that is all-too-often ignored: The trick is to not really move the 3D objects at all.

What!? No, I'm not kidding. The trick is to leave all of the 3D objects at the origin and not move them at all. Does that mess with your head? Okay, I'll explain. You know that a 3D object is made up of vertices (three for every triangle, to be exact). The key is to draw the 3D objects at a specified position, with a specified rotation and scaling value, without moving the "original" object itself. I don't mean that you should make a copy of it; instead, just draw it at the last instant before refreshing the screen. Do you remember how you were able to draw many sprites on the screen with only a single sprite image? It's sort of like that, only you're just drawing a 3D object based on the original "image," so to speak, and the original does not change. By leaving the source objects at the origin, you can rotate them around what is called a *local origin* for each object, which preserves the objects.

So, how do you move a 3D object without moving it? The answer is by using matrices. A *matrix* is a 4 × 4 grid of numbers that represent a 3D object in "space." Each 3D object in your scene (or game) has its own matrix.

Advice

As you might have guessed, matrix math is beyond the scope of this book, but I encourage you to look into a more advanced Direct3D book if you want to learn what *really* happens in the world of polygons. The *best* on the subject, in my opinion, is Carl Granberg–author of two good books: *Programming An RTS Game In Direct3D* and *Character Animation in Direct3D* (both published by Charles River). I use these books in my advanced DirectX courses.

The result of using matrices to give each 3D object its own origin is that your 3D world has its own coordinate system—as do all of the objects in the scene—so you can manipulate objects independently of one another. You can even manipulate the entire scene without affecting these independent objects. For example, suppose you are working on a racing game, and you have cars racing around an oval track. You want each car to be as realistic as possible so that each car can rotate and move on its own, regardless of what the other cars are doing. At some point, of course, you want to add the code that will cause the cars to crash if they collide. You also want the cars to stay "flat" on the pavement of the track, which means calculating the angle of the track and positioning the four corners of the car appropriately.

Imagine taking it even further—think of the possibilities that arise when you can cause individual objects to contain subobjects, each with their own local origins, that follow along with the "parent" object. You can then position the subobjects with respect to the origin of the parent object and cause the subobjects to rotate on their own. Does this help you to visualize how you might program the wheels of a car to roll on their own while the car remains stationary? The wheels "follow along" with the car, meaning they translate/rotate/scale with the parent object, but they also have the ability to roll and turn left or right.

Pay Careful Attention to the Camera!

The most frustrating problem with 3D programming is not seeing anything come up on the screen after you have written what you believe to be clean code that "should work, dang it!" The number one most common mistake in 3D programming is forgetting about the camera and view transform. As you work through this chapter, keep the following points in mind.

The first thing you should set up in the scene is the perspective, camera, and view with a test poly or quad to make sure your scene is set up properly before proceeding. Once you know for sure that the view is good, you can move ahead with the rest of the code for your game. Another frequent problem involves the position of the camera, which might seem okay for your initial test but then may be too close to the object for it to show up, or the object may have moved off "the screen." One good test is to move the camera away from the origin (such as a Z of –100, for instance), and then make sure your target matrix points to the origin (0,0,0). That should clear up any viewing problems and allow you to get cracking on the game again.

The second thing you should do to initially set up the scene is check the lighting conditions of your scene. Do you have lighting enabled without any lights? Direct3D is really literal and will not create ambient light for you unless you tell it there will be no light sources!

Moving to the Third Dimension

I hope you are now getting the hang of the Cartesian coordinate system. Although it is crucial to the study of 3D graphics, I will not go into any more detail because the subject requires more theory and explanation than I have room for here. Instead, I'm going to just cover enough material to teach you what you need to know to write a few simple 3D games, after which you can decide which aspect of 3D programming you'd like to study further. It's always more fun to do what works first and work on an actual game rather than try to learn every nook and cranny of a library like Direct3D all at once.

Advice

We're going to learn how to render a simple textured cube in this chapter using very low-level graphics programming with a vertex buffer. When working with the vertices in this manner, you are digging into the inner core of Direct3D which is like *touching* the GPU (graphics processing unit). After we've finished exploring the low-level aspects of Direct3D, we'll focus on loading and drawing 3D mesh files from a .X file, which is a bit easier. If you do not want to learn about the heart of the Direct3D rendering pipeline in this manner, you may skip to the next chapter (but I strongly recommend you follow along here instead!).

Figure 12.7 shows the addition of a third dimension to the Cartesian coordinate system. All of the current rules that you have learned about the 2D coordinate system apply, but each point is now referred to with three values (X,Y,Z) instead of just the two.

Grabbing Hold of the 3D Pipeline

The first thing you need to learn before you can draw a single polygon on the screen is that Direct3D uses a custom vertex format that *you* define. Here is the struct that you'll be using in this chapter:

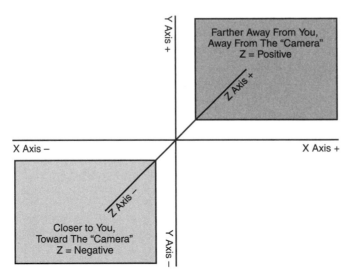

Figure 12.7
The Cartesian coordinate system with a third dimension.

```
struct VERTEX
{
    float x, y, z;
    float tu, tv;
};
```

The first three member variables are the position of the vertex, and the `tu` and `tv` variables are used to describe how a texture is drawn. Now you have an incredible amount of control over how the rendering process takes place. These two variables instruct Direct3D how to draw a texture on a surface, and Direct3D supports wrapping of a texture around the curve of a 3D object. You specify the upper-left corner of the texture with `tu = 0.0` and `tv = 0.0`, and then you specify the bottom-right corner of the texture using `tu = 1.0` and `tv = 1.0`. All the polygons in between these two will usually have zeroes for the texture coordinates, which tells Direct3D to just keep on stretching the texture over them.

Texturing is an advanced subject and there are a thousand options that you will discover as you explore 3D programming in more depth. For now, let's stick to stretching a texture over two triangles in a quad.

Introducing Quads

Using the `VERTEX` struct as a basis, you can then create a struct that will help with creating and keeping track of quads:

```
struct QUAD
{
    VERTEX vertices[4];
    LPDIRECT3DVERTEXBUFFER9 buffer;
    LPDIRECT3DTEXTURE9 texture;
};
```

The QUAD struct is completely self-contained as far as the data goes. Here you have the four vertices for the four corners of the quad (made up of two triangles); you have the vertex buffer for this single quad (more on that in a minute) and you have the texture that is mapped onto the two triangles. Pretty cool, huh? The only thing missing is the code that actually creates a quad and fills the vertices with real 3D points. First, let's write a function to create a single vertex. That can then be used to create the four vertices of the quad:

```
VERTEX CreateVertex(float x, float y, float z, float tu, float tv)
{
    VERTEX vertex;
    vertex.x = x;
    vertex.y = y;
    vertex.z = z;
    vertex.tu = tu;
    vertex.tv = tv;
    return vertex;
}
```

This function just declares a temporary VERTEX variable, fills it in with the values passed to it via parameters, and then returns it. This is very convenient because there are five member variables in the VERTEX struct. I'll show you how to create and draw a quad in a bit. But first you need to learn about the vertex buffer.

Vertex Buffers

The vertex buffer is not as scary as it might sound. My first impression of a vertex buffer was that it was some kind of surface onto which the 3D objects are drawn before being sent to the screen, sort of like a double buffer for 3D. I couldn't have been more wrong! A vertex buffer is just a place where you store the points that make up a polygon so that Direct3D can draw it. You *can* technically have many vertex buffers in your program—one for each triangle if you want.

For the sake of clarity and for illustrative purposes, I will be showing you how to get 3D objects on the screen by giving each object its own vertex buffer. As I'm basing this chapter on the concept of a quad (made up of two triangles arranged in a "strip"), it makes sense to create a vertex buffer for each quad in the scene, to help you understand what's going on, and it really helps when you are just learning this material for the first time. Having a vertex buffer for each quad makes it crystal-clear what's going on when a quad is rendered.

The vertex buffer is the subject of much discussion regarding optimization and efficiency. In fact, most 3D engines employ what is called a *vertex buffer cache* that contains *all* of the vertices that will be visible in the camera's view. Powerful 3D engines also use what's called a *texture cache* so that textures are re-used by polygons that share them. In case you are curious as to why this is the case, understand that a 3D card can only "use" one texture at a time. Therefore, it is more efficient to tell Direct3D to *use* a texture only once—and then use that texture throughout the scene on any polygon that needs it before going to the next texture. This is where a texture cache comes in handy, as it will take care of these kinds of issues.

Creating a Vertex Buffer

To get started, you must define a variable for the vertex buffer:

```
LPDIRECT3DVERTEXBUFFER9 buffer;
```

Next, you can create the vertex buffer by using the `CreateVertexBuffer` function. It has this format:

```
HRESULT CreateVertexBuffer(
    UINT Length,
    DWORD Usage,
    DWORD FVF,
    D3DPOOL Pool,
    IDirect3DVertexBuffer9** ppVertexBuffer,
    HANDLE* pSharedHandle
);
```

The first parameter specifies the size of the vertex buffer, which should be big enough to hold all of the vertices for the polygons you want to render. The second parameter specifies the way in which you plan to access the vertex buffer, which is usually write-only. The third parameter specifies the vertex stream type that Direct3D expects to receive. You should pass the values corresponding to the type of vertex struct you have created. Here, we have just the position and texture coordinates in each vertex, so this value will be D3DFVF_XYZ | D3DFVF_TEX1 (note that values are combined with *or*). Here is how I define the vertex format:

```
#define D3DFVF_MYVERTEX (D3DFVF_XYZ | D3DFVF_TEX1)
```

The fifth parameter specifies the vertex buffer pointer, and the last parameter is not needed. How about an example? Here y'go:

```
d3ddev->CreateVertexBuffer(
    4*sizeof(VERTEX),
    D3DUSAGE_WRITEONLY,
    D3DFVF_MYVERTEX,
    D3DPOOL_DEFAULT,
    &buffer,
    NULL);
```

As you can see, the first parameter receives an integer that is sizeof(VERTEX) times four (because there are four vertices in a quad). If you are drawing just a single triangle, you would specify 3 * sizeof(VERTEX), and so on for however many vertices are in your 3D object. The only really important parameters, then, are the vertex buffer length and pointer (first and fifth, respectively).

Filling the Vertex Buffer

The last step in creating a vertex buffer is to fill it with the actual vertices of your polygons. This step must follow any code that generates or loads the vertex array, as it will plug the data into the vertex buffer. For reference, here is the definition for the QUAD struct once more (pay particular attention to the VERTEX array):

```
struct QUAD
{
    VERTEX vertices[4];
    LPDIRECT3DVERTEXBUFFER9 buffer;
    LPDIRECT3DTEXTURE9 texture;
};
```

You can use the CreateVertex function, for instance, to set up the default values for a quad:

```
vertices[0] = CreateVertex(-1.0f, 1.0f, 0.0f, 0.0f, 0.0f);
vertices[1] = CreateVertex(1.0f, 1.0f, 0.0f, 1.0f, 0.0f);
vertices[2] = CreateVertex(-1.0f,-1.0f, 0.0f, 0.0f, 1.0f);
vertices[3] = CreateVertex(1.0f,-1.0f, 0.0f, 1.0f, 1.0f);
```

That is just one way to fill the vertices with data. You might define a different type of polygon somewhere in your program or load a 3D shape from a file (more on that in the next chapter!).

After you have your vertex data, you can plug it into the vertex buffer. To do so, you must Lock the vertex buffer, copy your vertices into the vertex buffer, and then Unlock the vertex buffer. Doing so requires a temporary pointer. Here is how you set up the vertex buffer with data that Direct3D can use:

```
void *temp = NULL;
buffer->Lock( 0, sizeof(vertices), (void**)&temp, 0 );
memcpy(temp,vertices, sizeof(vertices) );
buffer->Unlock();
```

For reference, here is the Lock definition. The second and third parameters are the important ones; they specify the length of the buffer and a pointer to it.

```
HRESULT Lock(
    UINT OffsetToLock,
    UINT SizeToLock,
    VOID **ppbData,
    DWORD Flags
);
```

Rendering the Vertex Buffer

After initializing the vertex buffer, it will be ready for the Direct3D graphics pipeline and your source vertices will no longer matter. This is called the "setup," and it is one of the features that have been moved out of the Direct3D drivers and into the GPU in recent years. Streaming the vertices and textures from the vertex buffer into the scene is handled much more quickly by a hard-coded chip than it is by software.

In the end, it's all about rendering what's inside the vertex buffer, so let's learn how to do just that. To send the vertex buffer that you're currently working on to the screen, set the stream source for the Direct3D device so that it points to your vertex buffer, and then call the DrawPrimitive function. Before doing this, you must first set the texture to be used. This is one of the most confusing aspects of 3D graphics, especially for a beginner. Direct3D deals with just one texture at a time, so you have to tell it which texture to use each time it changes or Direct3D will just use the last-defined texture for the entire scene! Kind of weird, huh? Well, it makes sense if you think about it. There is no pre-programmed way to tell Direct3D to use "this" texture for one polygon and "that" texture for the next polygon. You just have to write this code yourself each time the texture needs to be changed.

Well, in the case of a quad, we're just dealing with a single texture for each quad, so the concept is easier to grasp. You can create any size vertex buffer you want, but you will find it easier to understand how 3D rendering works by giving each quad its own vertex buffer. This is not the most efficient way to draw 3D objects on the screen, but it works great while you are learning the basics! Each quad can have a vertex buffer as well as a texture, and the source code to render a quad is therefore easy to grasp. As you can imagine, this makes things a lot easier to deal with because you can write a function to draw a quad, with its vertex buffer and texture easily accessible in the QUAD struct.

First, set the texture for this quad:

```
d3ddev->SetTexture(0, texture);
```

Next, set the stream source so that Direct3D knows where the vertices come from and how many need to be rendered:

```
d3ddev->SetStreamSource(0, q.buffer, 0, sizeof(VERTEX));
```

Finally, draw the primitive specified by the stream source, including the rendering method, starting vertex, and number of polys to draw:

```
d3ddev->DrawPrimitive(D3DPT_TRIANGLESTRIP, 0, 2);
```

Obviously, these three functions can be put into a reusable Draw function together (more on that shortly).

Creating a Quad

I don't know if *quad* is an official term, but it doesn't matter, because the term describes what I want to do on two levels. The first aspect of the term *quad* is that it represents four corners of a rectangle, which is the building block of most 3D scenes. You can build almost anything with a bunch of cubes (each of which is made up of six quads). As you might have guessed, those corners are represented as vertices. The second aspect of a quad is that it represents the four vertices of a triangle strip.

Drawing Triangles

There are two ways you can draw objects (all of which are made up of triangles):

- A triangle list draws every single polygon independently, each with a set of three vertices.

- A triangle strip draws many polygons that are connected with shared vertices.

Obviously, the second method is more efficient and, therefore, preferable, and it helps to speed up rendering because fewer vertices must be used. But you can't render the entire scene with triangle strips because most objects are not connected to each other. Now, triangle strips work great for things like ground terrain, buildings, and other large objects. It also works well for smaller objects like the characters in your game. But what helps here is an understanding that Direct3D will render the scene at the same speed regardless of whether all the triangles are in a single vertex buffer or in multiple vertex buffers. Think of it as a series of `for` loops. Tell me which one of these two sections of code is faster. Ignore the `num++` part and just assume that "something useful" is happening inside the loop.

```
for (int n=0; n<1000; n++) num++;
```

or

```
(for int n=0; n<250; n++) num++;
(for int n=0; n<250; n++) num++;
(for int n=0; n<250; n++) num++;
(for int n=0; n<250; n++) num++;
```

What do you think? It might seem obvious that the first code is faster because there are fewer calls. Someone who is into optimization might think the second code listing is faster because perhaps it avoids a few `if` statements here and there (it's always faster to unroll a loop and put `if` statements outside of them).

Unrolling a Loop

What do I mean when I say *unrolling a loop*? (This is not directly related to 3D, but helpful nonetheless.) Take a look at the following two groups of code (from a fictional line-drawing function, assume x and y have already been defined):

```
for (x=0; x<639; x++)
    if (x % 2 == 0)
        DrawPixel(x, y, BLUE);
    else
        DrawPixel(x, y, RED);
and
for (x=0; x<639; x+=2)
    DrawPixel(x, y, BLUE);
for (x=1; x<639; x+=2)
    DrawPixel(x, y, RED);
```

The second snippet of code is probably twice as fast as the first one because the loops have been unrolled and the if statement has been removed. Try to think about optimization issues like this as you work on a game because loops should be coded carefully. The for loop doesn't actually take up any processor time itself; it's the code executed *by* the for loop that is important to consider.

A quad is made up of two triangles. The quad requires only four vertices because the triangles will be drawn as a triangle strip. Check out Figure 12.8 to see the difference between the two types of triangle rendering methods.

Figure 12.9 shows some other possibilities for triangle strips. You can join any two vertices that share a side.

Creating a Quad

Creating a quad requires even less effort than creating two attached triangles, thanks to the triangle strip rendering process. To draw any polygon, whether it is a triangle, quad, or complete model, there are two basic steps involved.

First, you must copy the vertices into a Direct3D vertex stream. To do this, you first lock the vertex buffer, then copy the vertices to a temporary storage location with a pointer variable, then unlock the vertex buffer.

```
void *temp = NULL;
quad->buffer->Lock(0, sizeof(quad->vertices), (void**)&temp, 0);
memcpy(temp, quad->vertices, sizeof(quad->vertices));
quad->buffer->Unlock();
```

Triangle List

Triangle Strip
(V1 and V3 are shared)

Figure 12.8
Triangle list and triangle strip rendering methods compared and contrasted.

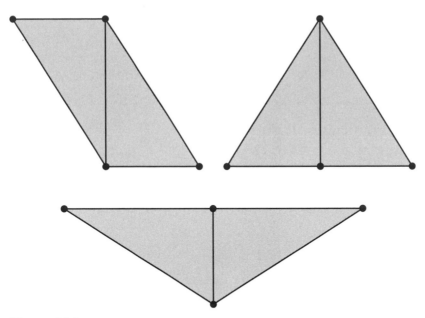

Figure 12.9
A triangle strip can take many forms. Note also that many more than two polygons can be used.

The next step is to set the texture, tell Direct3D where to find the stream source containing vertices, and then call on the DrawPrimitive function to draw the polygons specified in the vertex buffer stream. I like to think of this as a *Star Trek-esque* transporter. The polygons are transported from the vertex buffer into the stream and re-assembled on the screen!

```
d3ddev->SetTexture(0, quad->texture);
d3ddev->SetStreamSource(0, quad->buffer, 0, sizeof(VERTEX));
d3ddev->DrawPrimitive(D3DPT_TRIANGLESTRIP, 0, 2);
```

Advice
_____

Now that you have a working understanding of how to create and render individual polygons comprised of vertices using the very low-level 3D graphics programming features of Direct3D (namely, by manipulating and rendering a vertex buffer), you have gotten your hands greasy (so to speak) on the inner workings of 3D rendering. You should feel good about that! Not everyone has the ability to grasp 3D graphics programming, let alone master it and produce quality scenes.

The good news is that we will not be working with vertex buffers beyond this chapter. I will go over one complete example with you (the Textured Cube demo, covered shortly), but then we'll move on to loading and rendering mesh files using the .X file format.
_____

The Textured Cube Demo

Let's get realistic here. No one cares about drawing shaded and colored triangles, so I'm not going to waste time on the subject. Are you going to create a complete 3D game by programming triangles to assemble themselves into objects and then move them around and do collision checking and so on? Of course not, so why spend time learning about it? Triangles are critical to a 3D system, but not very useful in the singular sense. Only when you combine triangles do things get interesting.

The really interesting thing about modern 3D APIs is that it is easier to create a textured quad than one with shading. I will avoid the subject of dynamic lighting because it is beyond the scope of this book; ambient lighting will suffice for our purposes here. We will explore camera and lighting in more detail in an upcoming chapter.

The Textured_Cube program (shown in Figure 12.10) draws a textured cube on the screen and rotates it in the x and z axes.

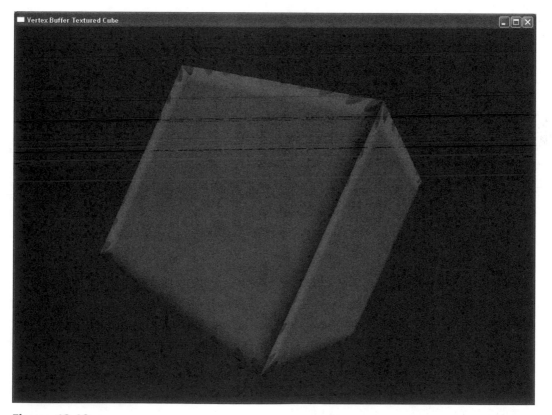

Figure 12.10
The Textured_Cube program demonstrates how to render a cube based on a vertex buffer created from scratch (i.e. the "hard way").

While it might seem like there are only eight vertices in a cube (refer to Figure 12.11), there are actually many more, because each triangle must have its own set of three vertices. But as you learned recently, a triangle strip works well to produce a quad with only four vertices.

As you have just worked with triangles and quads up to this point, a short introduction to cubes is in order. A cube is considered one of the simplest 3D objects you can create, and is a good shape to use as an example because it has six equal sides. As all objects in a 3D environment must be made up of triangles, it follows that a cube must also be made up of triangles. In fact, each side of a cube (which is a rectangle) is really two right triangles positioned side by side with the two right angles at opposing corners. See Figure 12.12.

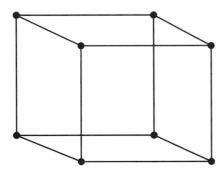

Figure 12.11
A cube has eight corners, each of which is represented by a vertex.

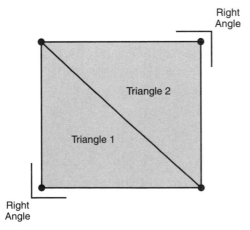

Figure 12.12
A rectangle is made up of two right triangles.

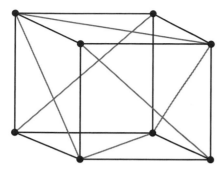

Figure 12.13
A cube is made up of six sides, with twelve triangles in all.

Advice

A right triangle is a triangle that has one 90-degree angle and is the preferred shape for 3D graphics. If you do not supply a right triangle to the video card, it will break up your oddly-shaped triangle into two or more right triangles—yes, it's that important!

After you have put together a cube using triangles, you end up with something like Figure 12.13. This figure shows the cube subdivided into triangles.

MyGame.cpp

Now it's time for the Textured_Cube program source code. I encourage you to load the project off the CD-ROM (which should be copied to your hard drive for convenience). If you think it's strange to create a 3D model using code as shown below, you would be right on the mark. This is indeed odd, but it is helpful at this point to illustrate how vertices are used to build polygons, which then make up models (also called meshes). It would be very difficult to create any type of complex 3D model using code like this, so it's only really useful for a simple example. Soon we'll learn how to load a mesh file into memory and render a complex mesh with lighting.

Advice

The complete source code for the Textured_Cube program is included here in this one listing. No changes to any of our support files are needed at this time.

```cpp
#include "MyDirectX.h"
using namespace std;

const string APPTITLE = "Vertex Buffer Textured Cube";
```

```
const int SCREENW = 1024;
const int SCREENH = 768;

DWORD screentimer = timeGetTime();

//vertex and quad definitions
#define D3DFVF_MYVERTEX (D3DFVF_XYZ | D3DFVF_TEX1)
struct VERTEX
{
    float x, y, z;
    float tu, tv;
};
struct QUAD
{
    VERTEX vertices[4];
    LPDIRECT3DVERTEXBUFFER9 buffer;
    LPDIRECT3DTEXTURE9 texture;
};

VERTEX cube[] = {
    {-1.0f, 1.0f,-1.0f, 0.0f,0.0f},    //side 1
    { 1.0f, 1.0f,-1.0f, 1.0f,0.0f },
    {-1.0f,-1.0f,-1.0f, 0.0f,1.0f },
    { 1.0f,-1.0f,-1.0f, 1.0f,1.0f },

    {-1.0f, 1.0f, 1.0f, 1.0f,0.0f },    //side 2
    {-1.0f,-1.0f, 1.0f, 1.0f,1.0f },
    { 1.0f, 1.0f, 1.0f, 0.0f,0.0f },
    { 1.0f,-1.0f, 1.0f, 0.0f,1.0f },

    {-1.0f, 1.0f, 1.0f, 0.0f,0.0f },    //side 3
    { 1.0f, 1.0f, 1.0f, 1.0f,0.0f },
    {-1.0f, 1.0f,-1.0f, 0.0f,1.0f },
    { 1.0f, 1.0f,-1.0f, 1.0f,1.0f },

    {-1.0f,-1.0f, 1.0f, 0.0f,0.0f },    //side 4
    {-1.0f,-1.0f,-1.0f, 1.0f,0.0f },
    { 1.0f,-1.0f, 1.0f, 0.0f,1.0f },
    { 1.0f,-1.0f,-1.0f, 1.0f,1.0f },

    { 1.0f, 1.0f,-1.0f, 0.0f,0.0f },    //side 5
    { 1.0f, 1.0f, 1.0f, 1.0f,0.0f },
    { 1.0f,-1.0f,-1.0f, 0.0f,1.0f },
    { 1.0f,-1.0f, 1.0f, 1.0f,1.0f },
```

```
    {-1.0f, 1.0f,-1.0f, 1.0f,0.0f },     //side 6
    {-1.0f,-1.0f,-1.0f, 1.0f,1.0f },
    {-1.0f, 1.0f, 1.0f, 0.0f,0.0f },
    {-1.0f,-1.0f, 1.0f, 0.0f,1.0f }
};

QUAD *quads[6];
D3DXVECTOR3 cameraSource;
D3DXVECTOR3 cameraTarget;


void SetPosition(QUAD *quad, int ivert, float x, float y, float z)
{
    quad->vertices[ivert].x = x;
    quad->vertices[ivert].y = y;
    quad->vertices[ivert].z = z;
}

void SetVertex(QUAD *quad, int ivert, float x, float y, float z, float tu, float tv)
{
    SetPosition(quad, ivert, x, y, z);
    quad->vertices[ivert].tu = tu;
    quad->vertices[ivert].tv = tv;
}

VERTEX CreateVertex(float x, float y, float z, float tu, float tv)
{
    VERTEX vertex;
    vertex.x = x;
    vertex.y = y;
    vertex.z = z;
    vertex.tu = tu;
    vertex.tv = tv;
    return vertex;
}

QUAD *CreateQuad(char *textureFilename)
{
    QUAD *quad = (QUAD*)malloc(sizeof(QUAD));

    //load the texture
    D3DXCreateTextureFromFile(d3ddev, textureFilename, &quad->texture);
```

```
    //create the vertex buffer for this quad
      d3ddev->CreateVertexBuffer(
        4*sizeof(VERTEX),
        0,
        D3DFVF_MYVERTEX, D3DPOOL_DEFAULT,
        &quad->buffer,
        NULL);

    //create the four corners of this dual triangle strip
    //each vertex is X,Y,Z and the texture coordinates U,V
    quad->vertices[0] = CreateVertex(-1.0f, 1.0f, 0.0f, 0.0f, 0.0f);
    quad->vertices[1] = CreateVertex( 1.0f, 1.0f, 0.0f, 1.0f, 0.0f);
    quad->vertices[2] = CreateVertex(-1.0f,-1.0f, 0.0f, 0.0f, 1.0f);
    quad->vertices[3] = CreateVertex( 1.0f,-1.0f, 0.0f, 1.0f, 1.0f);

    return quad;
}

void DeleteQuad(QUAD *quad)
{
    if (quad == NULL)
        return;

    //free the vertex buffer
    if (quad->buffer != NULL)
        quad->buffer->Release();

    //free the texture
    if (quad->texture != NULL)
        quad->texture->Release();

    //free the quad
    free(quad);
}

void DrawQuad(QUAD *quad)
{
    //fill vertex buffer with this quad's vertices
    void *temp = NULL;
    quad->buffer->Lock(0, sizeof(quad->vertices), (void**)&temp, 0);
    memcpy(temp, quad->vertices, sizeof(quad->vertices));
    quad->buffer->Unlock();
```

```
    //draw the textured dual triangle strip
    d3ddev->SetTexture(0, quad->texture);
    d3ddev->SetStreamSource(0, quad->buffer, 0, sizeof(VERTEX));
      d3ddev->DrawPrimitive(D3DPT_TRIANGLESTRIP, 0, 2);
}

void SetIdentity()
{
    //set default position, scale, and rotation
    D3DXMATRIX matWorld;
    D3DXMatrixTranslation(&matWorld, 0.0f, 0.0f, 0.0f);
    d3ddev->SetTransform(D3DTS_WORLD, &matWorld);
}

void ClearScene(D3DXCOLOR color)
{
    d3ddev->Clear(0, NULL, D3DCLEAR_TARGET | D3DCLEAR_ZBUFFER, color, 1.0f, 0 );
}

void SetCamera(float x, float y, float z, float lookx, float looky, float lookz)
{
    D3DXMATRIX matView;
    D3DXVECTOR3 updir(0.0f,1.0f,0.0f);

    //move the camera
    cameraSource.x = x;
    cameraSource.y = y;
    cameraSource.z = z;

    //point the camera
    cameraTarget.x = lookx;
    cameraTarget.y = looky;
    cameraTarget.z = lookz;

    //set up the camera view matrix
    D3DXMatrixLookAtLH(&matView, &cameraSource, &cameraTarget, &updir);
    d3ddev->SetTransform(D3DTS_VIEW, &matView);
}

void SetPerspective(float fieldOfView, float aspectRatio, float nearRange,
float farRange)
{
```

```
        //set the perspective so things in the distance will look smaller
        D3DXMATRIX matProj;
        D3DXMatrixPerspectiveFovLH(&matProj, fieldOfView, aspectRatio,
            nearRange, farRange);
        d3ddev->SetTransform(D3DTS_PROJECTION, &matProj);
    }


    void init_cube()
    {
        for (int q=0; q<6; q++)
        {
            int i = q*4; //little shortcut into cube array
            quads[q] = CreateQuad("cube.bmp");
            for (int v=0; v<4; v++)
            {
                quads[q]->vertices[v] = CreateVertex(
                    cube[i].x, cube[i].y, cube[i].z,      //position
                    cube[i].tu, cube[i].tv);              //texture coords
                i++;    //next vertex
            }
        }
    }

    bool Game_Init(HWND window)
    {
        srand(time(NULL));

        //initialize Direct3D
        if (!Direct3D_Init(window, SCREENW, SCREENH, false))
        {
            MessageBox(window,"Error initializing Direct3D",APPTITLE.c_str(),0);
            return false;
        }

        //initialize DirectInput
        if (!DirectInput_Init(window))
        {
            MessageBox(window,"Error initializing DirectInput",
            APPTITLE.c_str(),0);
            return false;
        }
        //initialize DirectSound
```

```
    if (!DirectSound_Init(window))
    {
        MessageBox(window,"Error initializing DirectSound",
        APPTITLE.c_str(),0);
        return false;
    }


    //position the camera
    SetCamera(0.0f, 2.0f, -3.0f, 0, 0, 0);

    float ratio = (float)SCREENW / (float)SCREENH;
    SetPerspective(45.0f, ratio, 0.1f, 10000.0f);

    //turn dynamic lighting off, z-buffering on
    d3ddev->SetRenderState(D3DRS_LIGHTING, FALSE);
    d3ddev->SetRenderState(D3DRS_ZENABLE, TRUE);

    //set the Direct3D stream to use the custom vertex
    d3ddev->SetFVF(D3DFVF_MYVERTEX);

    //convert the cube values into quads
    init_cube();

    return true;
}


void rotate_cube()
{
    static float xrot = 0.0f;
    static float yrot = 0.0f;
    static float zrot = 0.0f;

    //rotate the x and y axes
    xrot += 0.05f;
    yrot += 0.05f;


    //create the matrices
    D3DXMATRIX matWorld;
    D3DXMATRIX matTrans;
    D3DXMATRIX matRot;
```

```
        //get an identity matrix
        D3DXMatrixTranslation(&matTrans, 0.0f, 0.0f, 0.0f);

        //rotate the cube
        D3DXMatrixRotationYawPitchRoll(&matRot,
                            D3DXToRadian(xrot),
                            D3DXToRadian(yrot),
                            D3DXToRadian(zrot));
    matWorld = matRot * matTrans;

        //complete the operation
        d3ddev->SetTransform(D3DTS_WORLD, &matWorld);
}

void Game_Run(HWND window)
{
    if (!d3ddev) return;
    DirectInput_Update();
    d3ddev->Clear(0, NULL, D3DCLEAR_TARGET | D3DCLEAR_ZBUFFER,
        D3DCOLOR_XRGB(0,0,100), 1.0f, 0);

    // slow rendering to approximately 60 fps
    if (timeGetTime() > screentimer + 14)
    {
        screentimer = GetTickCount();

        rotate_cube();

        //start rendering
        if (d3ddev->BeginScene())
        {
            for (int n=0; n<6; n++)
                DrawQuad(quads[n]);

            //stop rendering
            d3ddev->EndScene();
            d3ddev->Present(NULL, NULL, NULL, NULL);
        }
    }

    //exit with escape key or controller Back button
    if (KEY_DOWN(VK_ESCAPE)) gameover = true;
    if (controllers[0].wButtons & XINPUT_GAMEPAD_BACK) gameover = true;
```

```
}

void Game_End()
{
    for (int q=0; q<6; q++)
        DeleteQuad(quads[q]);

    DirectSound_Shutdown();
    DirectInput_Shutdown();
    Direct3D_Shutdown();
}
```

What You Have Learned

This chapter has given you an overview of 3D graphics programming. You have learned a lot about Direct3D, and have seen a textured cube demo. Here are the key points:

- You learned what vertices are and how they make up a triangle.

- You learned how to create a vertex structure.

- You learned about triangle strips and triangle lists.

- You learned how to create a vertex buffer and fill it with vertices.

- You learned about quads and how to create them.

- You learned about texture mapping.

- You learned how to create a spinning cube.

Review Questions

The following questions will help to reinforce the information you have learned in this chapter.

1. What is a vertex?

2. What is the vertex buffer used for?

3. How many vertices are there in a quad?

4. How many triangles make up a quad?

5. What is the name of the Direct3D function that draws a polygon?

6. What is the flexible vertex buffer used for?

7. What is the most common data type used to represent the X,Y,Z values of a vertex?

8. What is the DirectX function that converts an angle from degrees to radians?

9. What C function do we normally use to copy large amounts of vertex data into the vertex buffer?

10. Which standard matrix represents what we see through the virtual camera?

On Your Own

The following exercises will help to challenge your retention of the information in this chapter.

Exercise 1. The Textured_Cube program creates a rotating cube that is textured. Modify the program so that the cube spins faster or slower based on keyboard input.

Exercise 2. Modify the Textured_Cube program so that each of the six sides of the cube has a different texture. Hint: You may need to copy the code from DrawQuad into your main source code file in order to use different textures.

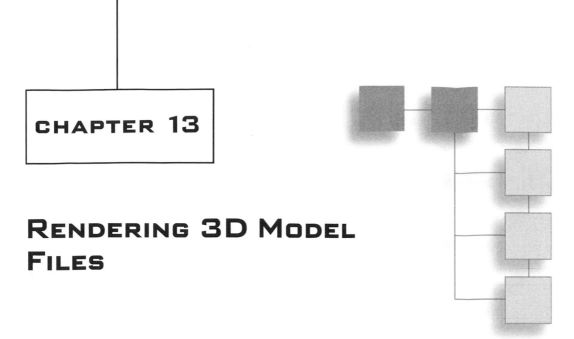

CHAPTER 13

RENDERING 3D MODEL FILES

This chapter is a natural follow-up to Chapter 12, in which you learned how to create and render a 3D textured cube from scratch using a raw vertex buffer. That was a good learning experience, but there's only so much you can do with a hand-coded mesh like a cube. This chapter takes it a step further, teaching you how to create stock 3D meshes at runtime using special Direct3D functions (which generate mesh shapes such as a cube, sphere, and cylinder), as well as how to load a mesh file from .X into memory and render it with texturing. We will be using just ambient lighting in this chapter.

Here is what you will learn in this chapter:

- How to create and render a stock mesh.

- How to load a mesh file into memory.

- How to transform and render a mesh.

Creating and Rendering Stock Meshes

I find it helpful to begin a study of 3D mesh rendering by exploring Direct3D's stock mesh functions. We have the ability to create a "runtime" mesh— that is, a mesh that is not loaded from file, but created algorithmically when the program runs. I call them stock meshes because they're built in to Direct3D and can be created at any time. In fact, stock meshes are incredibly helpful when making certain types of games that need to generate objects on the fly; for instance, the bullets in a scrolling shooter.

Advice
A *mesh* is a 3D object made up of vertices. The term "3D model" is deprecated.

Creating Stock Meshes

Direct3D has a number of stock mesh objects that it can create dynamically with functions that return an ID3DXMesh object. Here are some of the stock meshes we can create at runtime with Direct3D:

- Cube

- Sphere

- Cylinder

- Torus

- Teapot

There exists a function in Direct3D for creating each of these stock meshes. (There is also a function for creating 3D text and a simple polygon that I am not covering here.) When calling these functions, we will pass a pointer to a ID3DXMesh object that can be defined like so:

```
LPD3DXMESH mesh;
```

Please note that LPD3DXMESH is just a predefined pointer to a ID3DXMesh object and is defined by Direct3D as:

```
#define LPD3DXMESH *ID3DXMesh;
```

You can use either LPD3DXMESH or *ID3DXMesh when defining a mesh object, as the result is the same. I tend to use the former version since it's a little more consistent of a naming convention.

Advice

Although direct lights and shaders are much more impressive, these subjects are beyond the scope of the book, and would require several more chapters to properly explain! For this reason, I refer you to Appendix B for a list of books for further study. In addition, several examples of lighting and shaders are provided on the CD-ROM (look in \sources\AppendixD) and displayed in Appendix D for further study. These examples may not follow the book's format of using the "MyDirectX" files, but they share many of the same functions featured in this book.

Creating a Cube

Assuming you have defined your mesh object as explained above, you can create the vertices for a cube with the D3DXCreateBox function. Later in this chapter, I'll go over an example program called Stock_Mesh that demonstrates how to create and render stock meshes using these very functions. The output of this version of the program is shown in Figure 13.1.

```
D3DXCreateBox(d3ddev, 1.0f, 1.0f, 1.0f, &mesh, NULL);
```

Creating a Sphere

A sphere can be created dynamically at runtime with the D3DXCreateSphere function. The output of this version of the Stock_Mesh program is shown in Figure 13.2.

```
D3DXCreateSphere(d3ddev, 1.0f, 20, 20, &mesh, NULL);
```

Creating a Cylinder

To create a cylinder, which is quite a bit more complex than either of the two previous stock objects, you can use the D3DXCreateCylinder function, the output of which is shown in Figure 13.3.

```
D3DXCreateCylinder(d3ddev, 1.0f, 1.0f, 2.0f, 20, 20, &mesh, NULL);
```

Figure 13.1
Rendering a cube generated as a stock mesh.

Figure 13.2
Rendering a sphere generated as a stock mesh.

Figure 13.3
Rendering a cylinder generated as a stock mesh.

Figure 13.4
Rendering a torus generated as a stock mesh.

Creating a Torus

A torus is sort of a donut or wheel tube shaped object that can be created with the D3DXCreateTorus function. This is my favorite of the stock meshes because it demonstrates lighting so well (in a fully lit environment). The output is shown in Figure 13.4.

```
D3DXCreateTorus(d3ddev, 0.5f, 1.0f, 20, 20, &mesh, NULL);
```

Creating a Teapot

Finally, we have a real-world object that can be created dynamically: a teapot. This mesh has been featured in hundreds of books, articles, and websites over the years, so it's a bit of a celebrity. The output is shown in Figure 13.5.

```
D3DXCreateTeapot(d3ddev, &mesh, NULL);
```

Figure 13.5
Rendering a teapot generated as a stock mesh.

Rendering Stock Meshes

Although each of the stock meshes is created with a function that requires different sets of parameters, all of the stock mesh functions fill the same ID3DXMesh object with vertex data. This means these meshes are all treated in the same manner after they have been created. To render a mesh without concern for materials or textures, use the ID3DXMesh::DrawSubset function like so:

```
mesh->DrawSubset(0);
```

The Stock_Mesh Program

Let's create a working example that demonstrates how to create a stock mesh using one of the aforementioned functions and then render it (with rotation for good measure).

```
#include "MyDirectX.h"
using namespace std;

const string APPTITLE = "Stock Mesh Demo";
const int SCREENW = 1024;
const int SCREENH = 768;

DWORD screentimer = 0;

LPD3DXMESH mesh;


void SetCamera(float posx, float posy, float posz,
```

```
        float lookx = 0.0f, float looky=0.0f, float lookz=0.0f)
{
    float fov = D3DX_PI / 4.0;
    float aspectRatio = SCREENW / SCREENH;
    float nearRange = 1.0;
    float farRange = 2000.0;
    D3DXVECTOR3 updir = D3DXVECTOR3(0.0f, 1.0f, 0.0f);
    D3DXVECTOR3 position = D3DXVECTOR3(posx, posy, posz);
    D3DXVECTOR3 target = D3DXVECTOR3(lookx, looky, lookz);

    //set the perspective
    D3DXMATRIX matProj;
    D3DXMatrixPerspectiveFovLH(&matProj, fov, aspectRatio, nearRange, farRange);
    d3ddev->SetTransform(D3DTS_PROJECTION, &matProj);

    //set up the camera view matrix
    D3DXMATRIX matView;
    D3DXMatrixLookAtLH(&matView, &position, &target, &updir);
    d3ddev->SetTransform(D3DTS_VIEW, &matView);
}

bool Game_Init(HWND window)
{
    //initialize Direct3D
    if (!Direct3D_Init(window, SCREENW, SCREENH, false))
    {
        MessageBox(window,"Error initializing Direct3D",APPTITLE.c_str(),0);
        return false;
    }

    //initialize DirectInput
    if (!DirectInput_Init(window))
    {
        MessageBox(window,"Error initializing DirectInput",
        APPTITLE.c_str(),0);
        return false;
    }

    //initialize DirectSound
    if (!DirectSound_Init(window))
    {
        MessageBox(window,"Error initializing DirectSound",
        APPTITLE.c_str(),0);
```

```
            return false;
        }

    //set the camera position
    SetCamera( 0.0f, 1.0f, -4.0f );

    //use ambient lighting and z-buffering
    d3ddev->SetRenderState(D3DRS_ZENABLE, true);
    d3ddev->SetRenderState(D3DRS_LIGHTING, false);


    /**
     * create a stock 3D mesh: uncomment only one line at a time
     * and re-run the program to see each shape separately
     **/
    //D3DXCreateBox(d3ddev, 1.0f, 1.0f, 1.0f, &mesh, NULL);
    //D3DXCreateSphere(d3ddev, 1.0f, 20, 20, &mesh, NULL);
    //D3DXCreateCylinder(d3ddev, 1.0f, 1.0f, 2.0f, 20, 20, &mesh, NULL);
    D3DXCreateTorus(d3ddev, 0.5f, 1.0f, 20, 20, &mesh, NULL);
    //D3DXCreateTeapot(d3ddev, &mesh, NULL);

    return true;
}

void Game_Run(HWND window)
{
    if (!d3ddev) return;
    DirectInput_Update();
    d3ddev->Clear(0, NULL, D3DCLEAR_TARGET | D3DCLEAR_ZBUFFER,
        D3DCOLOR_XRGB(0,0,100), 1.0f, 0);


    // slow rendering to approximately 60 fps
    if (timeGetTime() > screentimer + 14)
    {
        screentimer = GetTickCount();

        //start rendering
        if (d3ddev->BeginScene())
        {
            //rotate the view
            D3DXMATRIX matWorld;
            D3DXMatrixRotationY(&matWorld, timeGetTime()/1000.0f);
            d3ddev->SetTransform(D3DTS_WORLD, &matWorld);
```

```
            //draw the mesh
            mesh->DrawSubset(0);

            //stop rendering
            d3ddev->EndScene();
            d3ddev->Present(NULL, NULL, NULL, NULL);
        }
    }

    //exit with escape key or controller Back button
    if (KEY_DOWN(VK_ESCAPE)) gameover = true;
    if (controllers[0].wButtons & XINPUT_GAMEPAD_BACK) gameover = true;
}

void Game_End()
{
    //free memory and shut down
    mesh->Release();

    DirectSound_Shutdown();
    DirectInput_Shutdown();
    Direct3D_Shutdown();
}
```

Loading and Rendering a Model File

Stock meshes can be very handy in a demo or a game. For example, I have used small spheres as bullets in a scrolling shooter! What we need to learn how to do next, though, is to read a 3D model out of a mesh file and render it. Are you ready? I said, *are you ready*!? Let's get to it, then.

Loading an .X File

Direct3D provides a function to create a mesh out of an .X file that is loaded, and that makes it very simple to read in any model file into your own games. We'll take it slowly, examining each step in detail, and end up with several reusable functions by the end of the chapter.

Defining a New MODEL Structure

First, we need a new struct to deal with model files that are to be loaded:

```
struct MODEL
{
```

```
    LPD3DXMESH mesh;
    D3DMATERIAL9* materials;
    LPDIRECT3DTEXTURE9* textures;
    DWORD material_count;
};
```

Some programmers and modelers prefer to call them "mesh" files, but I prefer the more descriptive "3D model" since it's easier for a beginner to understand. The MODEL struct contains the primary objects needed to load and render a model file. First, you have the mesh data (made up of vertices). Next, there is a D3DMATERIAL9 pointer variable that will be loaded with an array of materials defined in the model file. LPDIRECT3DTEXTURE9 should already be familiar to you after working with sprites, so no surprises here, except that a model may use multiple textures. These textures are not stored in the model file itself, but in separate bitmap files—only the texture *filenames* are stored in the model file.

Finally, there is a member variable that holds the number of materials in the model, which is used during rendering. There may be many materials in a model, but not every one is required to have a texture. However, a texture *must* be defined within a material. Hence, we have a material_count variable, but there is no need to keep track of the number of textures.

Loading a Mesh

The key to loading a model file resides in the D3DXLoadMeshFromX function:

```
HRESULT WINAPI D3DXLoadMeshFromX(
    LPCTSTR pFilename,
    DWORD Options,
    LPDIRECT3DDEVICE9 pDevice,
    LPD3DXBUFFER *ppAdjacency,
    LPD3DXBUFFER *ppMaterials,
    LPD3DXBUFFER *ppEffectInstances,
    DWORD *pNumMaterials,
    LPD3DXMESH *ppMesh
);
```

The parameters for this function are filled with either defaults (in one form or another) or NULLs, with key parameters being the filename, Direct3D device, material buffer, material count, and mesh object. First, you need a material buffer to load the materials into:

```
LPD3DXBUFFER matbuffer;
```

Let's also assume that a pointer to the MODEL struct has already been created:

```
MODEL *model = (MODEL*)malloc(sizeof(MODEL));
```

The struct is allocated in memory and returned by the LoadModel function (which I'll cover in a moment). Then you can read the model file and load the materials and meshes at the same time. Here is sample code that calls this function:

```
result = D3DXLoadMeshFromX(
    filename,                  //filename
    D3DXMESH_SYSTEMMEM,        //mesh options
    d3ddev,                    //Direct3D device
    NULL,                      //adjacency buffer
    &matbuffer,                //material buffer
    NULL,                      //special effects
    &model->material_count,    //number of materials
    &model->mesh);             //resulting mesh
```

Loading Materials and Textures

The materials are stored in the material buffer, but they need to be converted into Direct3D materials and textures before the model can be rendered. You are familiar with the texture object, but the material object, LPD3DXMATERIAL, is new.

Here is how you copy the materials and textures out of the material buffer and into individual material and texture arrays. First, let's create the arrays:

```
D3DXMATERIAL* d3dxMaterials = (LPD3DXMATERIAL)matbuffer->GetBufferPointer();
model->materials = new D3DMATERIAL9[model->material_count];
model->textures  = new LPDIRECT3DTEXTURE9[model->material_count];
```

The next step is to iterate through the materials and grab them out of the material buffer. For each material, the ambient color is set and the texture is loaded into the texture object. As these are dynamically allocated arrays, a model is limited only by available memory and the ability of your video card to render it. You could have a model with millions of faces, each with a different material.

```
//create the materials and textures
for(DWORD i=0; i<model->material_count; i++)
{
    //grab the material
    model->materials[i] = d3dxMaterials[i].MatD3D;

    //set ambient color for material
```

```
model->materials[i].Ambient = model->materials[i].Diffuse;

model->textures[i] = NULL;
if (d3dxMaterials[i].pTextureFilename != NULL)
{
    string filename = d3dxMaterials[i].pTextureFilename;
    if( FindFile(&filename) )
    {
        result = D3DXCreateTextureFromFile(
            d3ddev, filename.c_str(), &model->textures[i]);

        if (result != D3D_OK) {
            MessageBox(0,"Could not find texture",APPTITLE.c_str(),0);
            return false;
        }
    }
}
}
```

Did you notice the unknown function call, FindFile, in the code listing above? If you didn't, you should have been paying attention! That's a helper function that is really essential to loading textures in Direct3D. Very commonly, mesh files have embedded texture filenames with a complete path to the texture file hard-coded. When you load a mesh file and try to parse the texture filenames, you will get hard-coded pathnames representing the modeler's computer system that makes no sense in your game project.

(This is just a very common problem due to the way Maya and 3ds max in particular store texture filenames unless the modeler modifies the filenames manually.) So, we have to work around the problem. For example, Figure 13.6 shows the Fokker aircraft model file loaded into the DirectX Viewer. Note that it has no texture! This is because the texture file has a hard-coded path.

The texture file referenced by the Fokker.x file is Fokker.bmp and is shown in Figure 13.7. Note that most .X files are binary so you can't just open them and edit the texture pathname! Direct3D does support a text version of the .X file format but it is seldom used.

There are three functions here that work together to locate a texture file when a filename is encountered in a mesh. First, we have the FindFile function, which is embedded in our LoadMesh function. FindFile also needs two helper functions: DoesFileExist and SplitPath, which do pretty much what their names imply.

Figure 13.6
Viewing the Fokker aircraft model in the DirectX Viewer program.

Figure 13.7
The texture for the Fokker aircraft model.

```
void SplitPath(const string& inputPath, string* pathOnly, string* filenameOnly)
{
    string fullPath( inputPath );
    replace( fullPath.begin(), fullPath.end(), '\\', '/');
    string::size_type lastSlashPos = fullPath.find_last_of('/');

    // check for there being no path element in the input
    if (lastSlashPos == string::npos)
    {
        *pathOnly="";
        *filenameOnly = fullPath;
    }
    else {
        if (pathOnly) {
            *pathOnly = fullPath.substr(0, lastSlashPos);
        }
        if (filenameOnly)
        {
            *filenameOnly = fullPath.substr(
                lastSlashPos + 1,
                fullPath.size() - lastSlashPos - 1 );
        }
    }
}


bool DoesFileExist(const string &filename)
{
    return (_access(filename.c_str(), 0) != -1);
}


bool FindFile(string *filename)
{
    if (!filename) return false;

    //look for file using original filename and path
    if (DoesFileExist(*filename)) return true;

    //since the file was not found, try removing the path
    string pathOnly;
    string filenameOnly;
    SplitPath( *filename, &pathOnly, &filenameOnly);

    //is file found in current folder, without the path?
```

```
if (DoesFileExist(filenameOnly))
{
    *filename=filenameOnly;
    return true;
}

//not found
return false;
}
```

Rendering a Complete Model

Drawing the model is a piece of cake after it has been loaded. I'll admit, the code to load a model is not exactly easy to understand until you've walked through it line by line a few times. The rendering code is much easier, and should be quite understandable, as you have used the DrawPrimitive function already. Remember the Textured_Cube program in the previous chapter? That was just a simple example of what you must do now to render a 3D model.

First, you set the material, the texture, and then called DrawPrimitive to display that polygon (face). The biggest difference is that now you must iterate through the model and render each face individually using the material_count value and the DrawSubset function. The code is smart enough to skip the materials if there are none. Here is how it works:

```
//any materials in this mesh?
if (model->material_count == 0)
{
    model->mesh->DrawSubset(0);
}
else {
    //draw each mesh subset
    for( DWORD i=0; i < model->material_count; i++ )
    {
        // Set the material and texture for this subset
        d3ddev->SetMaterial( &model->materials[i] );

        if (model->textures[i])
        {
            if (model->textures[i]->GetType() == D3DRTYPE_TEXTURE)
            {
                D3DSURFACE_DESC desc;
                model->textures[i]->GetLevelDesc(0, &desc);
```

```
            if (desc.Width > 0) {
                d3ddev->SetTexture( 0, model->textures[i] );
            }
        }
    }

    // Draw the mesh subset
    model->mesh->DrawSubset( i );
    }
}
```

Deleting a Model from Memory

After you have finished with a MODEL object, you must free its resources or you could introduce a memory leak into your program. The assets in a game are usually released when the game is shutting down.

```
//remove materials from memory
if( model->materials != NULL )
    delete[] model->materials;

//remove textures from memory
if (model->textures != NULL)
{
    for( DWORD i = 0; i < model->material_count; i++)
    {
        if (model->textures[i] != NULL)
            model->textures[i]->Release();
    }
    delete[] model->textures;
}

//remove mesh from memory
if (model->mesh != NULL)
    model->mesh->Release();

//remove model struct from memory
if (model != NULL) free(model);
```

The Render_Mesh Program

I have written a complete program to load a mesh file (with an extension of .X) and render it fully shaded on the screen, and will now go over the source code for

Figure 13.8
The Render_Mesh program loads and renders a mesh from a .X file.

this program with you. Figure 13.8 shows the Render_Mesh program running. Pretty cool, isn't it?

Modifying MyDirectX.h

We will add some new functionality to the MyDirectX files now that we have some reusable 3D mesh loading and rendering code available. This code can be appended to the bottom of the file. I realize these DirectX helper files are growing a bit now, and contain a lot of code from different components, but it's very convenient this way. Note that the MODEL struct has evolved a bit from the early example we looked at earlier in the chapter, and it also includes a constructor that initializes its property variables. (Note: The MODEL struct and related function prototypes have already been added to the DirectX_Project template on the CD.)

```
//define the MODEL struct
struct MODEL
```

```
{
    LPD3DXMESH mesh;
    D3DMATERIAL9* materials;
    LPDIRECT3DTEXTURE9* textures;
    DWORD material_count;
    D3DXVECTOR3 translate;
    D3DXVECTOR3 rotate;
    D3DXVECTOR3 scale;

    MODEL()
    {
        material_count = 0;
        mesh = NULL;
        materials = NULL;
        textures = NULL;
        translate = D3DXVECTOR3(0.0f,0.0f,0.0f);
        rotate = D3DXVECTOR3(0.0f,0.0f,0.0f);
        scale = D3DXVECTOR3(1.0f,1.0f,1.0f);
    }
};


//3D mesh function prototypes
void DrawModel(MODEL *model);
void DeleteModel(MODEL *model);
MODEL *LoadModel(string filename);
bool FindFile(string *filename);
bool DoesFileExist(const string &filename);
void SplitPath(const string& inputPath, string* pathOnly, string* filenameOnly);
void SetCamera(float posx, float posy, float posz,
    float lookx = 0.0f, float looky=0.0f, float lookz=0.0f);
```

Modifying MyDirectX.cpp

Now we must make the following additions to the MyDirectX.cpp file. These are mainly reusable functions from existing code that I have shown you already. Just add this code to MyDirectX.cpp or open the finished project to examine the final result. (Note: These functions have already been added to the DirectX_Project template on the CD.)

```
void SetCamera(float posx, float posy, float posz,
    float lookx, float looky, float lookz)
{
    float fov = D3DX_PI / 4.0;
```

```
    float aspectRatio = SCREENW / SCREENH;
    float nearRange = 1.0;
    float farRange = 2000.0;
    D3DXVECTOR3 updir = D3DXVECTOR3(0.0f, 1.0f, 0.0f);
    D3DXVECTOR3 position = D3DXVECTOR3(posx, posy, posz);
    D3DXVECTOR3 target = D3DXVECTOR3(lookx, looky, lookz);

    //set the perspective
    D3DXMATRIX matProj;
    D3DXMatrixPerspectiveFovLH(&matProj, fov, aspectRatio, nearRange,
farRange);
    d3ddev->SetTransform(D3DTS_PROJECTION, &matProj);

    //set up the camera view matrix
    D3DXMATRIX matView;
    D3DXMatrixLookAtLH(&matView, &position, &target, &updir);
    d3ddev->SetTransform(D3DTS_VIEW, &matView);
}


void SplitPath(const string& inputPath, string* pathOnly, string* filenameOnly)
{
    string fullPath( inputPath );
    replace( fullPath.begin(), fullPath.end(), '\\', '/');
    string::size_type lastSlashPos = fullPath.find_last_of('/');

    // check for there being no path element in the input
    if (lastSlashPos == string::npos)
    {
        *pathOnly="";
        *filenameOnly = fullPath;
    }
    else {
        if (pathOnly) {
            *pathOnly = fullPath.substr(0, lastSlashPos);
        }
        if (filenameOnly)
        {
            *filenameOnly = fullPath.substr(
                lastSlashPos + 1,
                fullPath.size() - lastSlashPos - 1 );
        }
    }
}
```

```
}

bool DoesFileExist(const string &filename)
{
    return (_access(filename.c_str(), 0) != -1);
}

bool FindFile(string *filename)
{
    if (!filename) return false;

    //look for file using original filename and path
    if (DoesFileExist(*filename)) return true;

    //since the file was not found, try removing the path
    string pathOnly;
    string filenameOnly;
    SplitPath(*filename,&pathOnly,&filenameOnly);

    //is file found in current folder, without the path?
    if (DoesFileExist(filenameOnly))
    {
        *filename=filenameOnly;
        return true;
    }

    //not found
    return false;
}

MODEL *LoadModel(string filename)
{
    MODEL *model = (MODEL*)malloc(sizeof(MODEL));
    LPD3DXBUFFER matbuffer;
    HRESULT result;

    //load mesh from the specified file
    result = D3DXLoadMeshFromX(
        filename.c_str(),               //filename
        D3DXMESH_SYSTEMMEM,     //mesh options
        d3ddev,                 //Direct3D device
        NULL,                   //adjacency buffer
        &matbuffer,             //material buffer
        NULL,                   //special effects
```

```
        &model->material_count, //number of materials
        &model->mesh);          //resulting mesh

    if (result != D3D_OK)
    {
        MessageBox(0, "Error loading model file", APPTITLE.c_str(), 0);
        return NULL;
    }


    //extract material properties and texture names from material buffer
    LPD3DXMATERIAL d3dxMaterials = (LPD3DXMATERIAL)matbuffer->
    GetBufferPointer();
    model->materials = new D3DMATERIAL9[model->material_count];
    model->textures  = new LPDIRECT3DTEXTURE9[model->material_count];

    //create the materials and textures
    for(DWORD i=0; i<model->material_count; i++)
    {
        //grab the material
        model->materials[i] = d3dxMaterials[i].MatD3D;

        //set ambient color for material
        model->materials[i].Ambient = model->materials[i].Diffuse;

        model->textures[i] = NULL;
        if (d3dxMaterials[i].pTextureFilename != NULL)
        {
            string filename = d3dxMaterials[i].pTextureFilename;
            if( FindFile(&filename) )
            {
                result = D3DXCreateTextureFromFile(
                    d3ddev, filename.c_str(), &model->textures[i]);
                if (result != D3D_OK)
                {
                    MessageBox(0,"Could not find texture",
                        APPTITLE.c_str(),0);
                    return false;
                }
            }
        }
    }

    //done using material buffer
```

```
    matbuffer->Release();

    return model;
}

void DeleteModel(MODEL *model)
{
    //remove materials from memory
    if( model->materials != NULL )
        delete[] model->materials;

    //remove textures from memory
    if (model->textures != NULL)
    {
        for( DWORD i = 0; i < model->material_count; i++)
        {
            if (model->textures[i] != NULL)
                model->textures[i]->Release();
        }
        delete[] model->textures;
    }

    //remove mesh from memory
    if (model->mesh != NULL)
        model->mesh->Release();

    //remove model struct from memory
    if (model != NULL)
        free(model);
}

void DrawModel(MODEL *model)
{
    //any materials in this mesh?
    if (model->material_count == 0)
    {
        model->mesh->DrawSubset(0);
    }
    else {
        //draw each mesh subset
        for( DWORD i=0; i < model->material_count; i++ )
        {
            // Set the material and texture for this subset
```

```
            d3ddev->SetMaterial( &model->materials[i] );

            if (model->textures[i])
            {
                if (model->textures[i]->GetType() == D3DRTYPE_TEXTURE)
                {
                    D3DSURFACE_DESC desc;
                    model->textures[i]->GetLevelDesc(0, &desc);
                    if (desc.Width > 0) {
                        d3ddev->SetTexture( 0, model->textures[i] );
                    }
                }
            }

            // Draw the mesh subset
            model->mesh->DrawSubset( i );
        }
    }
}
```

The Render_Mesh Source Code (MyGame.cpp)

Now that the MyDirectX files have been updated with our reusable mesh code we can address the issue of the main source code for the demo program.

```
#include "MyDirectX.h"
using namespace std;

const string APPTITLE = "Render Mesh Demo";
const int SCREENW = 1024;
const int SCREENH = 768;

DWORD screentimer = timeGetTime();

MODEL *mesh=NULL;


bool Game_Init(HWND window)
{
    srand( (int)time(NULL) );

    //initialize Direct3D
    if (!Direct3D_Init(window, SCREENW, SCREENH, false))
    {
```

```
            MessageBox(window,"Error initializing Direct3D",APPTITLE.c_str(),0);
            return false;
        }

        //initialize DirectInput
        if (!DirectInput_Init(window))
        {
            MessageBox(window,"Error initializing DirectInput",
            APPTITLE.c_str(),0);
            return false;
        }

        //initialize DirectSound
        if (!DirectSound_Init(window))
        {
            MessageBox(window,"Error initializing DirectSound",
            APPTITLE.c_str(),0);
            return false;
        }


    //set the camera position
    SetCamera( 0.0f, -800.0f, -200.0f );

    //use ambient lighting and z-buffering
    d3ddev->SetRenderState(D3DRS_ZENABLE, true);
    d3ddev->SetRenderState(D3DRS_LIGHTING, false);

    //load the mesh file
    mesh = LoadModel("Fokker.X");
    if (mesh == NULL)
    {
        MessageBox(window, "Error loading mesh", APPTITLE.c_str(), MB_OK);
        return 0;
    }

    return true;
}

void Game_Run(HWND window)
{
    if (!d3ddev) return;
    DirectInput_Update();
    d3ddev->Clear(0, NULL, D3DCLEAR_TARGET | D3DCLEAR_ZBUFFER,
```

```
            D3DCOLOR_XRGB(0,0,100), 1.0f, 0);

    /*
     * slow rendering to approximately 60 fps
     */
    if (timeGetTime() > screentimer + 14)
    {
        screentimer = GetTickCount();

        //start rendering
        if (d3ddev->BeginScene())
        {
            //rotate the view
            D3DXMATRIX matWorld;
            D3DXMatrixRotationY(&matWorld, timeGetTime()/1000.0f);
            d3ddev->SetTransform(D3DTS_WORLD, &matWorld);

            //draw the model
            DrawModel(mesh);

            //stop rendering
            d3ddev->EndScene();
            d3ddev->Present(NULL, NULL, NULL, NULL);
        }
    }

    //exit with escape key or controller Back button
    if (KEY_DOWN(VK_ESCAPE)) gameover = true;
    if (controllers[0].wButtons & XINPUT_GAMEPAD_BACK) gameover = true;
}

void Game_End()
{
    //free memory and shut down
    DeleteModel(mesh);

    DirectSound_Shutdown();
    DirectInput_Shutdown();
    Direct3D_Shutdown();
}
```

You now have the ability to load a mesh file into your own game! There's so much potential here for what you can do now that it boggles the mind. The sky's the limit, really! Whatever kind of 3D game you can imagine—you now have the power to make it happen. There are, obviously, a lot of details to fill in along the way, but this is a terrific start. As usual, a ready-to-use project has already been provided for you to modify (see "DirectX_Project" in \sources\chapter13 on the CD-ROM).

What You Have Learned

This chapter has given you the information you need to load a model file into memory and render it with Direct3D! Here are the key points:

- You learned how to create and render stock objects at runtime.

- You learned how to load and render a mesh from an X file.

Review Questions

The following review questions will help you to determine if you grasped all of the information in this chapter.

1. What is the name of the Direct3D object that represents a mesh?

2. Which Direct3D function renders each face of a mesh one by one while our program iterates through the materials?

3. What is the name of the function you can use to load an X file into a Direct3D mesh?

4. What function would you use to draw each of the polygons in a model?

5. What is the Direct3D data type used to represent a texture in memory?

6. What is the name of the Direct3D data type used to store a matrix?

7. Which Direct3D function rotates a mesh on the Y axis?

8. Which standard matrix normally represents the current object being transformed and rendered in the scene?

9. Which standard matrix do we use to specify rendering properties such as the aspect ratio?

10. Which standard matrix represents the camera view?

On Your Own

The following exercises will help you to learn even more about the information in this chapter.

Exercise 1. Modify the Stock_Mesh program so that it draws two stock meshes at the same time on the screen.

Exercise 2. The Render_Mesh program demonstrates how to load an X file and render it on the screen. Modify the program so that it uses the keyboard or mouse to rotate the model rather than just watching it rotate on its own.

PART III

GAME PROJECT

The final part includes a single chapter that presents a nearly complete game for you to study, revise, tweak, and experiment on as an exercise in learning how a large-scale game, with a wide assortment of objects on the screen at once—moving and animating and interacting—is constructed.

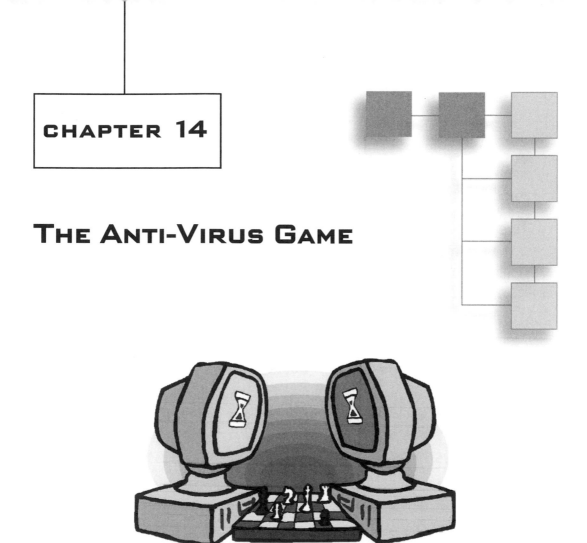

CHAPTER 14

THE ANTI-VIRUS GAME

This chapter is devoted to a single game project that effectively demonstrates all of the concepts we have studied in the previous 13 chapters! This single game is a prototype or work-in-progress which has been purposefully left in a simple state so that you can study it without being distracted or confused by the complexities of advanced gameplay, which tends to increase the size of a project by ten-fold in my experience. This game prototype weighs in at about 1,100 lines of well-spaced, well-commented code. I encourage you to study the code presented and explained in this chapter, and to open up the project on the CD, and enhance the game based on your own imagination! Here is what you will learn in this chapter:

- Creating the game project.

- Writing the source code.

The Anti-Virus Game

The Anti-Virus game featured in this chapter has been intentionally kept sparse on detail and function to encourage you to take it to the next level! The game features a scrolling background, a high-speed game loop that transforms and draws hundreds of sprites per frame, keyboard and Xbox 360 controller support, and some very interesting sound effects!

A d v i c e

All of the sound effects featured in the Anti-Virus game were created from sine waves, square waves, and saw waves using Audacity, a sound-editing program. Be sure to play the game with the speakers turned up!

The Anti-Virus game has a basic story and plot, but no formal game design document, so let me briefly explain the story to you. If this pseudo-game is to be turned into a formal game project, it will need a 30-second "elevator pitch":

NASA's supercomputer responsible for handling the Mars exploration rovers has been invaded by an alien computer virus transmitted from the rovers through their radio signals back to Earth. The alien virus is of a type never before encountered, and seems to behave more like a lifeform than a computer program.

The alien virus was able to translate itself to our computer systems after being downloaded. Now the virus is destroying all of the Mars data stored in the supercomputer! NASA engineers are worried that the alien computer virus might spread to other systems, so the infected supercomputer has been isolated. All known forms of anti-virus software and network security countermeasures have failed!

Until now! A new generation of nano-robotics has allowed us to construct a tiny remote-controlled robot. Your mission is simple: Enter the supercomputer's core memory and eradicate the alien menace!

Your nano-robot's codename is "R.A.I.N.e.R.": Remote-controlled Artificially Intelligent Nano-Robot. RAINeR is a completely self-contained, self-sustaining machine, but it does require energy to continue to function for long periods, especially with the extra virus-eradication gear installed. The core computer memory is filled with fragments of old programs and data that you can use to recharge your nanobot.

*Your mission is simple: Enter the supercomputer's memory through an aux-
iliary communication line, make your way through firewalls and stages of
memory toward the computer's core. Once there, you will destroy the first alien
virus— the "mother"— and gain access to its identity codes. Only then will we
be able to build a defense against its spread.*

Good luck!

Playing the Game

The Anti-Virus game already has many interesting gameplay features that simply
need to be connected together into a synergistic experience. For instance, the
game has support for weapon upgrades, but does not currently spawn any
power-ups for the player to pick up. In order to change the nanobot's firepower
upgrade level, you can press the F1 to F5 keys, with F1 being the default weapon
and F5 being the fully upgraded version.

Firepower 1

Figure 14.1 shows the first weapon, which is the default.

To fire a single shot, we still need to implement an array for the bullets and keep
track of timing so they don't come out of the nanobot like a fire hose! The code
for firing bullets is found in the player_shoot() function, in which there is a
switch statement that triggers code based on the firepower level of the nanobot.

```
case 1:
{
    //create a bullet
    int b1 = find_bullet();
    if (b1 == -1) return;
    bullets[b1].alive = true;
    bullets[b1].rotation = 0.0;
    bullets[b1].velx = 12.0f;
    bullets[b1].vely = 0.0f;
    bullets[b1].x = player.x + player.width/2;
    bullets[b1].y = player.y + player.height/2
        - bullets[b1].height/2;
}
break;
```

The bullet is positioned relative to the player's position with minor adjustments
so the bullets will appear right in front of the center of the nanobot. The other

Figure 14.1
Firing a single shot at a time with normal firepower.

four variations of firepower are based on this code. The graphical user interface (GUI) is a bit sparse but already taking shape, in the form of the energy bar at the top, and the computer's health bar at the bottom of the screen. As the game progresses, the alien virus will be doing damage to the computer and you must not only defeat the alien menace but also fix damage to the computer's systems as well (perhaps via short mini-games or objects that must be collected—the possibilities are endless!).

Firepower 2

The second firepower level is shown in Figure 14.2, and features two bullets streaming out of the nanobot toward the enemy virus programs (which are represented as translucent circles reminiscent of biological cells). You can engage this level with the F2 debug key.

Figure 14.2
Firing a double shot at a time with firepower level 2.

```
case 2:
{
    //create bullet 1
    int b1 = find_bullet();
    if (b1 == -1) return;
    bullets[b1].alive = true;
    bullets[b1].rotation = 0.0;
    bullets[b1].velx = 12.0f;
    bullets[b1].vely = 0.0f;
    bullets[b1].x = player.x + player.width/2;
    bullets[b1].y = player.y + player.height/2
        - bullets[b1].height/2;
    bullets[b1].y -= 10;

    //create bullet 2
    int b2 = find_bullet();
```

```
    if (b2 == -1) return;
    bullets[b2].alive = true;
    bullets[b2].rotation = 0.0;
    bullets[b2].velx = 12.0f;
    bullets[b2].vely = 0.0f;
    bullets[b2].x = player.x + player.width/2;
    bullets[b2].y = player.y + player.height/2
        - bullets[b2].height/2;
    bullets[b2].y += 10;
}
break;
```

Firepower 3

The third firepower level is shown in Figure 14.3, and features three bullets streaming out of the nanobot toward the enemy virus programs. While the second firepower level had the two bullets emerge at an equal distance apart from the

Figure 14.3
Firing a triple shot at a time with firepower level 3.

center of the nanobot, this third level features a center bullet with one bullet above and one below. Study the code that positions each bullet to understand how you might modify these firepower levels with your own custom bullet configurations.

```
case 3:
{
    //create bullet 1
    int b1 = find_bullet();
    if (b1 == -1) return;
    bullets[b1].alive = true;
    bullets[b1].rotation = 0.0;
    bullets[b1].velx = 12.0f;
    bullets[b1].vely = 0.0f;
    bullets[b1].x = player.x + player.width/2;
    bullets[b1].y = player.y + player.height/2
        - bullets[b1].height/2;

    //create bullet 2
    int b2 = find_bullet();
    if (b2 == -1) return;
    bullets[b2].alive = true;
    bullets[b2].rotation = 0.0;
    bullets[b2].velx = 12.0f;
    bullets[b2].vely = 0.0f;
    bullets[b2].x = player.x + player.width/2;
    bullets[b2].y = player.y + player.height/2
        - bullets[b2].height/2;
    bullets[b2].y -= 16;

    //create bullet 3
    int b3 = find_bullet();
    if (b3 == -1) return;
    bullets[b3].alive = true;
    bullets[b3].rotation = 0.0;
    bullets[b3].velx = 12.0f;
    bullets[b3].vely = 0.0f;
    bullets[b3].x = player.x + player.width/2;
    bullets[b3].y = player.y + player.height/2
        - bullets[b3].height/2;
    bullets[b3].y += 16;

}
break;
```

Firepower 4

The fourth weapon powerup features four bullets that truly look impressive, as you can see in Figure 14.4. This is the last of the powerups with just forward-facing bullets; we'll go in a different direction with the next powerup (pun intended!). Note how each of the four bullets below in the code listing are positioned and "fired" independently. Even though we see four bullets emerge together as a group, they are moving and interacting with the environment independent of each other. This is an important gameplay concept that I want you to grasp, so study the code! Most game code is just like this, taking a brute force approach with very simple code that is repeated as needed. If you are ever tempted to write a fancy algorithm or put these four bullets into a loop by some means, I encourage you to *not* do such a thing! Fancy algorithms do not translate into faster code, due to the way modern processor architectures have been designed, with long pipelines that handle sequences much better than algorithms.

Figure 14.4
Firing four shots at a time with firepower level 4.

```
case 4:
{
    //create bullet 1
    int b1 = find_bullet();
    if (b1 == -1) return;
    bullets[b1].alive = true;
    bullets[b1].rotation = 0.0;
    bullets[b1].velx = 12.0f;
    bullets[b1].vely = 0.0f;
    bullets[b1].x = player.x + player.width/2;
    bullets[b1].x += 8;
    bullets[b1].y = player.y + player.height/2
        - bullets[b1].height/2;
    bullets[b1].y -= 12;

    //create bullet 2
    int b2 = find_bullet();
    if (b2 == -1) return;
    bullets[b2].alive = true;
    bullets[b2].rotation = 0.0;
    bullets[b2].velx = 12.0f;
    bullets[b2].vely = 0.0f;
    bullets[b2].x = player.x + player.width/2;
    bullets[b2].x += 8;
    bullets[b2].y = player.y + player.height/2
        - bullets[b2].height/2;
    bullets[b2].y += 12;

    //create bullet 3
    int b3 = find_bullet();
    if (b3 == -1) return;
    bullets[b3].alive = true;
    bullets[b3].rotation = 0.0;
    bullets[b3].velx = 12.0f;
    bullets[b3].vely = 0.0f;
    bullets[b3].x = player.x + player.width/2;
    bullets[b3].y = player.y + player.height/2
        - bullets[b3].height/2;
    bullets[b3].y -= 32;

    //create bullet 4
    int b4 = find_bullet();
    if (b4 == -1) return;
```

```
        bullets[b4].alive = true;
        bullets[b4].rotation = 0.0;
        bullets[b4].velx = 12.0f;
        bullets[b4].vely = 0.0f;
        bullets[b4].x = player.x + player.width/2;
        bullets[b4].y = player.y + player.height/2
            - bullets[b4].height/2;
        bullets[b4].y += 32;
    }
    break;
```

Firepower 5

The fifth and final firepower upgrade is level five, and this one diverges from the pattern we've used in the previous four. In this one, we'll be firing bullets at an *angle* away from the nanobot rather than straight ahead. From this point onward, you can get as creative as you want with the firepower—I'll give you the necessary code and let you come up with some creative new possibilities! For starters, look at Figure 14.5.

Before you take the following code for granted, look more closely because it's a bit different from the previous firepower code! Let me show you what I mean. There are two new functions being used in this case. I'll highlight the function calls for you.

```
case 5:
{
    //create bullet 1
    int b1 = find_bullet();
    if (b1 == -1) return;
    bullets[b1].alive = true;
    bullets[b1].rotation = 0.0;
    bullets[b1].velx = 12.0f;
    bullets[b1].vely = 0.0f;
    bullets[b1].x = player.x + player.width/2;
    bullets[b1].y = player.y + player.height/2
        - bullets[b1].height/2;
    bullets[b1].y -= 12;

    //create bullet 2
    int b2 = find_bullet();
    if (b2 == -1) return;
```

Figure 14.5
Firing five shots at a time with firepower level 5.

```
bullets[b2].alive = true;
bullets[b2].rotation = 0.0;
bullets[b2].velx = 12.0f;
bullets[b2].vely = 0.0f;
bullets[b2].x = player.x + player.width/2;
bullets[b2].y = player.y + player.height/2
    - bullets[b2].height/2;
bullets[b2].y += 12;

//create bullet 3
int b3 = find_bullet();
if (b3 == -1) return;
bullets[b3].alive = true;
bullets[b3].rotation = -4.0;
    bullets[b3].velx = (float) (12.0 *
        LinearVelocityX( bullets[b3].rotation ));
```

```
        bullets[b3].vely = (float) (12.0 *
            LinearVelocityY( bullets[b3].rotation ));
    bullets[b3].x = player.x + player.width/2;
    bullets[b3].y = player.y + player.height/2
        - bullets[b3].height/2;
    bullets[b3].y -= 20;

    //create bullet 4
    int b4 = find_bullet();
    if (b4 == -1) return;
    bullets[b4].alive = true;
    bullets[b4].rotation = 4.0;
        bullets[b4].velx = (float) (12.0 *
            LinearVelocityX( bullets[b4].rotation ));
        bullets[b4].vely = (float) (12.0 *
            LinearVelocityY( bullets[b4].rotation ));
    bullets[b4].x = player.x + player.width/2;
    bullets[b4].y = player.y + player.height/2
        - bullets[b4].height/2;
    bullets[b4].y += 20;
}
break;
```

There are two forward-facing bullets and two that veer off at an angle, greatly increasing the potency of the shots since more of the screen is covered by this type of firepower! The key is in two functions: LinearVelocityX() and LinearVelocityY().

```
const double PI = 3.1415926535;
const double PI_over_180 = PI / 180.0f;

double LinearVelocityX(double angle)
{
    if (angle < 0) angle = 360 + angle;
    return cos( angle * PI_over_180);
}

double LinearVelocityY(double angle)
{
    if (angle < 0) angle = 360 + angle;
    return sin( angle * PI_over_180);
}
```

When you call either of these functions, you will need to pass the desired angle *in degrees.* The functions will convert degrees to radians internally, since the `sin()` and `cos()` (which calculate sine and cosine, respectively) deal only in radians. Pass your desired angle to `LinearVelocityX()`, and it will calculate the X velocity for a sprite that will need to move in that direction. Likewise, pass your desired angle to `LinearVelocityY()`, and it will calculate the Y velocity for a sprite. Together, you can cause a sprite (such as a bullet?) to move in the desired direction on the screen. The values will usually be small, in the range of 0.0 to 1.0, so if you want a sprite to move more quickly you can use a multiplier.

Advice

Remember that zero degrees, in the Cartesian coordinate system, is *to the right*, not *straight up* like a compass! Straight up is actually – 90 degrees, or +270 degrees (if you go around the circle clockwise). Straight down is +90 degrees.

Charging the Nanobot

All of this crazy firepower actually does have a cost—it consumes vast quantities of energy, and our little nanobot can only hold so much in its microscopic capacitors. So, a recharge is needed, and frequently! Fortunately, there are program fragments floating around in computer memory that you can consume. Press the keyboard X button or the controller X button to engage the recharge system, shown in Figure 14.6.

Overloading the Weapons System!

In addition to the normal levels of firepower, the RAINER nanobot can overload its weapon's system to produce a massive explosion of bullets all at once—handy for clearing the way when too many alien viri get too close! See Figure 14.7 for the overload sequence, and Figure 14.8 for the resulting energy storm of bullets blasted away! Due to the dangerous nature of overloading the weapon's system in this manner, the failsafe system will discharge the shots when the nanobot's energy capacitor reaches 50%. So, you must gain a full recharge for the most effective overload shot.

The Game's Source Code

Here is the complete source code for the game. What you will not find in this chapter is any code we've previously covered in the MyDirectX files and so forth.

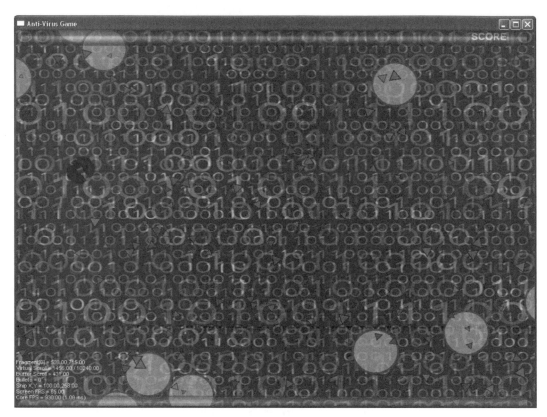

Figure 14.6
Charging the nanobot's capacitors by sucking in the geometric power nodes.

Even so, without any of the framework code we're looking at a pretty hefty 1,100 lines of code here—and this is only a *prototype* or *pseudo-game*, not the real Anti-Virus game! Throughout the source code listing, I will highlight important lines of code in bold that I want you to pay special attention to—because those lines of code are where you can make the most important changes to the game in the short term. As for the long term, well, we'll have to see how this game eventually turns out. Will *you* be the one who completes it?

```
/*
    Beginning Game Programming, Third Edition
    Anti-Virus Game
    MyGame.cpp
*/

#include "MyDirectX.h"
#include <sstream>
```

Figure 14.7
Preparing for an overload shot!

```
using namespace std;

const string APPTITLE = "Anti-Virus Game";
const int SCREENW = 1024;
const int SCREENH = 768;

//font variables
LPD3DXFONT font;
LPD3DXFONT debugfont;

//timing variables
bool paused = false;
DWORD refresh = 0;
DWORD screentime = 0;
double screenfps = 0.0;
double screencount = 0.0;
DWORD coretime = 0;
```

Figure 14.8
Launching the overload shot wipes out almost everything in sight!

```
double corefps = 0.0;
double corecount = 0.0;
DWORD currenttime;

//background scrolling variables
const int BUFFERW = SCREENW * 2;
const int BUFFERH = SCREENH;
double scrollx=0;
double scrolly=0;
LPDIRECT3DSURFACE9 background = NULL;
const double virtual_level_size = BUFFERW * 5;
double virtual_scrollx = 0;

//player variables
LPDIRECT3DTEXTURE9 player_ship;
SPRITE player;
enum PLAYER_STATES
```

```
{
    NORMAL = 0,
    PHASING = 1,
    CHARGING = 2,
    OVERLOADING = 3
};
PLAYER_STATES player_state = NORMAL;
PLAYER_STATES player_state_previous = NORMAL;
D3DXVECTOR2 position_history[8];
int position_history_index = 0;
DWORD position_history_timer = 0;
double charge_angle = 0.0;
double charge_tweak = 0.0;
double charge_tweak_dir = 1.0;
double energy = 100.0;
double health = 100.0;

//enemy virus objects
const int VIRUSES = 100;
LPDIRECT3DTEXTURE9 virus1_image;
SPRITE viruses[VIRUSES];

const int FRAGMENTS = 300;
LPDIRECT3DTEXTURE9 fragment_image;
SPRITE fragments[FRAGMENTS];

//bullet variables
LPDIRECT3DTEXTURE9 purple_fire;
const int BULLETS = 300;
SPRITE bullets[BULLETS];
int player_shoot_timer = 0;
int firepower = 1;
int bulletcount = 0;

//sound effects
CSound *tisk=NULL;
CSound *foom=NULL;
CSound *charging=NULL;


//GUI elements
LPDIRECT3DTEXTURE9 energy_slice;
LPDIRECT3DTEXTURE9 health_slice;
```

```
//controller vibration
int vibrating = 0;
int vibration = 100;


/**
 ** Game initialization
 **/
bool Game_Init(HWND window)
{
    Direct3D_Init(window, SCREENW, SCREENH, false);
    DirectInput_Init(window);
    DirectSound_Init(window);


    //create a font
    font = MakeFont("Arial Bold", 24);
    debugfont = MakeFont("Arial", 14);

    //load background
    LPDIRECT3DSURFACE9 image = NULL;
    image = LoadSurface("binary.bmp");
    if (!image) return false;


    //load player sprite
    player_ship = LoadTexture("ufo.png");
    player.x = 100;
    player.y = 350;
    player.width = player.height = 64;

    for (int n=0; n<4; n++)
        position_history[n] = D3DXVECTOR2(-100,0);

    //load bullets
    purple_fire = LoadTexture("purplefire.tga");
    for (int n=0; n<BULLETS; n++)
    {
        bullets[n].alive = false;
        bullets[n].x = 0;
        bullets[n].y = 0;
        bullets[n].width = 55;
        bullets[n].height = 16;
    }
```

```
//load enemy viruses
virus1_image = LoadTexture("virus1.tga");
for (int n=0; n<VIRUSES; n++)
{
    viruses[n].alive = true;
    viruses[n].width = 96;
    viruses[n].height = 96;
    viruses[n].x = (float)( 1000 + rand() % BUFFERW );
    viruses[n].y = (float)( rand() % SCREENH );
    viruses[n].velx = (float)((rand() % 8) * -1);
    viruses[n].vely = (float)(rand() % 2 - 1);
}


//load gui elements
energy_slice = LoadTexture("energyslice.tga");
health_slice = LoadTexture("healthslice.tga");


//load audio files
tisk = LoadSound("clip.wav");
foom = LoadSound("longfoom.wav");
charging = LoadSound("charging.wav");


//load memory fragments (energy)
fragment_image = LoadTexture("fragment.tga");
for (int n=0; n<FRAGMENTS; n++)
{
    fragments[n].alive = true;
    D3DCOLOR fragmentcolor = D3DCOLOR_ARGB(
        200 + rand() % 55,
        150 + rand() % 100,
        150 + rand() % 100,
        150 + rand() % 100);
    fragments[n].color = fragmentcolor;
    fragments[n].width = 128;
    fragments[n].height = 128;
    fragments[n].scaling = (float)(rand() % 20 + 10) / 150.0f;
    fragments[n].rotation = (float)( rand() % 360 );
    fragments[n].velx = (float)(rand() % 4 + 1) * -1.0f;
    fragments[n].vely = (float)(rand() % 10 - 5) / 10.0f;
    fragments[n].x = (float)( rand() % BUFFERW );
```

```
        fragments[n].y = (float)( rand() % SCREENH );
    }



    //create background for scroller
    HRESULT result =
    d3ddev->CreateOffscreenPlainSurface(
        BUFFERW,
        BUFFERH,
        D3DFMT_X8R8G8B8,
        D3DPOOL_DEFAULT,
        &background,
        NULL);
    if (result != D3D_OK) return false;

    //copy image to upper left corner of background
    RECT source_rect = {0, 0, SCREENW, SCREENH };
    RECT dest_ul = { 0, 0, SCREENW, SCREENH };

    d3ddev->StretchRect(
        image,
        &source_rect,
        background,
        &dest_ul,
        D3DTEXF_NONE);

    //copy image to upper right corner of background
    RECT dest_ur = { SCREENW, 0, SCREENW*2, SCREENH };

    d3ddev->StretchRect(
        image,
        &source_rect,
        background,
        &dest_ur,
        D3DTEXF_NONE);

    //get pointer to the back buffer
    d3ddev->GetBackBuffer(0, 0, D3DBACKBUFFER_TYPE_MONO,
        &backbuffer);


    //remove scratch image
    image->Release();
```

```
        return true;
}

/**
 ** Game shutdown
 **/
void Game_End()
{
        background->Release();
        font->Release();
        debugfont->Release();
        fragment_image->Release();
        delete charging;
        delete foom;
        delete tisk;
        energy_slice->Release();
        health_slice->Release();
        virus1_image->Release();
        purple_fire->Release();
        player_ship->Release();

        DirectSound_Shutdown();
        DirectInput_Shutdown();
        Direct3D_Shutdown();
}

/**
 ** Helper function used to print out variables
 **/
template <class T>
std::string static ToString(const T & t, int places = 2)
{
        ostringstream oss;
        oss.precision(places);
        oss.setf(ios_base::fixed);
        oss << t;
        return oss.str();
}

/**
 ** Updates the player's position
 **/
void move_player(float movex, float movey)
```

```
{
    //cannot move while overloading!
    if (player_state == OVERLOADING
        || player_state_previous == OVERLOADING)
        return;

    float multi = 4.0f;
    player.x += movex * multi;
    player.y += movey * multi;
}


/**
 ** Math helper functions
 **/
const double PI = 3.1415926535;
const double PI_under_180 = 180.0f / PI;
const double PI_over_180 = PI / 180.0f;

double toRadians(double degrees)
{
    return degrees * PI_over_180;
}

double toDegrees(double radians)
{
    return radians * PI_under_180;
}

double wrap(double value, double bounds)
{
    double result = fmod(value, bounds);
    if (result < 0) result += bounds;
    return result;
}

double wrapAngleDegs(double degs)
{
    return wrap(degs, 360.0);
}

double LinearVelocityX(double angle)
{
```

```
    //angle -= 90;
    if (angle < 0) angle = 360 + angle;
    return cos( angle * PI_over_180);
}

double LinearVelocityY(double angle)
{
    //angle -= 90;
    if (angle < 0) angle = 360 + angle;
    return sin( angle * PI_over_180);
}

/**
 ** Increases the energy capacitor level
 **/
void add_energy(double value)
{
    energy += value;
    if (energy < 0.0) energy = 0.0;
    if (energy > 100.0) energy = 100.0;
}

/**
 ** Handles vibrating the controller; most importantly,
 ** this function also helps to stop the vibration
 **/
void Vibrate(int contnum, int amount, int length)
{
    vibrating = 1;
    vibration = length;
    XInput_Vibrate(contnum, amount);
}

/**
 ** Look for an unused bullet in the array
 **/
int find_bullet()
{
    int bullet = -1;
    for (int n=0; n<BULLETS; n++)
    {
        if (!bullets[n].alive)
        {
```

```
                bullet = n;
                break;
            }
        }
    return bullet;
}


/**
 ** Add a bullet to the overload group
 **/
bool player_overload()
{
    //disallow overoad unless energy is at 100%
    if (energy < 50.0) return false;

    //reduce energy for this shot
    add_energy(-0.5);
    if (energy < 0.0)
    {
        energy = 0.0;
        return false;
    }

    //play charging sound
    PlaySound(charging);

    //vibrate controller
    Vibrate(0, 20000, 20);

    int b1 = find_bullet();
    if (b1 == -1) return true;
    bullets[b1].alive = true;
    bullets[b1].velx = 0.0f;
    bullets[b1].vely = 0.0f;
    bullets[b1].rotation = (float)(rand() % 360);
    bullets[b1].x = player.x + player.width;
    bullets[b1].y = player.y + player.height/2
        - bullets[b1].height/2;
    bullets[b1].y += (float)(rand() % 20 - 10);

    return true;
}
```

```
/**
 ** Fire a shot with firepower upgrades
 **/
void player_shoot()
{
    //limit firing rate
    if ((int)timeGetTime() < player_shoot_timer + 100) return;
    player_shoot_timer = timeGetTime();

    //reduce energy for this shot
    add_energy(-1.0);
    if (energy < 1.0)
    {
        energy = 0.0;
        return;
    }

    //play firing sound
    PlaySound(tisk);

    Vibrate(0, 25000, 10);

    //launch bullets based on firepower level
    switch(firepower)
    {
        case 1:
        {
            //create a bullet
            int b1 = find_bullet();
            if (b1 == -1) return;
            bullets[b1].alive = true;
            bullets[b1].rotation = 0.0;
            bullets[b1].velx = 12.0f;
            bullets[b1].vely = 0.0f;
            bullets[b1].x = player.x + player.width/2;
            bullets[b1].y = player.y + player.height/2
                - bullets[b1].height/2;
        }
        break;
        case 2:
        {
            //create bullet 1
            int b1 = find_bullet();
```

```
        if (b1 == -1) return;
        bullets[b1].alive = true;
        bullets[b1].rotation = 0.0;
        bullets[b1].velx = 12.0f;
        bullets[b1].vely = 0.0f;
        bullets[b1].x = player.x + player.width/2;
        bullets[b1].y = player.y + player.height/2
            - bullets[b1].height/2;
        bullets[b1].y -= 10;

        //create bullet 2
        int b2 = find_bullet();
        if (b2 == -1) return;
        bullets[b2].alive = true;
        bullets[b2].rotation = 0.0;
        bullets[b2].velx = 12.0f;
        bullets[b2].vely = 0.0f;
        bullets[b2].x = player.x + player.width/2;
        bullets[b2].y = player.y + player.height/2
            - bullets[b2].height/2;
        bullets[b2].y += 10;
    }
    break;

    case 3:
    {
        //create bullet 1
        int b1 = find_bullet();
        if (b1 == -1) return;
        bullets[b1].alive = true;
        bullets[b1].rotation = 0.0;
        bullets[b1].velx = 12.0f;
        bullets[b1].vely = 0.0f;
        bullets[b1].x = player.x + player.width/2;
        bullets[b1].y = player.y + player.height/2
            - bullets[b1].height/2;

        //create bullet 2
        int b2 = find_bullet();
        if (b2 == -1) return;
        bullets[b2].alive = true;
        bullets[b2].rotation = 0.0;
        bullets[b2].velx = 12.0f;
        bullets[b2].vely = 0.0f;
```

```
    bullets[b2].x = player.x + player.width/2;
    bullets[b2].y = player.y + player.height/2
        - bullets[b2].height/2;
    bullets[b2].y -= 16;

    //create bullet 3
    int b3 = find_bullet();
    if (b3 == -1) return;
    bullets[b3].alive = true;
    bullets[b3].rotation = 0.0;
    bullets[b3].velx = 12.0f;
    bullets[b3].vely = 0.0f;
    bullets[b3].x = player.x + player.width/2;
    bullets[b3].y = player.y + player.height/2
        - bullets[b3].height/2;
    bullets[b3].y += 16;

}
break;

case 4:
{
    //create bullet 1
    int b1 = find_bullet();
    if (b1 == -1) return;
    bullets[b1].alive = true;
    bullets[b1].rotation = 0.0;
    bullets[b1].velx = 12.0f;
    bullets[b1].vely = 0.0f;
    bullets[b1].x = player.x + player.width/2;
    bullets[b1].x += 8;
    bullets[b1].y = player.y + player.height/2
        - bullets[b1].height/2;
    bullets[b1].y -= 12;

    //create bullet 2
    int b2 = find_bullet();
    if (b2 == -1) return;
    bullets[b2].alive = true;
    bullets[b2].rotation = 0.0;
    bullets[b2].velx = 12.0f;
    bullets[b2].vely = 0.0f;
    bullets[b2].x = player.x + player.width/2;
    bullets[b2].x += 8;
```

```
            bullets[b2].y = player.y + player.height/2
                - bullets[b2].height/2;
            bullets[b2].y += 12;

            //create bullet 3
            int b3 = find_bullet();
            if (b3 == -1) return;
            bullets[b3].alive = true;
            bullets[b3].rotation = 0.0;
            bullets[b3].velx = 12.0f;
            bullets[b3].vely = 0.0f;
            bullets[b3].x = player.x + player.width/2;
            bullets[b3].y = player.y + player.height/2
                - bullets[b3].height/2;
            bullets[b3].y -= 32;

            //create bullet 4
            int b4 = find_bullet();
            if (b4 == -1) return;
            bullets[b4].alive = true;
            bullets[b4].rotation = 0.0;
            bullets[b4].velx = 12.0f;
            bullets[b4].vely = 0.0f;
            bullets[b4].x = player.x + player.width/2;
            bullets[b4].y = player.y + player.height/2
                - bullets[b4].height/2;
            bullets[b4].y += 32;
        }
        break;

    case 5:
        {
            //create bullet 1
            int b1 = find_bullet();
            if (b1 == -1) return;
            bullets[b1].alive = true;
            bullets[b1].rotation = 0.0;
            bullets[b1].velx = 12.0f;
            bullets[b1].vely = 0.0f;
            bullets[b1].x = player.x + player.width/2;
            bullets[b1].y = player.y + player.height/2
                - bullets[b1].height/2;
            bullets[b1].y -= 12;
```

```
            //create bullet 2
            int b2 = find_bullet();
            if (b2 == -1) return;
            bullets[b2].alive = true;
            bullets[b2].rotation = 0.0;
            bullets[b2].velx = 12.0f;
            bullets[b2].vely = 0.0f;
            bullets[b2].x = player.x + player.width/2;
            bullets[b2].y = player.y + player.height/2
                - bullets[b2].height/2;
            bullets[b2].y += 12;

            //create bullet 3
            int b3 = find_bullet();
            if (b3 == -1) return;
            bullets[b3].alive = true;
            bullets[b3].rotation = -4.0;// 86.0;
            bullets[b3].velx = (float) (12.0 *
                LinearVelocityX( bullets[b3].rotation ));
            bullets[b3].vely = (float) (12.0 *
                LinearVelocityY( bullets[b3].rotation ));
            bullets[b3].x = player.x + player.width/2;
            bullets[b3].y = player.y + player.height/2
                - bullets[b3].height/2;
            bullets[b3].y -= 20;

            //create bullet 4
            int b4 = find_bullet();
            if (b4 == -1) return;
            bullets[b4].alive = true;
            bullets[b4].rotation = 4.0;// 94.0;
            bullets[b4].velx = (float) (12.0 *
                LinearVelocityX( bullets[b4].rotation ));
            bullets[b4].vely = (float) (12.0 *
                LinearVelocityY( bullets[b4].rotation ));
            bullets[b4].x = player.x + player.width/2;
            bullets[b4].y = player.y + player.height/2
                - bullets[b4].height/2;
            bullets[b4].y += 20;
        }
        break;
    }
}
```

Due to the large size of this program, the remaining portion of the source code for the Anti-Virus game has been removed, and is available for your perusal on the CD-ROM. Please open the project to review the rest of the source code. If you do not have the CD-ROM, please visit www.jharbour.com/forum to download the projects.

What You Have Learned

That wraps up the Anti-Virus game. There is such huge potential in this game! The real question here is not what this pseudo-game can do, but what it *can't* do! We have a great storyline, some very good gameplay already (with just a need for more design), and very functional firing code already working. This is one side-scrolling shooter that needs to be taken by someone who is talented and willing to spend a little time on it to turn it into the great game it was meant to be! Will that be you?

Review Questions

The following review questions will help you to determine if you grasped all of the information in this chapter.

1. How many levels of firepower are currently featured in the game?

2. What trigonometric function do we call to calculate the X velocity of a sprite based on a given angle?

3. What trigonometric function do we call to calculate the Y velocity of a sprite based on a given angle?

4. What type of Direct3D object is this game using for the scrolling background: a surface or a texture?

5. Which function handles firing of bullets based on the firepower level of the nanobot?

6. What shape do the program fragments take in the game?

7. What are the program fragments used for in the game?

8. Do the enemy viruses attack the player in the game? Why or why not?

9. Briefly explain how the game handles all of the sprites being rendered at one time.

10. What is the name of the font printing function?

On Your Own

I'm just going to make two suggestions here for the Anti-Virus game, although I can easily come up with 30 off the top of my head very quickly.

Exercise 1. The Anti-Virus game features enemy virus objects that do not seem to affect the player's nanobot in any way. Modify the program so that the enemy virus sprites are dangerous to the player, so that a collision will damage or destroy the nanobot.

Exercise 2. Modify the Anti-Virus game further by causing the enemy viruses to explode into smaller particles that are each dangerous to the player's nanobot, and which must be avoided or destroyed.

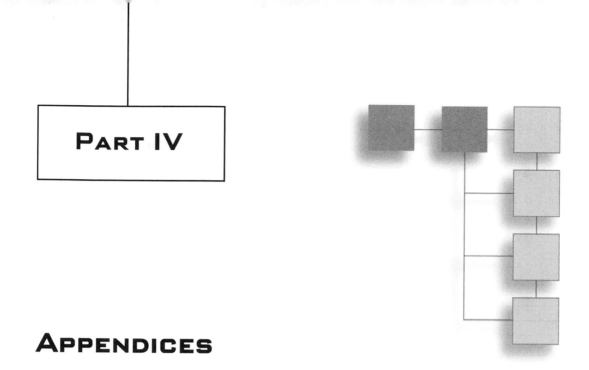

PART IV

APPENDICES

The following appendices will provide the extra resources either not covered in the text (to improve flow and readability) or supplemental to the text (such as the Chapter Quiz Answers). Appendix D provides additional examples that I wanted to include in the book but which had to be cut, either due to time constraints or due to the difficulty level of some subjects. There are four appendices:

- Appendix A: Configuring Visual C++

- Appendix B: Resources for Further Study

- Appendix C: Chapter Quiz Answers

- Appendix D: Additional Examples

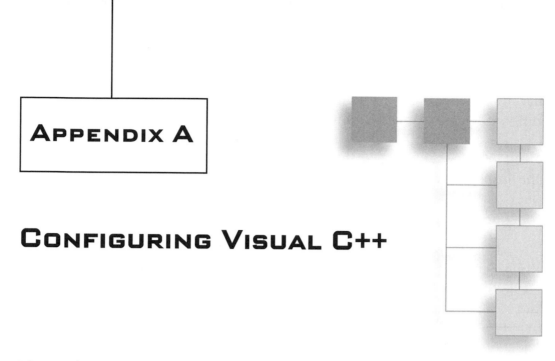

APPENDIX A

CONFIGURING VISUAL C++

I have taken a more general approach to compiler project configuration in this book to simplify things, since the average beginner (based on my experience with my first-time DirectX students) has a hard time understanding where files belong. Let's face it, Visual C++ 2008 is a complex development environment with many, many options—which can seem daunting to a beginner, even for someone who is fairly experienced with the C++ language.

To keep project configuration simple, first of all, we'll just store all project assets (that's the bitmap files, audio files, etc.) in the *project folder*. Now, the project folder is not the same as the *solution folder*. The solution file, which has a .SLN extension, is usually in the main folder when you create a new project in Visual C++ 2008. The *project folder*, which contains the project file (with an extension of .VCPROJ) will be in a subfolder under the solution folder. Whew! Put all of your game's assets in the *project folder*, and then when you debug in Visual C++ (with the F5 key), it will be able to find your assets.

Setting Folders Manually

It's important that you install Visual C++ 2008 *before* you install DirectX. There are two versions of DirectX that you can download from Microsoft: the *runtime* and the *software development kit* (or SDK). You want to download and install the DirectX SDK, which includes the runtime too. If you just install the runtime—which comes with most new games—then you won't be able to compile any DirectX code in the book. Make sure you have installed Visual C++ 2008 first, then go to http://msdn.microsoft.com/directx/ to download and install the DirectX SDK. (The latest version at the time of this writing is March 2009.) Be sure to install DirectX *after* Visual C++ so that it will be configured properly.

If you installed DirectX *first*, no problem—just re-install DirectX SDK again after Visual C++. This is necessary because the DirectX installer will configure Visual C++ automatically, telling it where to find the DirectX SDK files when you compile your DirectX code. Otherwise, you have to add the DirectX folders manually. Should you need to do that, for whatever reason, you can configure the folders by opening the Tools menu, selecting Options, then Projects and Solutions, and then VC++ Directories. From the Show directories for drop-down list, choose Include files and add the DirectX include folder (normally in the C:\Program Files\Microsoft DirectX SDK (Month Year) folder). Do the same for the Library files, adding a reference to the DirectX SDK\Lib\x86 folder.

Creating a New Project

First, let's see how to create a new project. Open Visual C++ 2008. If you have not downloaded and installed it yet, just hop over to http://www.microsoft.com/Express/vc/, download, and install Visual C++ 2008. It's a cinch! When you run Visual C++ 2008, the integrated development environment (IDE) will come up as shown in Figure A.1.

Open the File menu, choose New, Project. The New Project dialog appears, as shown in Figure A.2. In this example, I am using the Professional edition, which has more project types than the Express edition, which you may be using. Open the Visual C++ list item, and then choose Win32. You will see (normally) two Win32 project templates, one for a console project, and another called "Win32 Project." Choose the latter for all of your DirectX projects. Type in a name for the new project and choose a location.

Next up is the Win32 Application Wizard dialog, shown in Figure A.3. Below the Overview page link on the left select Application Settings. By default, the "Windows application" type will be selected.

Figure A.1
The Visual C++ 2008 IDE.

This is where things can (and often do) go *very wrong*! So if you are a complete beginner, please pay attention to this important step!

Check the Empty project checkbox to disable the default project that Visual C++ will create for you if you do not. If you forget to check this option, you will get a *huge* project filled with all kinds of files and resources. This option is helpful when you want to quickly create an application, but for a DirectX program, we don't need any of those application features. If you accidentally leave the Empty option off, you will get a project that looks like the one in Figure A.4.

Figure A.2
The New Project dialog in Visual C++ 2008.

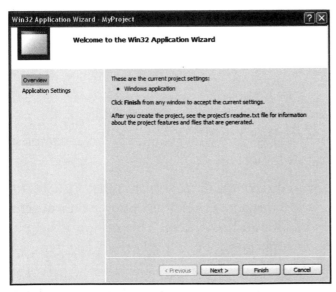

Figure A.3
The Win32 Application Wizard in Visual C++ 2008.

Figure A.4
A large sample project generated by the Win32 Application Wizard (which we don't want!).

By checking the Empty project option, you will be presented with a much more agreeable project. Now that we have a clean but empty project, we need to add a source code file. Open the Project menu and select Add New Item as shown in Figure A.5. This brings up the Add New Item dialog shown in Figure A.6.

From this dialog, choose C++ File (.cpp) as the file type, and enter a filename into the Name field. I have entered main.cpp in the example shown.

After adding the new main.cpp file to the project, your environment will resemble the one shown in Figure A.7. Since all of the code presented in this book uses a #pragma statement to add library files to the project (such as d3d9.lib), we

Figure A.5
Adding a new source code file via the Project menu.

Figure A.6
Adding a new C++ File to the project with the Add New Item dialog.

Figure A.7
The new project is ready for your DirectX code!

don't need to make any more configuration changes to compile DirectX code! You're done!

Changing the Character Set

There is one recurring problem that often crops up for beginners that I would like to address: the default character set. By default, new projects are configured with the Unicode character set, which means you must use Unicode string conversion functions when working with all of your string data. This can be quite a pain and tends to "ugly up" your DirectX game code—not to mention making the code non-standard so it likely will not compile with another compiler (such as Dev-C++ or Turbo C++ 2006—both of which do support DirectX 9).

Figure A.8
Changing the default character set to multi-byte.

Changing the character set is a cinch. Open the Project menu, choose Project Properties at the bottom. Next, the Project Property Pages dialog will appear (see Figure A.8). Open the Configuration Properties list item, and then select General. Near the bottom of the General property page is the Character Set property. Change this to multi-byte. Problem solved!

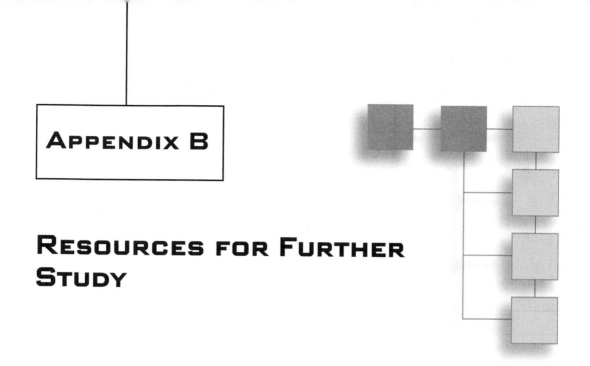

APPENDIX B

RESOURCES FOR FURTHER STUDY

Game Development Websites

Here are some excellent game development sites on the web that I visit frequently:

Allegro Home Site: http://www.talula.demon.co.uk/allegro/

GameDev LCC: http://www.gamedev.net

MSDN DirectX: http://msdn.microsoft.com/directx

MSDN Visual C++: http://msdn.microsoft.com/visualc

Game Development Search Engine: http://www.gdse.com

CodeGuru: http://www.codeguru.com

Programmers Heaven: http://www.programmersheaven.com

AngelCode.com: http://www.angelcode.com

OpenGL: http://www.opengl.org

NeHe Productions: http://nehe.gamedev.net

NeXe: http://nexe.gamedev.net

Game Institute: http://www.gameinstitute.com

Wotsit's Format: http://www.wotsit.org

Publishing, Game Reviews, and Download Sites

Keeping up with all that is happening is a daunting task, to say the least. New things happen every minute all over the world, and hopefully, the next set of links will help you keep up to date with it all.

Course Technology: http://www.courseptr.com

Games Domain: http://www.gamesdomain.com

Blue's News: http://www.bluesnews.com

Download.com: http://www.download.com

Tucows: http://www.tucows.com

Slashdot: http://slashdot.org

Imagine Games Network (IGN): http://www.ign.com

Industry

If you want to be in the business, you need to know the business. Reading magazines and visiting association meetings will help you for sure.

Game Developers Magazine: http://www.gdmag.com

GamaSutra: http://www.gamasutra.com

International Game Developers Association: http://www.igda.com

Game Developers Conference: http://www.gdconf.com

Association of Shareware Professionals: http://www.asp-shareware.org

RealGames: http://www.real.com/games

Computer Humor

Here are some great sites to visit when you are looking for a good laugh.

Homestar Runner (Strong Bad!): http://www.homestarrunner.com/

User Friendly: http://www.userfriendly.org

Geeks!: http://www.happychaos.com/geeks

Off the Mark: http://www.offthemark.com/computers.htm

Player Versus Player: http://www.pvponline.com

Recommended Books

I've provided a short description for each of the books in this list because they are either books I have written (plug!) or that I highly recommend and have found useful, relaxing, funny, or essential on many an occasion. You will find this list of recommended books useful as references to the C language and as complementary titles and references to subjects covered in this book.

Advanced 2D Game Development

Jonathan Harbour; Course Technology; ISBN 1598633422

This is my most recent book and a good follow-up book after you have completed the beginning book. Advanced 2D goes into game engine design from the ground up, with the intermediate programmer in mind, and explains in detail how to create a 2D game engine. The most important topics in 2D games are covered, but it is not a "game project" book, more of an engine book to help get you to the next level in DirectX experience.

Introduction to 3D Game Programming with DirectX 9.0c: A Shader Approach

Frank Luna; Wordware; ISBN 1598220160

This is a comprehensive book on 3D graphics programming with Direct3D 9, but was not intended for beginners so you will need a solid grasp of C++ and at least a working knowledge of DirectX before this book will be beneficial to you. As an intermediate-advanced level book, it will teach you the most useful techniques used in game projects today such as 3D terrain, character animation, and shader programming.

Programming an RTS Game with Direct3D

Carl Granberg; Charles River; ISBN 1584504986

The real-time strategy game developed in this book is an extraordinary example of the genre and a fantastic learning tool for any intermediate-advanced level DirectX programmer. The chapters on 3D terrain and animation are indispensable. Although the shader code is presented in HLSL 2.0 file format, the shader programs still compile and run, and can easily be copied into a .fx file for 3.0 support.

Character Animation with Direct3D

Carl Granberg; Charles River; ISBN 1584505702

This is *the* book to get on 3D mesh animation techniques with Direct3D, currently the only up to date book (i.e., with *working* source code examples) on the market. I highly recommend it! Just be forewarned—this is an extremely advanced book that should, at minimum, be read after one has read Granberg's RTS book (or another intermediate DirectX book).

AI Techniques for Game Programming

Mat Buckland; Premier Press; ISBN 193184108X

"[This book] takes the difficult topics of genetic algorithms and neural networks and explains them in plain English. Gone are the tortuous mathematic equations and abstract examples to be found in other books. Each chapter takes you through the theory a step at a time, explaining clearly how you can incorporate each technique into your own games."

DarkBASIC Pro Game Programming, Second Edition

Jonathan S. Harbour and Joshua R. Smith; Premier Press; ISBN 1598632876

This book provides a good introduction to programming Direct3D, the 3D graphics component of DirectX, using the C language.

Beginning C++ Game Programming

Michael Dawson; Premier Press; ISBN 1592002056

"If you're ready to jump into the world of programming for games, [this book] will get you started on your journey, providing you with a solid foundation in the game programming language of the professionals. As you cover each programming concept, you'll create small games that demonstrate your new skills. Wrap things up by combining each major concept to create an ambitious multiplayer game. Get ready to master the basics of game programming with C++!"

C++ Programming for the Absolute Beginner, 2nd Edition

Mark Lee and Dirk Henkenmans; Premier Press; ISBN 1592003532

If you are new to programming with C++ and you are looking for a solid introduction, this is the book for you. This book will teach you the skills you need for practical C++ programming applications and how you can put these skills to use in real-world scenarios.

Character Development and Storytelling for Games

Lee Sheldon; Premier Press; ISBN 1592003532

" [This book] begins with a history of dramatic writing and entertainment in other media. It then segues to writing for games, revealing that while proven techniques in linear media can be translated to games, games offer many new challenges on their own such as interactivity, non-linearity, player input, and more. It then moves beyond linear techniques to introduce the elements of the craft of writing that are particularly unique to interactive media. It takes us from the relatively secure confines of single-player games to the vast open spaces of virtual worlds and examines player-created stories, and shows how even here writers on the development team are necessary to the process, and what they can do to aid it."

Game Design: The Art and Business of Creating Games

Bob Bates; Premier Press; ISBN 0761531653

This very readable and informative book is a great resource for learning how to design games—the high-level process of planning the game prior to starting work on the source code or artwork.

High Score! The Illustrated History of Electronic Games

Rusel DeMaria and Johnny L. Wilson; McGraw-Hill/Osborne; ISBN 0072224282

This is a gem of a book that covers the entire video game industry, including arcade machines, consoles, and computer games. It is jam-packed with wonderful interviews with famous game developers and is chock full of color photographs.

Mathematics for Game Developers

Christopher Tremblay; Premier Press; ISBN 159200038X

"[This book] explores the branches of mathematics from the game developer's perspective, rejecting the abstract, theoretical approach in favor of demonstrating real, usable applications for each concept covered. Use of this book is not confined to users of a certain operating system or enthusiasts of particular game genres; the topics covered are universally applicable."

Programming Role Playing Games with DirectX, Second Edition

Jim Adams; Premier Press; ISBN 159200315X

"In the second edition of this popular book, you'll learn how to use DirectX9 to create a complete role-playing game. Everything you need to know is included! You'll begin by learning how to use the various components of DirectX 9. Once you have a basic understanding of DirectX 9, you can move on to building the basic functions needed to create a game—from drawing 2D and 3D graphics to creating a scripting system. Wrap things up as you see how to create an entire game—from start to finish!"

Swords & Circuitry: A Designer's Guide to Computer Role-Playing Games

Neal and Jana Hallford; Premier Press; ISBN 0761532994

This book is a fascinating overview of what it takes to develop a commercial-quality role-playing game, from design to programming to marketing. This is a helpful book if you would like to write a game like *Zelda*.

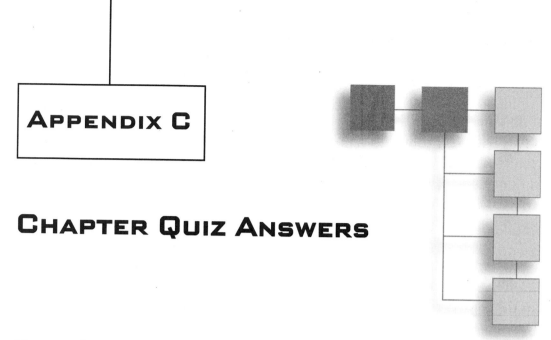

APPENDIX C

CHAPTER QUIZ ANSWERS

Here are the answers to the quizzes found at the end of each chapter, which are provided as a courtesy.

Chapter 1

1. What type of multi-tasking does Windows 2000 and XP use, preemptive or non pre-emptive?

Answer: Preemptive

2. What compiler is primarily featured in this book (although the programs are compatible with any Windows compiler)?

Answer: Visual C++ 2008

3. What scheme does Windows use to notify programs that events have occurred?

Answer: Messaging system

4. What is the process called wherein a program uses multiple, independent parts that might work together to accomplish a task (or that might perform completely independent tasks)?

Answer: Modular development

5. What is Direct3D?

Answer: The 3D component of DirectX

6. What does the hWnd variable represent?

Answer: Window handle

7. What does the hDC variable represent?

Answer: Device context of a window, used for drawing

8. What is the main function in a Windows program called?

Answer: WinMain

9. What is the name of the window event callback function?

Answer: WinProc

10. What function is used to display a message inside a program window?

Answer: DrawText (MessageBox is an acceptable answer)

Chapter 2

1. What does the WinMain function do?

Answer: WinMain is the entry point for a Windows program

2. What does the WinProc function do?

Answer: WinProc is the callback function that handles event messages

3. What is a program instance?

Answer: Represents the running instances of a program (there can be more than one)

4. What function can you use to draw pixels in a window?

Answer: SetPixel

5. What function is used to draw text inside a program window?

Answer: DrawText

6. What is a real-time game loop?

Answer: A loop that continues in real time while a game is running

7. Why do you need to use a real-time loop in a game?

Answer: To provide an interactive experience in real time (one possible answer)

8. What is the main helper function used to create a real-time loop?

Answer: `WinMain`, `InitInstance`, and `MyRegister` class are all acceptable answers

9. What Windows API function can you use to draw a bitmap onto the screen?

Answer: `BitBlt`

10. What does DC stand for?

Answer: Device context

Chapter 3

1. What is Direct3D?

Answer: The 3D component of DirectX

2. What is the Direct3D interface object called?

Answer: `IDirect3D9` (or `LPDIRECT3D9`)

3. What is the Direct3D device called?

Answer: `IDirect3DDevice9` (or `LPDIRECT3DDEVICE9`)

4. Which Direct3D function do you use to start rendering?

Answer: `BeginScene`

5. What function lets you read from the keyboard asynchronously?

Answer: `GetAsyncKeyState`

6. What is the name of the main Windows function, known as the "entry point" of the program?

Answer: `WinMain`

7. What is the common name for the event handling function in a Windows program?

Answer: WinProc

8. Which Direct3D function refreshes the screen after rendering is complete, by copying the back buffer onto the frame buffer in video memory?

Answer: Present

9. What version of DirectX are we using in this book?

Answer: 9.0c

10. What is the name of the Direct3D header file?

Answer: d3d.h

Chapter 4

1. What is the name of the primary Direct3D object?

Answer: IDirect3D9 (or LPDIRECT3D9)

2. What is the Direct3D device called?

Answer: IDirect3DDevice9 (or LPDIRECT3DDEVICE9)

3. What is the name of the Direct3D surface object?

Answer: IDirect3DSurface9

4. What function can you use to draw a Direct3D surface to the screen?

Answer: StretchRect

5. What is the term that describes copying images in memory?

Answer: bit block transfer (or blitting)

6. What is the name of the struct used to handle a Direct3D surface?

Answer: IDirect3DSurface9

7. What is the name of the long-pointer defined version of the same struct?

Answer: LPDIRECT3DSURFACE9

8. Which function returns a pointer to the Direct3D back buffer?

Answer: GetBackBuffer

9. Which Direct3D device function fills a surface with a given color?

Answer: ColorFill

10. Which function is used to load a bitmap file into a Direct3D surface in memory?

Answer: `D3DXLoadSurfaceFromFile`

Chapter 5

1. What is the name of the primary DirectInput object?

Answer: `IDirectInput8` (or `LPDIRECTINPUT8`)

2. What is the function that creates a DirectInput device?

Answer: `CreateDevice`

3. What is the name of the struct that contains mouse input data?

Answer: `DIMOUSESTATE`

4. What function do you call to poll the keyboard or mouse?

Answer: `GetDeviceState`

5. What is the name of the function that helps check for sprite collisions?

Answer: `IntersectRect`

6. What is the benefit of having concept drawings for a game?

Answer: Helps visualize the gameplay more effectively

7. What is the name of the surface object in Direct3D?

Answer: `IDirect3DSurface9` (or `LPDIRECT3DSURFACE9`)

8. What function should you use to draw a surface on the screen?

Answer: `StretchRect`

9. What D3DX helper function do you use to load a bitmap image into a surface?

Answer: `D3DXLoadSurfaceFromFile`

10. Where can you find a good collection of free sprites on the web?

Answer: SpriteLib at www.flyingyogi.com is a good resource

Chapter 6

1. What is the name of the DirectX object used to handle sprites?

Answer: ID3DXSprite (or LPD3DXSPRITE)

2. What function is used to load a bitmap image into a texture object?

Answer: D3DXCreateTextureFromFile (-Ex suffix is a variation)

3. What function do you use to create the sprite object?

Answer: D3DXCreateSprite

4. What is the name of the D3DX function that draws a sprite?

Answer: Draw

5. What is the Direct3D texture object called?

Answer: IDirect3DTexture9 (or LPDIRECT3DTEXTURE9)

6. Which function returns the size of an image contained in a bitmap file?

Answer: D3DXGetImageInfoFromFile

7. Which Windows API function provides a clock tick value used for timing?

Answer: GetTickCount or timeGetTime

8. What is the name of the function that must be called before drawing any sprites?

Answer: Begin (or ID3DXSprite::Begin)

9. What is the name of the function called when sprite drawing is finished?

Answer: End (or ID3DXSprite::End)

10. What is the data type used to specify the source rectangle in the sprite drawing function?

Answer: RECT

Chapter 7

1. What type of Direct3D object must we use for the source image of a sprite?

Answer: IDirect3DTexture9 (or LPDIRECT3DTEXTURE9)

2. Which function creates a matrix for transforming a 2D sprite based on rotation, scaling, and translation vectors passed to it?

Answer: `D3DXMatrixTransformation2D`

3. How are angles encoded when rotating a sprite, with degrees or radians?

Answer: `Radians`

4. What data type is used to hold a vector for sprite scaling?

Answer: `D3DXVECTOR2`

5. What data type is used to hold a vector for sprite movement?

Answer: `D3DXVECTOR2`

6. What data type is used to hold a value for sprite rotation?

Answer: `float`

7. Which `ID3DXSprite` function is used to apply a matrix to the sprite's transform?

Answer: `SetTransform`

8. What parameter is always passed to the `ID3DXSprite::Begin` function?

Answer: `D3DXSPRITE_ALPHABLEND`

9. Besides width, height, and frame number, what other value is needed for animation?

Answer: Columns

10. Which macro is used to encode a `D3DCOLOR` with an alpha color component?

Answer: `D3DCOLOR_ARGB`

Chapter 8

1. What type of object do we need to fill with the bounds of each sprite to use the `IntersectRect` function?

Answer: `RECT`

2. What is the first parameter passed to `IntersectRect` used for?

Answer: Filled with a rectangle representing the overlap of the two rectangles

3. What type of triangle do we use (conceptually) to calculate the distance between two points?

Answer: Right triangle

4. Briefly describe how the bounding box method handles sprite scaling.

Answer: The bounding box must be reduced or enlarged based on the sprite's scale in order to return accurate collision results

5. In a fast-paced arcade game with hundreds of sprites on the screen at once, where precision is not as important, which of the two collision-detection techniques should be used?

Answer: Bounding box is faster since Distance involves square root, which is one of the most difficult functions for a computer to process

6. In a slower game (such as an RPG) where precision is important to the gameplay, and few sprites will be on the screen at a time, which collision technique should be used?

Answer: Distance based collision is more precise

7. When calculating the distance between two sprites, where is the X,Y point on each sprite normally located?

Answer: The center of each sprite must be used since distance-based collision detection involves a *radius* from the center

8. After a collision between two sprites occurs, why would you want to move the sprites away from each other before the next frame?

Answer: So they will not get stuck by repeated collision events

9. What are the second and third parameters of the `IntersectRect` function?

Answer: Two `RECT` variables representing the two sprites

10. Briefly describe a situation in a game where you might want to use *both* collision techniques with the same two sprites to determine if they are touching.

Answer: Any valid answer such as: If a game has a *huge* amount of sprites, then it is beneficial to use the fast bounding box method first to cut down on distance calculations.

Chapter 9

1. What is the name of the font object used to print text on the screen?

Answer: `ID3DXFont`

2. What is the name of the long pointer version of the font object?

Answer: `LPD3DXFONT`

3. What is the name of the function used to print text on the screen?

Answer: `ID3DXFont::DrawText`

4. Which function is used to create a new font object based on certain font properties?

Answer: `D3DXCreateFontIndirect`

5. What is the name of the constant used to specify that text will be wrapped inside a supplied rectangular region on the screen?

Answer: `DT_WORDBREAK`

6. If the sprite object is not supplied to the font renderer, will it create its own sprite object for 2D output when rendering the font to the screen?

Answer: Yes

7. Which `std::string` function converts the string data into a C-style character array for use by functions such as `strcpy`?

Answer: `c_str`

8. Which `std::string` function returns the length of the string (i.e., the number of characters in the string)?

Answer: length

9. What Direct3D data type would you use to define a color for text output?

Answer: `D3DCOLOR`

10. Which function returns a Direct3D color with an alpha channel component?

Answer: `D3DCOLOR_ARGB`

Chapter 10

1. What was the resolution of the virtual scroll buffer used in the static scrolling program?

Answer: Width = 25 tiles × 64 pixels; Height = 18 tiles × 64 pixels

2. Likewise, what was the resolution of the buffer used in the dynamic scrolling program?

Answer: 16 × 64 by 24 × 64

3. What is the difference between the tile drawing code in the two example programs?

Answer: The scroll buffer is only the size of the screen in the dynamic scroller, while the scroll buffer is the size of the entire level in the static version.

4. How would you create a tile map using Mappy with a *gigantic* level with thousands of tiles?

Answer: This question is referring to the type of scroll buffer; in this case, the dynamic scroll buffer would allow gigantic levels to be rendered without consuming unrealistic amounts of memory (for the static version).

5. What is the effective limit on map size for a game that draws tiles dynamically?

Answer: Virtually unlimited (only limited by available memory)

6. What is the file extension for a native Mappy level file?

Answer: FMP

7. What type of export do we want to perform to convert a Mappy level file into a form usable in a DirectX program?

Answer: Text output or C-style array

8. How many times do we need to blit the source background image onto the scroll buffer for a bitmap scroller?

Answer: Only once during program startup

9. What term is used by Mappy to refer to individual tiles in a level?

Answer: Block

10. If you wanted to create a game similar to the old Mario platformer games, would you use a bitmap scroller or a tile scroller?

Answer: Tile scroller

Chapter 11

1. What is the name of the primary DirectSound class used in this chapter?

Answer: CSoundManager

2. What is a secondary sound buffer?

Answer: This refers to the audio data (i.e., the loaded wave file)

3. What is the secondary sound buffer called in DirectSound.h?

Answer: CSound

4. What is the option called that causes a sound to play with looping?

Answer: DSBPLAY_LOOPING

5. For reference, what is the name of the function that draws a texture (as a sprite)?

Answer: ID3DXSprite::Draw

6. Which DXUT helper class handles wave file loading?

Answer: CWaveFile

7. Which DXUT helper class do you need to use in order to create a secondary sound buffer?

Answer: CSound

8. Briefly explain how DirectSound handles sound mixing from a user's point of view.

Answer: It is automatically handled by DirectSound

9. Since DirectMusic is now defunct, what would be a good alternative for music playback in a game?

Answer: Short, looping audio clips or another audio library such as FMOD (which can play Ogg-Vorbis files)

10. Which function must be called to initialize DirectSound?

Answer: `Initialize`

Chapter 12

1. What is a vertex?

Answer: The basic 3D construct, containing X,Y,Z values

2. What is the vertex buffer used for?

Answer: The source of vertices for a 3D scene

3. How many vertices are there in a quad?

Answer: 4

4. How many triangles make up a quad?

Answer: 2

5. What is the name of the Direct3D function that draws a polygon?

Answer: `DrawPrimitive`

6. What is the flexible vertex buffer used for?

Answer: Defines the format of each vertex in a vertex buffer

7. What is the most common data type used to represent the X,Y,Z values of a vertex?

Answer: float

8. What is the DirectX function that converts an angle from degrees to radians?

Answer: `D3DXToRadian`

9. What C function do we normally use to copy large amounts of vertex data from into the vertex buffer?

Answer: `memcpy`

10. Which standard matrix represents what we see through the virtual camera?

Answer: View matrix

Chapter 13

1. What is the name of the Direct3D object that represents a mesh?

Answer: `ID3DXMesh`

2. Which Direct3D function renders each face of a mesh one by one while our program iterates through the materials?

Answer: `DrawSubset`

3. What is the name of the function you can use to load an X file into a Direct3D mesh?

Answer: `D3DXLoadMeshFromX`

4. What function would you use to draw each of the polygons in a model?

Answer: `DrawSubset`

5. What is the Direct3D data type used to represent a texture in memory?

Answer: `IDirect3DTexture9` (or `LPDIRECT3DTEXTURE9`)

6. What is the name of the Direct3D data type used to store a matrix?

Answer: `D3DXMATRIX`

7. Which Direct3D function rotates a mesh on the Y axis?

Answer: `D3DXMatrixRotationY`

8. Which standard matrix normally represents the current object being transformed and rendered in the scene?

Answer: World matrix

9. Which standard matrix do we use to specify rendering properties such as the aspect ratio?

Answer: Projection matrix

10. Which standard matrix represents the camera view?

Answer: View matrix

Chapter 14

1. How many levels of firepower are currently featured in the game?

Answer: 5

2. What trigonometric function do we call to calculate the X velocity of a sprite based on a given angle?

Answer: cosine

3. What trigonometric function do we call to calculate the Y velocity of a sprite based on a given angle?

Answer: sine

4. What type of Direct3D object is this game using for the scrolling background: a surface or a texture?

Answer: Surface

5. Which function handles firing of bullets based on the firepower level of the nanobot?

Answer: `player_shoot`

6. What shape do the program fragments take in the game?

Answer: Triangle

7. What are the program fragments used for in the game?

Answer: Energy

8. Do the enemy viruses attack the player in the game? Why or why not?

Answer: No. (Reasons will vary.) Because they have not been programmed to do anything more than move randomly.

9. Briefly explain how the game handles all of the sprites being rendered at one time.

Answer: (Answers will vary.) The sprites are handled with several arrays.

10. What is the name of the font printing function?

Answer: `FontPrint` (or `ID3DXFont::DrawText`)

APPENDIX D

ADDITIONAL EXAMPLES

On the CD-ROM in the \sources\extras folder are additional projects that did not make the cut, but which I wanted to share with you anyway. Many of these are projects I use in my DirectX courses as samples for demonstration in class. The complete source code for each of these projects is provided on the CD-ROM. Since these are used as classroom examples, the source code is not based on any engine (not even one of my own), but is presented like the projects in this book.

Point Light Demo

The lighting example shown in Figure D.1 demonstrates how to light a scene with direct lighting. In this particular example, there is a small point light just above the sphere in the scene.

Black Wireframe Vertex Shader Demo

The shader example shown in Figure D.2 demonstrates how to use a vertex shader to render a stock mesh as a wireframe. You can edit the color value, changing it from black to a different color.

Ambient-Diffuse Shader Demo

The shader example shown in Figure D.3 demonstrates how to use a vertex and pixel shader to render a mesh using two different color properties: ambient and

Figure D.1
Direct lighting.

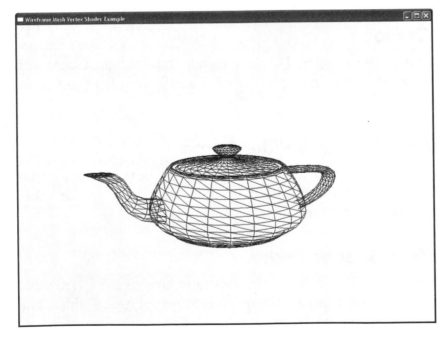

Figure D.2
Black wireframe vertex shader demo.

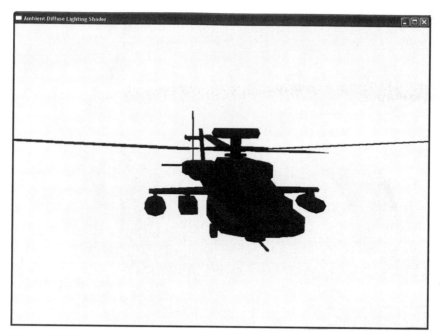

Figure D.3
Ambient-diffuse shader demo.

diffuse (which is "normal" color). The helicopter mesh was provided courtesy of Geo-Metricks (www.geo-metricks.com), an excellent source of royalty-free 3D models for use in your own game projects! (They are not free, but are affordably priced.)

INDEX